Pennsylvania

Hiking Pennsylvania

A Guide to the State's Greatest Hikes

Fourth Edition

John L. Young

FALCONGUIDES

GUILFORD, CONNECTICUT
HELENA, MONTANA

FALCONGUIDES®

An imprint of Rowman & Littlefield
Falcon, FalconGuides, and Outfit Your Mind are registered trademarks of Rowman & Littlefield.

Distributed by NATIONAL BOOK NETWORK

Copyright © 2001, 2008, 2015 by Rowman & Littlefield
Previously published as *Hike Pennsylvania* by Beachway Press Publishing, Inc. in 2001
Maps: Beachway Press © Rowman & Littlefield
All interior photos by John Young unless otherwise credited

British Library Cataloguing-in-Publication Information available

Library of Congress Cataloging-in-Publication Data available

ISBN 978-1-4930-0682-3 (paperback)
ISBN 978-1-4930-1440-8 (e-book)

∞™ The paper used in this publication meets the minimum requirements of American National Standard for Information Sciences—Permanence of Paper for Printed Library Materials, ANSI/NISO Z39.48-1992.

The author and Rowman & Littlefield assume no liability for accidents happening to, or injuries sustained by, readers who engage in the activities described in this book.

Contents

The Hikes

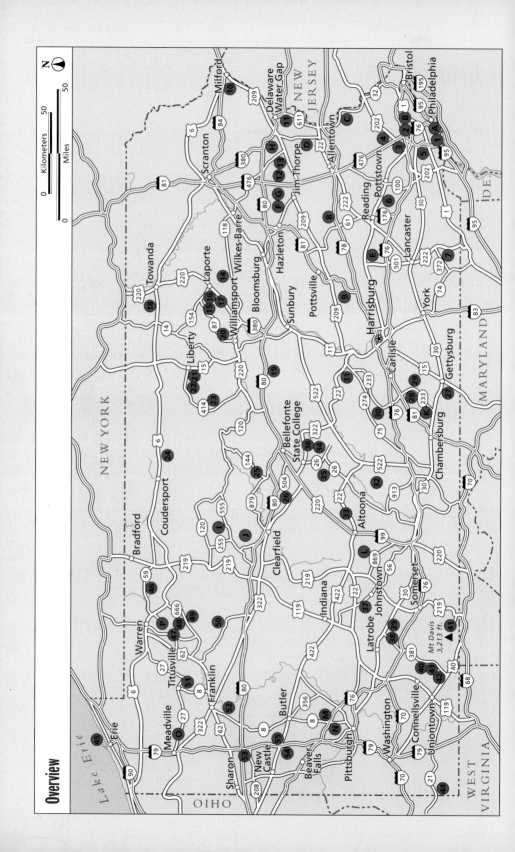

Overview

N

| Kilometers |
| 0 ... 50 |

| Miles |
| 0 ... 50 |

Acknowledgments

I would like to thank my wife, Debra, for her unbounded encouragement, support, and patience during the writing of this book.

I would like to thank the state park, state forest, state game lands, Department of Conservation & Natural Resources, US Wildlife Service, and National Park Service employees who answered many questions, returned my telephone calls, and mailed me materials. I honestly don't know of any other agencies where a person can get so much help for free.

And, finally, this book is dedicated to all the hiking clubs and volunteers who go out week after week, year after year, and sometimes decade after decade to maintain the trails of Pennsylvania.

Barefoot hiker eats lunch in the Haystacks Section of Loyalsock Creek.

Introduction

Hiking in Pennsylvania is an excellent example of the proverbial "best-kept secret." There are more than 3,000 miles of hiking trails, most on public lands. There are vast, remote areas where it's just you and Mother Nature. You can hike all day—sometimes for days—and not see another human being.

There are trails on abandoned railroad beds that are beautifully groomed and refreshingly level. And there are trails along ravines so steep that a water bottle dropped is a water bottle forever lost. Some trails are what I call SUC trails: straight uphill climbs. As soon as you step out of your vehicle, you're climbing. Most other trails, those that are more civilized, allow you a warm-up period . . . then they make you climb.

Ultimately, Pennsylvania hiking is about climbing mountains. This is not to be confused with mountain climbing. Because the highest point in the state is less than 3,500 feet above sea level, there's little need for oxygen canisters, crampons, Sherpa guides, or other exotic (and expensive) equipment. All you'll need to hike the trails in this guide are a good pair of hiking boots—and maybe a walking stick you've picked up along the way.

When I started out across the state, I wanted to see sights I'd never seen before, so I chose hikes I felt had at least one interesting feature. I also chose hikes that I had done many times before, like Rickett's Glen, and wanted to share with readers.

What will you see on the hikes in this guide? How about a hike with more than twenty-two waterfalls, one of which cascades 94 feet? Or a 1,200-year-old tree? How about a "ghost town" state park? If you think you can handle it, you'll have the opportunity to sway in the breeze at the top of an 80-foot fire tower or stand on a platform 480 feet above the Allegheny River. One of the hikes takes you past the first commercial oil well in the world; another offers a glimpse of the catastrophic Johnstown Flood that wiped out a city. Walk the rims of Pennsylvania's Grand Canyon, and watch an eagle as it swoops into the icy waters of Pine Creek and emerges with a fish in its talons.

You'll find that more than half the hikes are located in state parks. More people hike these park trails, and consequently this creates more resources that can be devoted to trail maintenance and other park features. Another reason state parks are a good place to hike is that many of them have preserved the history of their regions. Most of the remaining hikes are in state forests, national parks, and on state game lands; one is on land owned by the Western Pennsylvania Conservancy. These trails are cared for mostly by volunteers from regional and statewide trail clubs. If you want to get in shape, skip a Saturday at the gym and volunteer for trail maintenance. Carrying a chainsaw for 5 miles or so will give you the entire workout you need.

There is much to explore in Pennsylvania's outdoors. With this guidebook you'll be able to set out on your own adventure.

Pennsylvania Weather

Pennsylvania's mountain ranges, proximity to the Great Lakes, and position on the East Coast contribute to a wide range of weather patterns across the state. The state averages a modest annual rainfall of anywhere from 32 to 48 inches, but in the mountainous regions it often exceeds 48 inches. And while most of the state can expect 1 to 3 feet of snow each winter, the annual snowfall along the New York border and in the Snow Belt near the West Virginia border is frequently 60 inches or more.

Weather in the Appalachian Mountains tends to be more severe than anywhere else in the state; the mountains serve as a barrier for storm systems coming off the Great Lakes and in from the Midwest. Basically, the folks in the mountains take the brunt of it. An exception to this is in the northwest corner of the state. Here the moist air picked up over the Great Lakes can create major snowstorms. Pennsylvania also has its share of thunderstorms.

My father passed on to me an old saying among Pennsylvania deer hunters: "You can always take it off." I would offer the same advice to hikers: Overdress when you're out here in Pennsylvania; you can always remove a layer and be comfortable.

Flora and Fauna

When Europeans settled in Pennsylvania, the state was covered with trees. At the time, old-growth white pine and hemlocks accounted for about two-thirds of the forests. But in less than one hundred years, the logging industry had clear-cut the entire state. By the beginning of the twentieth century, the only hemlocks and white pines that remained were small pockets considered too difficult to log.

Today the dominant forest types are hardwoods. The mixed-hardwood forest is defined by a minimum 40 percent composition of sugar maple, beech, and yellow birch; the mixed-oak forest is defined as anywhere oak is the dominant tree. The other notable forest—though composing less than 10 percent of the state's forests—is the hemlock stand. Generally found along streambeds and in moist ravine bottoms

PENNSYLVANIA SYMBOLS

State dog: Great Dane

State insect: Firefly

State tree: Hemlock

State flower: Mountain laurel

State fish: Brook trout

State animal: White-tailed deer

State bird: Ruffed grouse

State beverage: Milk

State beautification plant: Crown vetch

State steam locomotive: K4s Steam

State electric locomotive: GG1 4859 Electric

State ship: United States Brig *Niagara*

State fossil: *Phacops rana*

State song: "Pennsylvania"

and slopes, the hemlock's shallow root system allows it to cling to the edge of cliffs and other precarious locations. The eastern hemlock is the state tree.

The state flower is the mountain laurel, which is far more like a bush or shrub than a flower (it grows from 5 to 8 feet tall). But when it blooms in early June, it decorates the forest with white and pink cup-shaped flowers. Except for an area in the northwest tip, it can be found throughout the state. The rhododendron, a cousin to the mountain laurel, thrives in moister locales, although it can be found in dry areas. It's not uncommon for these shrubs to grow to heights of 20 feet. Its peak blossom time is the first week of July: Look for large balls of either pink or white.

Wildflowers are abundant in the state. Some, like black-eyed Susans, Queen Anne's lace, wild bergamot, and common goldenrod, are in bloom all summer. (That's because they exist in meadows, where the sunlight is never blocked.) Others, those that grow under the forest canopy, bloom in spring, before the trees sprout their leaves. One of these is the trillium, a member of the lily family. It has a single flower that may be white, pink, dark red, yellow, or green.

DID YOU KNOW?

- Pennsylvania is the number-one source of potato chips in the United States, with revenues of $57 million a year.
- Pennsylvania's hardwood forests are the most productive in the nation, with revenues of $5.5 billion per year.
- During World War I, 400,000 Pennsylvania coal miners provided 227 million tons of coal a year to defense industries.
- If all the coal still underground in Pennsylvania were piled into a 1-square-mile area, it would be 5 miles high.
- Pennsylvania applies 5,640 paint-miles every year when it re-lines the Pennsylvania Turnpike.
- Pennsylvania's population in 2014 was 12,702,379.
- Native Pennsylvanians are more likely to stay in the state where they were born than residents anywhere else in the nation.
- One-third of Pennsylvania's residents live in rural surroundings, representing the largest nonurban population in the nation.
- More than half of Pennsylvania—17 million acres—is forest.
- No matter where you are in the state, you're never more than 25 miles from a state park.
- Pennsylvania has 739,200 acres of lakes, ponds, reservoirs, streams, and rivers. There are 57,000 bridges in Pennsylvania—more than any area on earth its size.

These Indian Pipes are white because they have no chlorophyll to make them green.
DEBRA YOUNG

More than sixty species of mammals live in Pennsylvania. The most noticeable is the white-tailed deer—if you hike in this state, you will see deer. (In fact, one theory holds that in sparsely populated Potter County, there are more deer than people.) There are also black bears, some weighing in at more than 500 pounds. But your chances of seeing one of these creatures in the wild are slim. You may never see a beaver either, but if you hike along streams and creeks, sooner or later you will see evidence of their existence in the heavily gnawed trees. And in the village of Benezette in Elk County, you can watch as elk from a herd of more than 500 wander into civilization foraging for food.

There are two world-class birding sites in the state. Gull Point, situated on the eastern tip of Presque Isle in Lake Erie, has designated a special management area to protect shorebird habitat. Hawk Mountain Wildlife Sanctuary, on the Kittatinny Ridge between Reading and Pottsville, is considered the premier site in North America to view migrating raptors. The best time to be there is October.

As you hike along the lakeshores and mountain streams, you may never see a fish, but there are more than 150 species here in Pennsylvania. You may never see the elusive wild turkey, either, but they're out there. More than likely you'll see a quail or a grouse or a ring-necked pheasant. If you're lucky, and know what to look for, you may see a northern river otter or a fisher, both of which had all but disappeared but have recently been successfully reintroduced.

Wilderness Restrictions/Regulations

There are no day-use or hiking fees in any of the 120 Pennsylvania state parks. (You should note that most day-use parks close at dusk, however.) Within the park system there are more than twenty-two natural areas—unique examples of natural history; there are no fees or restrictions associated with these areas. For more information call (888) PA-PARKS (888-727-2757).

In all, twenty state forests cover more than 2 million acres in forty-eight of Pennsylvania's sixty-seven counties. Within this system there are sixty-one natural areas set aside as examples of scenic beauty or a place of historical, ecological, or geological importance. There are no restrictions. For more information call (717) 787-2703.

The Pennsylvania Game Commission owns land in almost every county. There are no hiking restrictions on state game lands. For more information call (717) 787-9797.

Getting around Pennsylvania

Area Codes

The 814 area code covers Erie in the northwest and extends east to Williamsport. It runs south to include the State College–Altoona area. The city of Pittsburgh's area code is 412, with an 878 overlay. The area code for the Pittsburgh region is 724. For the Williamsport–Hazelton–Wilkes-Barre region the area code is 570. In Harrisburg and the Susquehanna Valley, the area code is 717. The area codes for the Lehigh Valley are 610 and 484. In Philadelphia the area code is 215; the surrounding area is 267.

Roads

For driving conditions on interstate highways, call (888) 783-6783. For driving conditions on the Pennsylvania Turnpike, call (800) 331-3414 or visit www.paturnpike .com.

By Air

Pennsylvania is served by two major airports: Philadelphia International Airport (PHL) and Pittsburgh International Airport (PIT). A number of smaller airports throughout the state have connections through these airports. A travel agent can best advise you on the cheapest and/or most direct way to connect from wherever you're departing. They can also arrange transportation from the airport to your final destination.

To book reservations online, check out your favorite airline's website or search one of the following travel sites for the best price: www.cheaptickets.com, www. expedia.com, www.priceline.com, http://travel.yahoo.com, www.travelocity.com, www.trip.com—just to name a few. Many of these sites can connect you with a shuttle or rental service to get you from the airport to your destination.

The Susquehannock River from the Wister Run Overlook in Susquehannock State Park.

By Bus

Most major towns and a few trailheads in Pennsylvania are served by bus. The major carriers are Greyhound, Capitol Trailways, Susquehanna Trailways, and Fullington Trailways. These bus companies share ticketing and terminals. Fares, schedules, and tickets can be accessed online at Greyhound's website: www.greyhound.com. In addition, frequent commuter buses that go to New York's Port Authority Bus Terminal serve points in eastern Pennsylvania. These include Martz Trailways, which serves Delaware Water Gap (on the Appalachian Trail) and the Poconos (570-821-3800, http://martztrailways.com); Beiber Tourways, which serves Reading (610-375-0839, www.beibertourways.com); and Trans-Bridge Lines, which serves Allentown and Doylestown (610-868-6001, www.transbridgebus.com).

By Train

Philadelphia is the hub of Amtrak's Acela service, offering frequent trains between Washington, New York, and Boston. Acela Regional trains run up to ten round-trips daily between Philadelphia, Lancaster, and Harrisburg. Three long-distance trains continue on to Johnstown, Pittsburgh, and Chicago. You can also connect to the buses at the Harrisburg Transportation Center. Erie is the lone Pennsylvania stop for the daily Lake Shore Limited between New York and Chicago. Amtrak information and reservations are available online at www.amtrak.com or by phone at (800) 872-7245.

Visitor Information

For visitor information or a travel brochure, call the Pennsylvania Vacation Guide at (800) 847-4872 or visit www.visitpa.com.

How to Use This Book

Take a close look and you'll find that this guidebook contains everything you'll need to choose, plan, and enjoy a hike in Pennsylvania. Stuffed with many pages of useful Pennsylvania-specific information, *Hiking Pennsylvania* features fifty-five mapped and cued hikes and sixteen honorable mentions, as well as everything from advice on getting into shape to tips on getting the most out of hiking with your children or your dog. And as you'd expect with any FalconGuide, you get the best maps man and technology can render. We've done everything but load your pack and tie up your bootlaces. With so much information, the only question you may have is: How do I sift through it all? Well, we answer that too.

We've designed our FalconGuide to be highly visual, for quick reference and ease of use. What this means is that the most pertinent information rises quickly to the top—you don't have to waste time poring through bulky hike descriptions to get mileage cues. They're set aside for you. And yet a FalconGuide doesn't read like a laundry list. Take the time to dive into a hike description and you'll realize that this guide is not just a good source of information; it's a good read. In the end you get the best of both worlds: a quick-reference guide and an engaging look at a region. Here's an outline of the guide's major components.

This little blue heron waits for his next meal in the John Heinz National Wildlife Refuge.

What You'll Find in a FalconGuide

Let's start with the individual chapter. To aid in quick decision making, we start each chapter with a hike summary. This short overview gives you a taste of the hiking adventure at hand. You'll learn about the trail terrain and what surprises the route has to offer. If your interest is piqued, you can read more. If not, skip to the next hike summary.

The hike specs are fairly self-explanatory. Here you'll find the quick, nitty-gritty details of the hike: where the trailhead is located, hike distance, average hiking time, difficulty rating, schedule and best season for hiking the trail, type of trail terrain, elevation gain, land status, the nearest town, what fees or permits might be required, what other trail users you may encounter, whether the hike is suitable for dogs, applicable USGS topo maps, and whom to contact for more information on the trail.

Our **Finding the trailhead** section gives you dependable directions from a nearby city right down to where you'll want to park.

The Hike description is the meat of the chapter. Detailed and honest, it's the author's carefully researched impression of the trail. While it's impossible to cover everything, you can rest assured that we won't miss what's important.

In our **Miles and Directions** section, we provide mileage cues to identify all turns and trail name changes, as well as points of interest.

Following each hike you'll find such additional information as sources for more in-depth information on the hike area, local events/attractions, accommodations and campgrounds, restaurants, hiking/trail organizations, and local outdoor retailers (for emergency trail supplies).

The **Honorable Mentions** section at the end of each region details hikes that didn't make the cut. In many cases it's not because they aren't great hikes but because they're overcrowded or environmentally sensitive to heavy traffic. Be sure to read through these. A jewel might be buried among them.

Thanks for purchasing *Hiking Pennsylvania*. The role of the writer is to make old things new and new things familiar. I hope I've done that for you in this book. See you out there.

Trail Finder

No.	Hike	Water features	Open vistas	Primitive camping	Campground or cabin	Snowshoeing	Suggested for kids	Autumn colors	No car sounds
1	John Heinz National Wildlife Refuge: Impoundment Loop	●					●		
2	Wissahickon Gorge North Loop	●					●		
3	Valley Forge National Historical Park						●		
4	Skippack Creek Trail	●				●	●	●	●
5	Ridley Creek State Park	●		●		●	●	●	●
6	French Creek State Park	●		●	●		●	●	
7	Susquehannock State Park	●	●	●			●	●	●
8	The Pinnacle		●						●
9	Swatara State Park	●					●	●	●
10	Dingmans Falls	●		●			●	●	●
11	Mount Minsi	●	●	●					●
12	Hawk Falls	●		●	●	●	●	●	●
13	Hickory Run Boulder Field			●	●	●	●	●	●
14	Ricketts Glen State Park	●		●	●		●	●	●
15	Canyon Vista	●	●	●	●	●			●
16	Worlds End State Park	●	●	●	●	●	●	●	●
17	Haystacks	●		●			●	●	●
18	Mount Pisgah State Park	●	●	●		●	●	●	●
19	R. B. Winter State Park	●	●		●	●	●	●	●

No.	Hike	Water features	Open vistas	Primitive camping	Campground or cabin	Snowshoeing	Suggested for kids	Autumn colors	No car sounds
20	Loyalsock Trail		•	•				•	•
21	Gillespie Point		•	•				•	•
22	Bohen Run Falls & West Rim Trail	•	•	•				•	•
23	Pine Trail & Hemlock Mountain		•	•				•	•
24	Splash Dam Hollow	•		•			•	•	•
25	Wykoff Run Natural Area	•		•			•	•	•
26	Black Moshannon State Park	•		•	•	•	•	•	
27	Gettysburg						•		
28	Sunset Rocks		•	•			•	•	•
29	Pole Steeple	•	•	•			•	•	•
30	Flat Rock		•	•			•	•	•
31	Little Buffalo State Park	•				•	•	•	•
32	Trough Creek State Park	•	•		•		•	•	•
33	Canoe Creek State Park	•			•		•	•	•
34	Greenwood Furnace State Park	•	•		•		•	•	•
35	Indian Steps		•	•				•	•
36	Alan Seeger Natural Area to Greenwood Fire Tower		•				•	•	•
37	Conemaugh Gorge	•	•	•			•	•	
38	Linn Run State Park	•	•	•		•	•	•	•

No.	Hike	Water features	Open vistas	Primitive camping	Campground or cabin	Snowshoeing	Suggested for kids	Autumn colors	No car sounds
39	Wolf Rocks Trail		●	●			●	●	●
40	Bear Run Nature Reserve	●	●	●			●	●	●
41	Mount Davis Natural Area		●				●	●	●
42	Ferncliff Peninsula Natural Area	●					●	●	●
43	Youghiogheny River Trail to Jonathan Run Falls	●					●	●	●
44	Ryerson Station State Park	●	●		●	●	●	●	●
45	Presque Isle State Park	●				●	●	●	●
46	Hemlock Run	●		●			●	●	●
47	Tom's Run	●		●	●		●	●	●
48	Minister Creek	●	●	●	●		●	●	●
49	Logan Falls	●		●			●	●	●
50	Cook Forest State Park	●	●	●	●	●	●	●	●
51	Oil Creek State Park	●	●	●			●	●	●
52	Allegheny Gorge	●	●	●					●
53	Schollard's Wetlands	●					●	●	●
54	McConnells Mill State Park	●		●			●	●	●
55	Moraine State Park	●		●	●	●	●	●	●

Map Legend

Municipal

≡80≡ Interstate Highway

≡220≡ US Highway

≡61≡ State Road

≡SR 2001≡ Local/County Road

≡FS 265≡ Forest Road

==== Unpaved Road

⊢—⊢—⊢ Railroad

— - — - State Boundary

•——•——• Power Line

——— Pipeline

Trails

████ Featured Trail

------ Trail

——— Paved Trail

·········· Off-Trail Hike

Water Features

Body of Water

Marsh

River/Creek

Intermittent Stream

Waterfall

Spring

Land Management

State/County Park

Symbols

✗ Airfield

Ⓐ Appalachian Trail

≍ Bridge

▲ Backcountry Campground

▥ Boardwalk/Steps

≈ Boat Launch

■ Building/Point of Interest

Λ Campground

✚ First Aid/Hospital

Ⓜ Food

⫯ Gate

✕ Mine/Quarry

Ⓟ Parking

▲ Peak/Elevation

Picnic Area

Ranger Station/Park Office

Restroom

Scenic View

Ski Area

Tower

○ Town

20 Trailhead

❓ Visitor/Information Center

◆◆ Most Difficult

◆ Difficult

This lone backpacker leaves civilization behind as he begins his trek up Hemlock Mountain.

Southeast Pennsylvania

ennsylvania: America starts here" was the state slogan some years back. But let's get specific: America really starts in southeastern Pennsylvania. Even if the region were as flat as a Kansas wheat field and there were no old-growth forests or crystal-clear streams or tidal wetlands or wildlife refuges or natural areas boasting 300-year-old trees, it would still be well worth your while to hike this region—just to soak up the history.

For example, at Valley Forge hikers can walk through the winter encampment of Gen. George Washington and his Continental Army, or they can step back in time to a year earlier and visit the site where Washington and his troops crossed the Delaware River. Hikers can visit the last remaining intact canal system of the great towpath-building era or spend a day on a circa 1700 Quaker farm.

Tired of people? Desk stress got you down? Need to get away? Spend some time with greater snow geese or migrating raptors. Really tired of people? Climb a rocky outcrop to one of the best views in the state, or spend a day exploring a fossil pit in an undeveloped state park.

Geologically speaking, the Southeast region provides a landscape as diverse as its population. The Coastal Plain is a narrow strip along the Delaware border that encompasses Philadelphia. Just west of the Coastal Plain, the Piedmont region begins. (A piedmont is a plateau near the foot of a mountain.) The Piedmont in southeastern Pennsylvania comprises the fertile farming region of the Lancaster Valley, from the Coastal Plain in the east to the great Appalachian Mountain system in the west. Just west of the Piedmont, the Blue Mountains extend into Pennsylvania, where they are known as South Mountain.

The Reading Prong stretches across the Susquehanna Valley; it's sometimes considered an extension of the Blue Ridge Mountains. The Great Valley—which is 20 miles wide and extends from the Maryland border in the south to the Delaware River in the northeast—begins west of the Reading Prong and South Mountain and ends where the Ridge and Valley Province of central Pennsylvania begins. In southeastern Pennsylvania, it's known as the Cumberland Valley.

What does all this mean to hikers eager to lace up and get out there? It means that the same geological forces that created these mountains and land formations also created a lot of exciting features, like stunning waterfalls, water gaps, wind gaps, deep gorges, and on and on. Simply put, it means where there's a lot of geological diversity, there will also be a lot of great hiking.

1 John Heinz National Wildlife Refuge: Impoundment Loop

Want a hike where you can take your children and your parents? This is it. Along this easy, flat hike, you're surrounded by nature's beauty and the excitement of spotting some of the 280 species of birds. In season you can check out the migratory birds as they make their spring and fall journeys. On this 1,200-acre refuge, you can bike, fish, or take a canoe and do your birding and amphibian and reptile sighting from the water. Once written off as a useless swamp, the refuge will surprise you with more than fifty species of wildflowers, an abundance of deciduous trees, and wildlife from white-tailed deer to turtles.

Start: Parking area near the John Heinz Visitor Contact Station
Distance: 3.5-mile loop
Hiking time: 1 to 2 hours
Difficulty: Easy, due to the level terrain
Schedule: Open every day, year-round, from sunrise to sunset
Seasons: Year-round
Trail surface: Wide, level dirt and gravel roads through a 1,200-acre marsh
Elevation gain: 28 feet

Land status: National wildlife refuge
Nearest town: Philadelphia
Fees and permits: No fees or permits required
Other trail users: Cyclists, joggers, birders
Canine compatibility: Leashed dogs permitted
Maps: USGS Lansdowne, PA, and Philadelphia, PA; John Heinz NWR map available at the visitor contact station
Trail contacts: John Heinz Visitor Center Station, Tinicum; (215) 365-3118; www.fws.gov/refuge/John_Heinz/

Finding the trailhead: From Philadelphia, drive south on I-95 to the Bartram Avenue exit. Drive west on Bartram Avenue to 84th Street. Turn right onto 84th Street and drive to Lindbergh Boulevard. Turn left onto Lindbergh Avenue and follow the signs to the John Heinz Visitor Contact Station. Park in the lot just beyond the visitor center. *DeLorme: Pennsylvania Atlas & Gazetteer:* Page 96 A1. GPS: N39 53.573' / W075 15.448'

By train: From Market East Station, take the SEPTA R1 Airport Line to Eastwick Station. Now on foot, leave the station and turn left on 84th Street. Follow the driving directions to the visitor contact station. (It's about a 0.75-mile walk to the trailhead from the train station.)

By bus: SEPTA bus routes 37 and 108 serve the corner of 84th Street and Lindbergh Boulevard. Follow the driving directions above from here. (It's a couple of blocks to the trailhead from the bus stop.)

The Hike

The Tinicum National Environmental Center was established by an act of Congress in 1972 to protect the last 200 acres of freshwater tidal marsh in Pennsylvania. In 1991 the name was changed to the John Heinz National Wildlife Refuge to honor the late senator who helped preserve Tinicum Marsh. The history of the marsh can be traced back to the mid-1600s when early settlers diked and drained part of the marsh for grazing. At that time the marsh was more than 5,700 acres, but with the rapid urbanization of the area that followed World War I, the marsh was reduced to a mere 200 acres.

In 1955 Gulf Oil donated 145 acres adjacent to the eastern end of the marsh, and the area soon became a haven for wildlife. But in 1969 plans were on the table to route I-95 right through the marsh. This started a series of injunctions and public hearings that ended in 1972 when Congress gave the secretary of the interior authorization to acquire the 1,200 acres that compose the marsh today.

One of the popular ways to explore the refuge is by canoe, on the 4.5-mile section of Darby Creek that winds through the marsh. If you've got a canoe, bring it; there's a canoe launch, but there are no canoe rentals. Also, keep in mind that the refuge waters are tidal and navigable only within two hours of high tide. If you plan to canoe, it's best to contact the visitor contact station. They can provide you with a canoe map and ten points of interest, or you can download the canoe map from the refuge's website, listed below. Fishing is permitted, and you can use the same map for fishing.

From your canoe you'll see a diversity of waterfowl, wildlife, and amphibians. You may come upon an eastern painted turtle or a state-endangered red-bellied turtle

The boardwalk provides visitors with an up close view of waterfowl.

sunning itself on a log. Chances are you'll see one of these ducks: hooded merganser, pintail, shoveler, or mallard. There are three nonvenomous snakes that call the marsh home: the northern water snake, the eastern garter snake, and the northern brown snake. Eight species of toads, frogs, and turtles have been identified here.

In addition to the indigenous population, the refuge is along the Atlantic Flyway and serves as a stopover for migratory birds in the spring and fall. Sightings have included great blue herons, Canada geese, egrets, killdeer, and sandpipers. More than 280 species of birds have been sighted, with 80 of those species recorded as nesting in or near the marsh. Bring your binoculars and birding book: You might just see a bird here you've never seen before, like a great crested flycatcher, a Philadelphia vireo, or a yellow-throated warbler.

There are a number of environmental education opportunities here for young and old. Educators and group leaders use the refuge as an outdoor classroom to enhance student learning. Field trips are free, but you need to reserve a place for your group in advance. It's recommended that anyone planning on leading an educational field trip meet with the refuge staff for an introduction to the refuge.

The refuge offers ongoing free programs with titles like Nature Photo Walk, Birding Basics, Waterfowl Wonderment, and Minnow Evolution. There are even free professional development workshops for educators offered throughout the year. Add to all this a resource library, located in the visitor contact station, with more than 200 activity guides, videos, and other resources, and you have the perfect place to spend a day.

Miles and Directions

0.0 Start from the parking area. Get on the Impoundment Trail toward the observation tower.
0.2 Pass a wooden footbridge on your left.
0.7 Arrive at the observation tower; continue straight.
1.3 Pass a spur trail to an observation blind. Continue straight.
1.4 Turn left at a trail junction, still following the Impoundment Trail.
1.9 The trail turns left.
2.5 The trail bears left.
3.5 Arrive back at the parking area.

Local Information

Philadelphia Convention & Visitors Bureau, 1601 Market St., Ste. 200, Philadelphia 19103; (215) 636-3300 or (800) 537-7676; www.discoverphl.com

Local Events/Attractions

Independence Mall, located between Fourth and Eighth Streets, Philadelphia—home of the Liberty Bell, Independence Hall, Congress Hall, and other points of interest
The Italian Market, Ninth Street and Passyunk Avenue, Philadelphia
South Street, between Third and Eighth Streets, Philadelphia

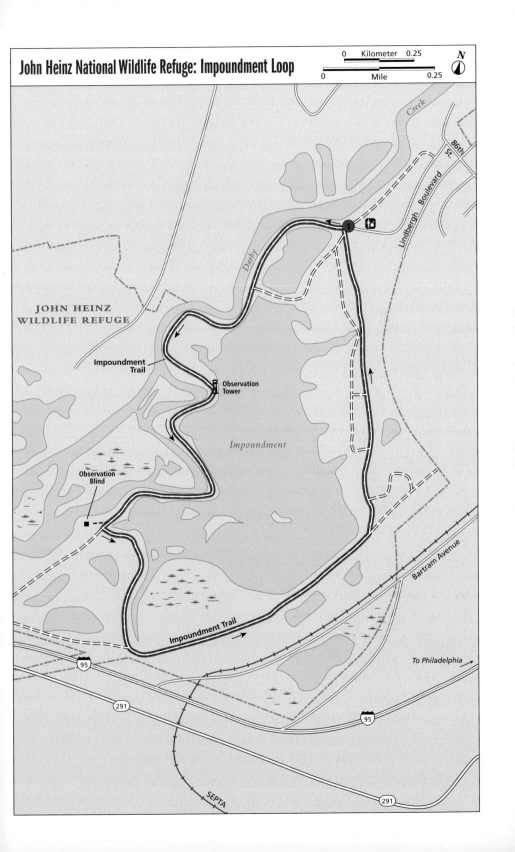

John Heinz National Wildlife Refuge: Impoundment Loop

0   Kilometer   0.25

0   Mile   0.25

N

Creek

86th St.

Lindbergh Boulevard

1

Darby

JOHN HEINZ
WILDLIFE REFUGE

Impoundment
Trail

Observation
Tower

Impoundment

Observation
Blind

Bartram Avenue

Impoundment Trail

To Philadelphia

95

95

291

SEPTA

291

Accommodations

Purcell Darrell House Bed & Breakfast, 315 N. Chester Rd., Swarthmore; (610) 690-4421; http://purcelldarrellhouse.com

Restaurants

Hibachi Grill & Supreme Buffett, Penrose Plaza, 3000 Island Ave., Philadelphia; (215) 365-8881; www.hibachibuffetpa.com

Organizations

Friends of Heinz Wildlife Refuge (FOHR), PO Box 333, Folcroft, PA 19032-0333; (215) 365-3118; www.friendsofheinzrefuge.org

2 Wissahickon Gorge North Loop

There are two major attractions on this hike that make this an absolute must for serious outdoor lovers. Hikers can investigate the history and historical significance of Northwest Philadelphia while they're overwhelmed by the natural history and majestic beauty of Wissahickon Gorge. Be sure to bring your camera. Centered on Wissahickon Gorge and wide-flowing Wissahickon Creek, which runs 7 miles through Fairmount Park, this hike leads you through a historic stone arch to Indian Rock, where the Lenni-Lenape Indians held council until they disappeared from the valley in the mid-eighteenth century. Here you can take a photo of the Kneeling Warrior, a stone statue of Tedyuscung. Explore a 97-foot-long covered bridge built in 1737, or take a break near a small dam that sends water cascading 5 feet over its crest. And be sure to get a photo of the giant tulip poplars—with diameters up to 4 feet, these are some of the largest in the state.

Start: Upper Valley Green parking area
Distance: 5.5-mile loop
Hiking time: About 3 hours
Difficulty: Moderate, due to a few strenuous sections
Schedule: Open year-round
Season: Spring, summer, fall
Trail surface: Gravel paths, rocky footpaths, dirt roads, and paved roads navigating a steep-sided gorge
Elevation gain: 365 feet
Land status: City park
Nearest town: Chestnut Hill

Fees and permits: No fees or permits required for hikers. Free permits are required for bicyclists and equestrians in certain sections of the park; call for details.
Other trail users: Cyclists, joggers, sightseers, equestrians
Canine compatibility: Leashed dogs permitted
Maps: USGS Germantown, PA
Trail contacts: Fairmount Park; (215) 683-0200; www.visitphilly.com/outdoor-activities/philadelphia/fairmount-park/
Fairmount Park Conservancy; (215) 988-9334; www.fairmountpark.org

Finding the trailhead: From Philadelphia, drive west on I-76 to I-476. Drive north on I-476 to the Germantown Avenue exit. Drive east on Germantown Avenue for 6.1 miles to Springfield Avenue. Turn right onto Springfield Avenue and travel 0.7 mile. Bear right on Valley Green Road and drive 0.4 mile to the parking area on your right. *DeLorme: Pennsylvania Atlas & Gazetteer:* Page 82 D2. GPS: N40 3.391' / W75 12.861'

   By train: From Market East Station, take the SEPTA R8 Chestnut Hill line to St. Martin's Station. Now on foot, leave the station and turn left on St. Martin's Lane. Turn right on Springfield Avenue and follow the driving directions to the Valley Green Inn. (It's about a 1-mile walk to the trailhead from the train station.)

The Hike

Fairmount Park stretches from the edge of downtown Philadelphia to the city's northwest corner, and at 4,500 acres it's the largest urban park in any city in the world. Before the land for the park was acquired by the City of Philadelphia in 1868, it was an industrial area composed mostly of mills—paper mills, sawmills, textile mills—run by waterwheels. The mill owners lived on top of the gorge and built roadways and paths so they could walk or take their buggies down to their factories. Many of those trails remain today. In fact, Forbidden Drive, the main thoroughfare that runs on the west side of Wissahickon Creek, was once a popular carriage road.

The world-famous Philadelphia Museum of Art lies at the southern end of Fairmount Park atop the Faire Mount plateau. The mammoth structure, modeled after ancient Greek temples, covers 10 acres and is home to 200 galleries housing an amazing 300,000 works of art—including Van Gogh, Renoir, Picasso, and Rubens, to name but a few. If you visit Philadelphia, this museum is a must-see.

There's a pretty good chance that you've already seen the museum. The 1976 film *Rocky*, written by and starring Sylvester Stallone, contains a now-famous scene where heavyweight contender Rocky Balboa runs up Benjamin Franklin Parkway to the front of the museum, continuing up the museum's ninety-nine steps to the terrace, where he raises both fists and exalts himself to "Gonna Fly Now," the highly recognizable *Rocky* theme song.

Meanwhile, back in the real world, you probably won't hear the *Rocky* theme as you continue your hike; but you may be enraptured by the tumbling waters of Wissahickon Creek as you make your way upstream, past outcrops and along the forested trails that rise up the gorge away from the creek. At the 2.6-mile mark, you have the option of crossing Bell's Mill Road at the crosswalk and walking north a little more than 0.5 mile to the Andorra Nature Center and Tree House Visitor Center.

The Andorra Natural Area is part of the old Andorra Nursery, once the largest nursery on the East Coast. The natural area, which is now a wooded plot that measures about 1 mile wide and a 0.5 mile long, is included in the National Natural Landmark designation that includes the entire Wissahickon Valley. Follow the signs to the visitor center and get a trail map so you can explore the area on your own. If you visit here in spring, you'll see Solomon's seal, skunk cabbage, mayapple, wild ginger, spring beauty, and smooth yellow violet in bloom.

Want to see a 250-year-old cucumber tree and some other enormous trees? Take the Central Loop to Cucumber Meadow. Here you'll find white-tailed deer and a bounty of birds, such as the northern cardinal, American redstart, red-bellied woodpecker, and scarlet tanager. On the way to Tulip Meadow, you'll walk under huge white birches, one more than one hundred years old. On the Azalea Loop you'll pass enormous American beech trees and a white oak that is more than 300 years old.

There are more than 230 species and 110 varieties of deciduous trees, evergreens, and shrubs left over from the nursery. Many of these, like the Japanese maple, are

Boulders along the trail

labeled. On the Big Tree Trail, you'll see some impressive trees—specifically, giant scarlet oaks, black oaks, and white oaks. When you get to the L. M. C. Smith Trail, you'll pass under the Great Beech.

After your visit to the Andorra Natural Area, retrace your steps to Bell's Mill Road and continue the North Loop Hike. *Note:* Your mileage walked to and from the natural area isn't included in the directional cues.

Miles and Directions

0.0 Start from the Upper Valley Green parking area. Walk to a trail at the end of the parking area; continue straight through the trail junction.

0.2 Turn right and begin a short uphill climb.

0.5 Turn right and head toward a trail junction.

0.7 The trail starts downhill as you pass over several water-bars.

1.1 The trail becomes rocky.

1.3 Cross a road and begin a steep climb to the Kneeling Warrior statue.

1.5 The Kneeling Warrior statue is on your left. Continue straight to steep steps that lead to a road.

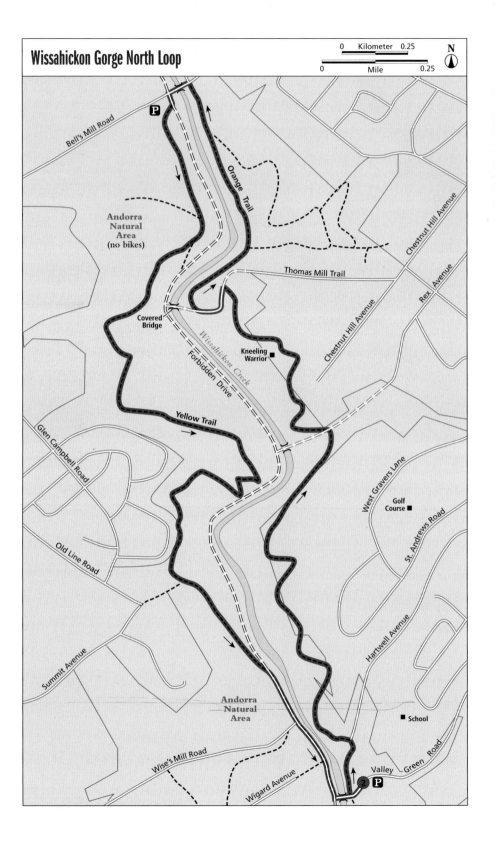

Wissahickon Gorge North Loop

0   Kilometer   0.25

0   Mile   0.25

N

Bell's Mill Road

P

Andorra
Natural
Area
(no bikes)

Orange Trail

Thomas Mill Trail

Covered
Bridge

Wissahickon Creek

Forbidden Drive

Kneeling
Warrior

Chestnut Hill Avenue

Chestnut Hill Avenue

Rex Avenue

Yellow Trail

Glen Campbell Road

Old Line Road

West Gravers Lane

Golf
Course

St. Andrews Road

Summit Avenue

Andorra
Natural
Area

Hartwell Avenue

School

Wise's Mill Road

Valley   Green   Road

Wigard Avenue

2 P

1.9 The trail turns right.

2.0 Turn left and begin descent to Bell's Mill Road.

2.6 Turn left and cross over a bridge to Forbidden Drive. (FYI: A right turn here will access the Andorra Natural Area.)

2.7 Turn left onto the Yellow Trail.

2.9 Turn left and head toward a trail junction.

3.1 Turn right toward a trail junction.

3.5 Turn right and begin an uphill climb to a trail junction.

3.7 Turn left to a trail junction.

4.1 Turn right again toward a bridge.

4.2 Cross the bridge to a trail junction.

4.6 Turn left and descend to Forbidden Drive.

5.2 Turn left, cross the Valley Green Bridge, and retrace your steps to the parking area.

5.5 Arrive back at the parking area.

Local Information

Philadelphia Convention & Visitors Bureau, 1601 Market St., Ste. 200, Philadelphia 19103; (215) 636-3300 or (800) 537-7676; www.discoverphl.com

Local Events/Attractions

Andorra Natural Areas, Tree House Visitor Center; (215) 247-0417; www.fow.org

Morris Arboretum, 100 E. Northwestern Ave., Philadelphia (Chestnut Hill); (215) 247-5777; www.upenn.edu/arboretum

Accommodations

Manayunk Terrace Bed & Breakfast, 3937 Terrace St., Philadelphia; (215) 483-0109; www.manayunkterrace.com

Restaurants

Valley Green Inn, Valley Green Road at Wissahickon, Philadelphia; (215) 247-1730; www.valleygreeninn.com

Organization

Friends of the Wissahickon, Philadelphia; (215) 247-0417; www.fow.org

3 Valley Forge National Historical Park

Visit one of the most important sites in American history. Walk through the encampment where Gen. George Washington and 11,000 of his patriot soldiers spent the harsh winter of 1777–1778 after suffering two crushing defeats in Philadelphia. Highlights are the reconstructed soldiers' huts, the Washington Memorial Chapel, the Memorial Arch, and the statue of Baron Frederic von Steuben, the Prussian military leader who volunteered to change Washington's army from a dissolute band of irregulars into a disciplined fighting machine.

Start: Washington Headquarters parking area
Distance: 6.7-mile lollipop
Hiking time: 3 to 4 hours
Difficulty: Easy, due to the level terrain
Schedule: Open year-round
Season: Spring, summer, fall
Trail surface: Asphalt path through rolling hills
Elevation gain: 432 feet
Land status: National park

Nearest town: King of Prussia
Fees and permits: No fees or permits required
Other trail users: Tourists, cyclists
Canine compatibility: Leashed dogs permitted
Maps: USGS Valley Forge, PA
Trail contacts: Valley Forge National Historical Park, 1400 N. Outer Line Dr., King of Prussia 19406; (610) 783-1000; www.nps.gov/vafo

Finding the trailhead: From Philadelphia, drive west on I-76 to King of Prussia and US 202. Take US 202 south to US 422 and drive west for 1.6 miles to PA 23. Turn left onto PA 23 and pass the Valley Forge Visitor Center. Continue west on PA 23 for 2.4 miles to the Washington Headquarters parking area, on the right. *DeLorme: Pennsylvania Atlas & Gazetteer:* Page 81 D7. GPS: N40 06.140' / W075 27.459'

The Hike

The chain of events that led to the Revolutionary War actually began with the French and Indian War (1754–1763) between France and Great Britain, which was fought mostly throughout the northern colonies. Although Britain won the war, it had accumulated a large debt in the process, which it hoped to pay off by imposing taxes on its American colonies. The first of these taxes came in 1765 with the Stamp Act, which set a levy on legal documents, pamphlets, newspapers, deeds, and even playing cards. The second tax was the Tea Act, which eliminated the customs duty on tea purchased from the East India Company, a British company, while maintaining the duty on teas imported from other countries. Frustrated to the point of revolt, the Tea Act motivated the colonists to hold the famous Boston Tea Party in December 1773.

It was nearly two years, however, before the revolution proper began: April 19, 1775. British troops were ordered to close the Massachusetts Assembly and capture a stockpile of colonial arms. The colonial militia opened fire on the Loyalists, first at Lexington and then at Concord, where the British had retreated. The skirmish was a

These replicas of the huts give visitors a glimpse of the soldier's life.

strong American victory, with the British suffering nearly three times the American losses. In June 1775 the Continental Congress commissioned George Washington to organize and lead a Continental Army.

General Washington's Valley Forge encampment began when Sir William Howe loaded 20,000 British troops onto 250 ships and landed in the upper end of the Chesapeake Bay. His objective was to capture Philadelphia, home of the Continental Congress. Although Congress had fled the city, Washington had little choice but to meet Howe and defend the city. Washington's 11,000 soldiers, outnumbered and poorly prepared, lost the Battle of Brandywine on September 11 and the Battle of Germantown on October 4. Howe and his troops occupied Philadelphia.

With winter setting in, the prospects for more campaigning diminished. Washington withdrew his forces 18 miles northwest of Philadelphia to set up camp at Valley Forge, where one of their first tasks was to build 1,000 huts to fight off the bitter winds and snow. But the huts did little to stave off the hunger and disease the men faced with the onset of winter. The troops' shoes and garments were so tattered that at one point more than 4,000 men were declared unfit for duty. More than 2,000 men died that winter from typhus, typhoid, dysentery, and pneumonia; about half the surviving men deserted.

But as weeks wore on and supplies and equipment and fresh troops trickled in, morale began to lift. Skilled Prussian drillmaster Baron Frederic von Steuben volunteered to drill and train the troops in military tactics. Von Steuben's training resulted in better discipline among the ranks and a renewed sense of ability and confidence in the men.

Gen. George Washington's headquarters at Valley Forge

With spring came the news that the French had signed an alliance with the colonists. Then word came that British troops had pulled out of Philadelphia and were heading to New York. But they would not make it in time. Because of Washington and his ragtag troops' efforts to save Philadelphia, Howe could not move his men north quickly enough. This, in turn, led to the defeat of the British at Saratoga, New York, considered by many scholars as a turning point for the American Revolution.

Hiking this trail is much more than making a simple loop over rolling fields; it will take you back in time, where you can walk through the encampment and immerse yourself in the history and drama of an American landmark. If you were to walk this trail at a normal pace, it might take less than 2 hours. But it's more than likely you'll want to stop, read the educational plaques, and linger at the displays; you may even want to stop for lunch in the picnic area or take a short break on the grass. For these reasons, it would be best to set aside 3 to 4 hours to complete this journey into American history.

Miles and Directions

0.0 Start by walking back to PA 23. Turn left onto the walking path and begin a gentle climb past several monuments and soldier huts on PA 23.

0.7 Cross PA 23. Veer left onto the path and pass the von Steuben statue.

1.2 Come to the Washington Memorial Chapel, on your left.

1.3 Cross a paved road.

2.1 Cross a second road and make a short climb to the visitor center.

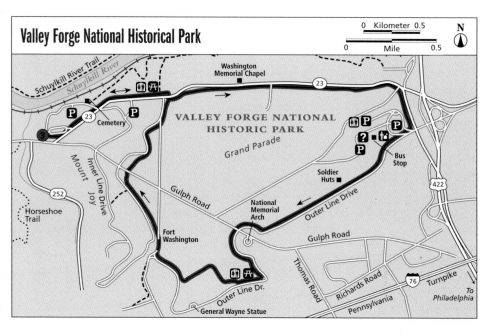

Valley Forge National Historical Park

2.4 The trail veers left past the visitor center and enters an open field.

2.8 Arrive at a cluster of soldier huts.

3.3 Pass the National Memorial Arch on your left. The trail turns right toward Wayne's Woods.

4.0 Arrive at Wayne's Woods and a picnic area.

4.8 Turn right at the fork in the trail.

5.9 Arrive back at the von Steuben statue. Retrace your steps back to the parking area.

6.7 Arrive back at the parking area.

Local Information

Valley Forge Convention and Visitors Bureau, 1000 First Ave., Ste. 101, King of Prussia 19406; (610) 834-1550; www.valleyforge.org

Local Events/Attractions

Schuylkill Center for Environmental Education, 8480 Hagy's Mill Rd., Philadelphia; (215) 482-7300; www.schuylkillcenter.org

Valley Forge Revolutionary 5-Mile Run, April; (610) 834-1550; www.valleyforge.org/revolutionary-run/

Accommodations

Brandywine Creek Campground, 1091 Creek Rd., Downington; (610) 942-9950; www.brandywinecreekcampground.com

4 Skippack Creek Trail

This trail is within the Evansburg State Park in Montgomery County, 6 miles north of Norristown. The 4.7-mile loop runs 2.5 miles along each side of picturesque Skippack Creek. The hike can include a nature trail and visits to the nature center and the Friedt Visitor Center, where you can see an herb garden, root cellar, and well—all built by German Mennonites in the early 1700s.

Start: Parking lot behind the picnic pavilion

Distance: 4.7-mile loop

Hiking time: 2.5 to 3 hours

Difficulty: Easy, due to mostly level terrain

Schedule: Open year-round

Season: Spring, summer, fall

Trail surface: Creek-side path, marshy areas, cliff-side path

Elevation gain: None

Land status: State park

Nearest town: Norristown

Fees and permits: No fees or permits required

Other trail users: Equestrians

Canine compatibility: Leashed dogs permitted

Maps: USGS Collegeville, PA

Trail contacts: Evansburg State Park, 851 May Hall Rd., Collegeville 19426; (610) 409-1150; www.dcnr.state.pa.us/stateparks/findapark/evansburg/

Finding the trailhead: From Allentown, drive south about 20 miles on I-476 and take exit 31. Drive east on PA 63 to PA 363; turn right on PA 363 and drive 8.5 miles to Germantown Pike. Make a right on Germantown Pike and drive 2.7 miles, crossing over Skippack Creek, and turn right onto Skippack Creek Road. Continue on Skippack Creek Road to Mill Road; at the Mill Road intersection, get on May Hall Road and follow it into the park. *DeLorme: Pennsylvania Atlas & Gazetteer.* Page 81 C7. GPS: N40 11.904' / W75 24.256'

The Hike

Evansburg State Park comprises just 3,349 acres, but what it lacks in size it more than makes up for in charm and history. It's hard to believe that in this, one of the state's most urbanized areas, there are pockets of serenity just a few turns off the main thoroughfares.

The centerpiece of this hike—Skippack Creek—is also the park's main attraction. Within the length of the park, the Skippack is wide at spots and, as you can see as you begin this hike, is prone to overflowing its western bank, making the area around the trail marshy and muddy. On the west bank there is also a tangle of debris that gets swept along the stream banks when the creek overflows. The trail, however, remains intact and is well marked and easy to follow.

On the western side of the Skippack, the trail is flat and essentially runs alongside the creek; from this vantage point you can see the cliffs that rise above the eastern bank of the stream. The stone bridge across Skippack Creek on Anders Road is the farthest northern reach of the trail. After crossing the stream you enter a brushy area

The trail at Skippack Creek

then begin your ascent of the cliffs that rise to form the stream's eastern side. There are rock quarries here that make the going a little rough, but this section is short-lived and you are soon back on level ground.

During the summer season, park visitors can visit the Friedt Visitor Center. The Freidts were early German Mennonite settlers who built their house in the early 1700s. The historic building has been kept just as it was when the Freidts lived and worked here. Outside on the grounds, you can explore the original root cellar, the well, and an herb garden. The area around the park was farmland, and soon mills sprang up along Skippack Creek and a highway was built to take their goods to Philadelphia.

Being on a main road to Philadelphia, the area, like nearby Valley Forge, was a resting site for Gen. George Washington and the Continental Army. They camped out along the Skippack before they entered the Battle of Germantown, and after they lost that battle, they retreated back to the banks of the Skippack. This was in the fall of 1777, and as the nights grew colder, the men took to tearing down the wooden fences of the nearby farms and using the wood to build fires to fight off the cold. According to one historical account of this period, after the Continental Army moved through an area, there wasn't a fence standing or a bag of flour to be found.

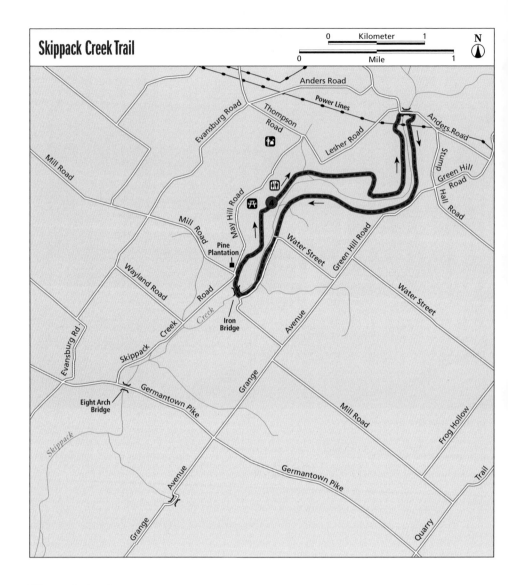

Skippack Creek Trail

0   Kilometer   1

0   Mile   1

N

Miles and Directions

0.0 Start from the parking lot behind the picnic pavilion and walk to the trail beside the restrooms. Cross a wooden bridge over a washout. Follow the white diamond blazes.

0.2 The Nature Trail goes off uphill; you bear right downhill.

0.4 Cross a footbridge. The Horse Trail connects for a few hundred feet and then your trail turns left uphill.

1.5 Pass under the power lines.

1.6 Turn right on Anders Run Road; cross over the stone bridge and turn right.

2.1 Turn left to ascend Hemlock Slope.

3.4 Turn right onto the paved Water Street.

3.9 Turn right across the Iron Bridge; turn right on the other side and cross the old millrace, now just a gulley.

4.0 Pass a pine plantation on your left.

4.7 Arrive back at the parking lot.

Local Information

Valley Forge Convention and Visitors Center, 1000 First Ave., Ste. 101, King of Prussia 19406; (610) 834-1550; www.valleyforge.org

Local Events/Attractions

John James Audubon Center at Mill Grove, 1201 Pawlings Rd., Audubon; (610) 666-5593; http://johnjames.audubon.org

Accommodations

Homestead Campground, 1150 Allentown Rd., Green Lane; (215) 257-7178; www.homesteadcampground.com

5 Ridley Creek State Park

This park is just 16 miles from downtown Philadelphia in Delaware County, but when you explore the colonial setting here, it feels like you're in another country. On this easy 4.3-mile loop hike, you have a chance to visit a circa 1700 Quaker farm, complete with period-dressed interpreters and farm animals. There's also the Tyler Arboretum, home to more than 1,000 varieties of native and exotic trees and shrubs. This hike is great for seniors and children.

Start: Parking lot at Picnic Area 17
Distance: 4.3-mile loop
Hiking time: 2.5 to 3 hours
Difficulty: Moderate, due to short climbs
Schedule: Open year-round
Season: Best in summer
Trail surface: Forest footpath through ravines and along a stream
Elevation gain: 400 feet
Land status: State park

Nearest town: Newton Square
Fees and permits: No fees or permits required
Other trail users: Cross-country skiers
Canine compatibility: Leashed dogs permitted
Maps: USGS Media, PA
Trail contacts: Ridley Creek State Park, 1023 Sycamore Mills Rd., Media 19063; (610) 892-3900; www.dcnr.state.pa.us/stateparks/findapark/ridleycreek/

Finding the trailhead: From Philadelphia, take US 1 to PA 252 (Providence Road) and turn right. Drive for 2.4 miles and turn left on Gradyville Road. Drive for 1.1 miles; bear left onto Sandy Flash Drive South and follow the signs to Picnic Area 17. *DeLorme: Pennsylvania Atlas & Gazetteer:* Page 95 A7. GPS: N40 11.904' / W75 24.256'

The Hike

Visitors to Ridley Creek State Park will be pleased to learn that aside from everything else you'd expect to find in a state park, this park has a fully restored eighteenth-century farm. Actually, the Colonial Pennsylvania Plantation has been in existence since before the Revolutionary War, and in the summer months visitors can tour the farm and watch volunteer reenactors work the farm and perform household chores.

Back in colonial days a small village was built around the mill that operated on Ridley Creek. The village buildings are gone now or used as private residences, but the area that was the hub of activity, now known as Sycamore Mills, has been listed on the National Register of Historic Places. Hikers or bicyclists can get on the paved multiuse trail and make their way to this site. The multiuse trail runs for 5 miles and essentially makes a loop around the center of the park.

In 1966, when the Commonwealth bought the 2,606 acres that were to become the park from the Jeffords family, the purchase included the Jeffords Estate mansion. The mansion was built between 1915 and 1918 in the middle of the property, and

Hikers can take a break at Ridley Creek before climbing out of the gorge.

it remains there today in its current incarnation as the park office. If you feel like exploring the grounds, self-guided tour directions, available in the office, lead you to the pump house, the old springhouse, the pond, the greenhouse, and a cistern where water was stored to a capacity of 20 feet deep. Water was pumped here from the pump house, and when a faucet was turned on in the house or barn, the water flowed out of the cistern and into the water pipes. There is only one pump house, but enough about history. Our hike is on the White Trail, and even though there are other colored trails—such as the Blue, Red, and Yellow—that intersect, connect, and overlap our trail, it's important to remember to follow the white blazes.

There are a few exceptionally pleasant sites on this trail. At a little over 1.0 mile, just after you've crossed the multiuse trail for the first time, there is a clearing next to Ridley Creek where a bench has been placed so that you can eat your lunch or take a few photos of the stream. Another nice site is the wooden footbridge that runs across a feeder stream that empties into Ridley Creek. You get to it at 2.4 miles. The stream is narrow here and noisy as its waters splash against the boulders on their way down into the valley.

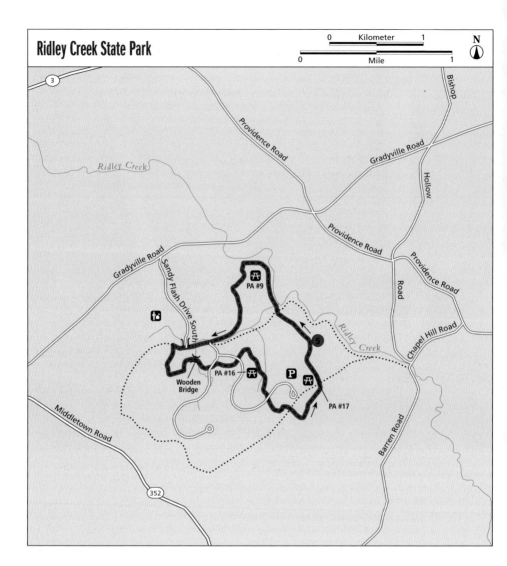

0   Kilometer   1

0   Mile   1

N

Miles and Directions

0.0   Start from Picnic Area 17. Walk to the multiuse trail and turn left to go downhill.

0.2   Turn left onto the White Trail (which is the trail we'll be following). The trail is also blazed yellow, but the Yellow Trail turns off to the left as the White Trail continues straight.

0.3   The Red Trail joins the White Trail from the left.

0.4   Cross the Yellow Trail.

0.8   Turn right onto the multiuse trail; then turn left onto the White Trail toward Ridley Creek.

1.2   The trail turns left, away from the stream, and you begin an uphill climb.

1.6   Arrive at Picnic Area 9. Turn right onto the paved road and follow the white markings painted on the very right-hand side of the road.

1.7 Turn left onto the trail at the white arrow painted on the road. Enter the forest.

1.9 Cross the Yellow Trail.

2.0 Turn right onto the multiuse trail and pass through a culvert under Sandy Flash Drive. Immediately after the culvert, turn left and begin an uphill climb. At two confusing trail intersections, turn left and then left again.

2.4 Cross a stream on a wooden bridge. Turn right and then cross the road.

2.6 Turn left, downhill, then right at the white blaze. Cross Sandy Flash Drive and arrive at Picnic Area 16; walk behind the restrooms.

3.4 Cross the road and turn left at a set of steps.

3.6 Turn left at a yellow arrow that points to the right, toward the Tyler Arboretum.

3.7 Turn left onto the multiuse trail.

4.3 Arrive back at Picnic Area 17.

Local Information

Brandywine Conference & Visitors Bureau, 1501 N. Providence Rd., Media 19063; (610) 565-3679 or (800) 343-3983; www.brandywinecountry.com

Local Events/Attractions

Longwood Gardens, 1001 Longwood Rd., Kennett Square; (610) 388-1000 or (800) 737-5500; http://longwoodgardens.org

Tyler Arboretum, 515 Painter Rd., Media; (610) 566-9134; www.tylerarboretum .org

Accommodations

Organized group tenting: Qualified organized groups can use the 120-person area from April to October. A restroom with flush toilets but no showers is available. Call (888) PA-PARKS (888-727-2757) for required reservations.

Organizations

Colonial Pennsylvania Plantation, 3900 N. Sandy Flash Dr., Newtown Square 19073; (610) 566-1725; www.colonialplantation.org

6 French Creek State Park

After you finish this 6.0-mile loop, you can visit historic Hopewell Furnace, a once-thriving industrial plantation built on the border of Berks and Chester Counties in 1771. See a restored ironworker's village, complete with implements and tools, sheds, furniture, and houses.

Start: Hopewell Lake Boat Launch parking lot
Distance: 6.0-mile loop
Hiking time: About 3 hours
Difficulty: Moderate, due to lengthy climbs
Schedule: Open year-round
Season: Spring, summer, fall
Trail surface: Park roads, typical forest footpath, stony washouts
Elevation gain: 350 feet
Land status: State park

Nearest town: Reading
Fees and permits: No fees or permits required
Other trail users: Equestrians, mountain bikers
Canine compatibility: Leashed dogs permitted
Maps: USGS Elverson, PA
Trail contacts: French Creek State Park, 843 Park Rd., Elverson 19520; (610) 582-9680; www.dcnr.state.pa.us/stateparks/findapark/frenchcreek

Finding the trailhead: From Harrisburg, drive east on I-76 about 50 miles and take exit 298. Drive east on PA 23 through Elverson and turn left onto PA 345. Drive north on PA 345 for 2.5 miles then turn left into the park at its south entrance. Drive 0.5 mile past the park office; turn right at the Hopewell Lake Boat Launch and drive to the parking lot. *DeLorme: Pennsylvania Atlas & Gazetteer:* Page 81 C4. GPS: N40 11.895' / W75 47.430'

The Hike

French Creek State Park is one of the top state parks in the system. Within its 7,475 acres there are 35 miles of well-marked and well-maintained hiking trails. One connector trail will even lead you to the Hopewell Furnace National Historic Site. At Hopewell Furnace you will learn how southeastern Pennsylvania—because of its combined natural resources of water power, iron ore, and abundant timber—played an important role in the fledgling colonies defeating the British in the Revolutionary War.

The iron ore was combined with the also-abundant mineral limestone and smelted into iron. The blast furnaces used a bellows system and charcoal to produce heats up to 3,000°F to forge the iron ore into iron. Local timber was harvested and stacked on pads that were then covered with dirt and left to smolder and make charcoal. The furnace at Hopewell used 800 bushels of charcoal a day.

When the war began, Hopewell owner and ironmaster Mark Bird switched from making stove plates to making cannons and shot for the Continental Army and Navy. After the war and throughout its life span, Hopewell suffered one setback after another as the technology to develop iron and steel shifted away from charcoal furnaces and the labor-intensive processes that accompanied them.

Hopewell Furnace and this restored homestead are National Historic Sites.

Hopewell did have one heyday, from 1816 to 1831, when it produced the popular Hopewell cast-iron stoves. But by the 1840s the flame of prosperity was extinguished for the final time.

The restoration of Hopewell Furnace reflects that period in the 1840s. Many of the buildings, houses, and barns stand today as they did then, and in summer reenactors lead visitors through the grounds and explain how the ironworkers' jobs were done, how the families lived on the compound, and how other workers did tasks that supported the ironworkers and their families.

There are also ongoing events throughout the year: Sheep Shearing Day in May, Fueling the Furnace Day in August, Harvest Time Day in September, Family Social Day in October, and Iron Plantation Christmas in December.

Our hike is on the Boone Trail. The loop was designed to allow hikers to see for themselves the highlights of this park, such as the swimming pool, Hopewell Lake and spillway, the campground, the group camping area, and the natural beauty of the hills surrounding the park proper.

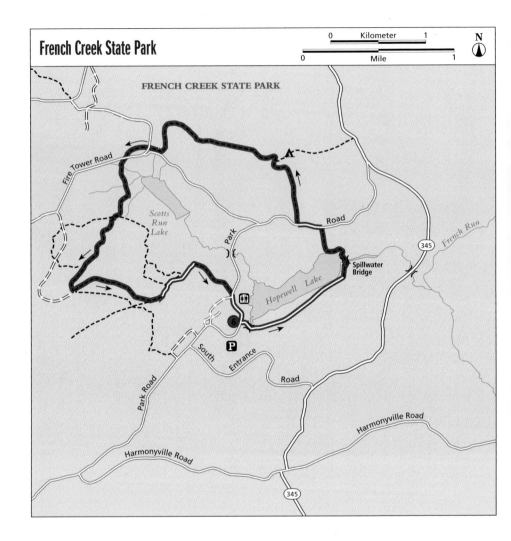

French Creek State Park

FRENCH CREEK STATE PARK

Fire Tower Road

Scotts Run Lake

Park Road

Road

345

French Run

Spillwater Bridge

Hopewell Lake

South Entrance Road

Park Road

Harmonyville Road

Harmonyville Road

345

Miles and Directions

0.0 Start from the far-left, back side of the parking lot. Walk through the opening in the trees and cross a bridge over a feeder stream. Turn left and follow the blue blazes. Pass through the picnic area and past the swimming pool.

0.7 Turn left at the corner of the lake.

0.8 Arrive at the spillway of the dam. Follow the blue blazes around the lake.

1.2 Turn right away from the lake and arrive at a trail intersection. Continue straight, following the blue blazes.

1.3 Turn left at Park Road.

1.5 Cross Park Road.

1.8 Cross the campground access road.

1.9 Pass the Green Trail and turn left, following the blue blazes.

3.0 Take a hairpin turn to the right.

3.2 Cross Fire Tower Road.

3.6 Cross Fire Tower Road a second time.

4.0 Arrive at an intersection with the Yellow Trail. Turn right and follow the blue blazes.

4.6 Trail turns left.

5.7 Turn right onto Park Road; then turn left on the lake access road.

6.0 Arrive back at the parking lot.

Local Information

Greater Reading Convention & Visitors Bureau, 2525 N. 12th St., Reading 19605; (610) 375-4085 or (800) 443-6610; www.gogreaterreading.com

Local Events/Attractions

Hopewell Furnace National Historic Site, 2 Mark Bird Ln., Elverson; (610) 582-8773; www.nps.gov/hofu

Daniel Boone Homestead, 400 Daniel Boone Rd., Birdsboro; (610) 582-4900; www.danielboonehomestead.org

Campgrounds

French Creek State Park, 843 Park Rd., Elverson; (610) 582-9680; (888) 727-2757 (camping information and reservations); www.dcnr.state.pa.us/stateparks/findapark/frenchcreek. Camping, cabins, group tent camping; open year-round.

7 Susquehannock State Park

The park overlooks the Lower Susquehanna River in southern Lancaster County. There are just 5 miles of hiking within this 224-acre park, but the Bureau of Parks includes this tiny park on its list of the best-kept secrets of the Pennsylvania State Park System. Highlights include panoramic, cliff-side views of the Susquehanna River and an optional visit to the Lock No. 12 Historic Area.

Start: Parking lot by the park office
Distance: 3.5-mile loop
Hiking time: About 2.5 hours
Difficulty: Moderate, due to short, steep climbs
Schedule: Open year-round
Season: Spring, summer, fall
Trail surface: Forest footpath, old roads, creek-side path
Elevation gain: 720 feet

Land status: State park
Nearest town: Lancaster
Fees and permits: No fees or permits required
Other trail users: Equestrians, tent campers
Canine compatibility: Leashed dogs permitted
Maps: USGS Holtwood, PA
Trail contacts: Susquehannock State Park, 1880 Park Dr., Drumore 17518; (717) 252-1134; www.dcnr.state.pa.us/stateparks/findapark/susquehanna/

Finding the trailhead: From Lancaster, drive south on US 222/PA 272 for approximately 15 miles to Buck. In Buck, turn right onto PA 372; drive west for 5 miles and turn left at the Susquehannock State Park sign. Drive 4 miles south on Susquehannock Drive and turn right at the sign for the park. Drive another 0.8 mile to the park office parking lot. *DeLorme: Pennsylvania Atlas & Gazetteer:* Page 93 B7. GPS: N39 48.362' / W76 17.009'

The Hike

Susquehannock State Park is small and a million miles from nowhere, but it's well worth a visit to do this hike, especially in mid-June to early July, when the rhododendron is in bloom. This hike takes you through miles of rhododendron, alongside a bubbling mountain stream, and out onto cliff-side viewing platforms that rise 380 feet above the Susquehanna River as it makes its way from Pennsylvania into Maryland. In Maryland the river is dammed and becomes the Conowingo Reservoir, which, aside from the hydroelectric energy it creates, provides recreational opportunities for pleasure boaters and anglers.

From the overlooks you can see a number of islands in the river. One of these, Mount Johnson Island, was the world's first bald eagle sanctuary. Eagles and other raptors still inhabit the islands and can be seen with the platform viewer or binoculars, cruising above the water in search of their next meal. At Hawk Point Overlook educational plaques explain the life of eagles to the novice.

Having a peculiar place-name in Pennsylvania is just about par for the course, but here in Lancaster County, place-names reach a new plateau, with names such as

The Hawk Point Overlook gives visitors a breathtaking view of the Susquehanna River as it makes its way into Maryland.   DEBRA YOUNG

Bird-in-Hand, Paradise, and Intercourse. The name Susquehannock is derived from the term "Sasquesahanough," which was given to Capt. John Smith by his Algonquian-speaking interpreter. Smith first encountered the Susquehannocks, part of the Iroquois Nation, in 1608; it is not known if this group of Indians called themselves Susquehannocks or not. But the name, which means "people at the falls," stuck because they lived near the Susquehanna River.

For modern history buffs there are two sites to explore after you've finished your hike and before you leave the area. The Landis House was built in 1850 and incorporates the craftsmanship of the era in its slate roof and the laid native stone and cement coving construction of its exterior. Inside, the floors are plank and the walls are plastered with a mixture of horsehair and sand.

Because of its proximity to the Susquehanna River, the house became a haven for runaway slaves from the South who made their escape up the river. The house's owner, Jacob Schoff, sheltered the runaways, and his home became one of many riverside stops on the Underground Railroad.

When you leave the park, drive north on Susquehannock Drive, turn left on PA 372, and cross the river on the Norman Wood Bridge. As soon as you get to the other side, look for the sign reading "Lock 12 Historic Site" and turn right into the parking lot.

Lock 12 is one of the most well-preserved locks of the old Susquehanna and Tidewater Canal, which was built between 1836 and 1839. It was used for commerce

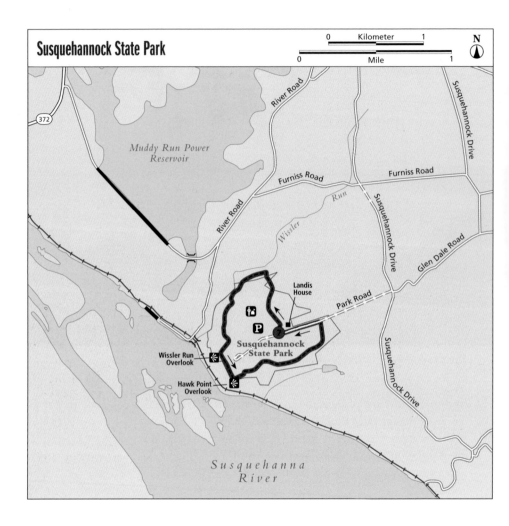

Muddy Run Power Reservoir

Landis House

Susquehannock State Park

Wissler Run Overlook

Hawk Point Overlook

Susquehanna River

between the Harrisburg area and Chesapeake Bay. Nearby, several hundred feet up Anderson's Run, is a restored double limekiln and the remains of a sawmill and its dam, pond, and millrace.

Miles and Directions

0.0 Start from the park office parking lot, and walk between the park office and the Landis House. Pass a hand pump for drinking water and get on the red-blazed Rhododendron Trail.

0.3 Turn right onto the Five Points Trail and cross a feeder stream.

0.6 Turn left onto the Five Points Trail.

0.9 Turn left at Wissler Run.

1.0 Turn right onto the Rhododendron Trail.

1.2 The trail turns left and uphill, away from Wissler Run.

1.6 The Rhododendron Trail turns left; the Phites Eddy Trail goes straight.

1.7 Turn right onto the Fire Trail and walk to the Wissler Run Overlook. Take the Overlook Trail to Hawk Point Overlook and continue on the Overlook Trail.

2.4 Turn right onto the Landis Trail.

2.9 Turn right onto the Chimney Trail.

3.2 Turn left onto Park Road.

3.5 Arrive back at the parking lot.

Local Information

Pennsylvania Dutch Convention & Visitors Bureau, 501 Greenfield Rd., Lancaster 17601; (800) 723-8824; www.padutchcountry.com

Local Events/Attractions

The Amish Village, 199 Hartman Bridge Rd., Ronks; (717) 687-8511; theamish village.net

Campgrounds

Susquehannock State Park, 1880 Park Dr., Drumore; (717) 252-1134; www.dcnr .state.pa.us/stateparks/findapark/susquehanna/. Qualified adult and youth groups may reserve space in the organized group tenting area for overnight use. The organized group campsites can accommodate groups up to a maximum of 300 people.

Tucquan Park Family Campground, 917 River Rd., Holtwood; (717) 284-2156; http://camptucquanpark.com

Restaurants

Good 'N Plenty, Route 896, Smokestown; (717) 394-7111; www.goodnplenty.com

8 The Pinnacle

Walk the Appalachian Trail for spectacular views of Hawk Mountain, the Lehigh Valley, and Blue Rocks. Many Appalachian Trail thru-hikers claim the views at The Pinnacle are the best views on the Pennsylvania stretch of the Appalachian Trail. On this hike you'll get a vigorous workout climbing up the rocky path to the top then get a reprieve as you make a gentle descent on a wide dirt road. This is an extremely popular trail.

Start: Parking area at the Hamburg Reservoir
Distance: 8.7-mile loop
Hiking time: About 5 hours
Difficulty: Moderate, due to the steep, rocky climbs
Schedule: Open year-round
Season: Spring, summer, fall
Trail surface: Rocky forest footpaths and abandoned roads following forested mountain trails and mountain streams to a ridgetop boulder outcrop
Elevation gain: 868 feet

Land status: Private and state game lands
Nearest town: Hamburg
Fees and permits: No fees or permits required
Other trail users: Thru-hikers, cyclists, hunters (in season)
Canine compatibility: Leashed dogs permitted
Maps: USGS Hamburg, PA
Trail contacts: Pennsylvania Game Commission, Southeast Region, 448 Snyder Rd., Reading 19605; (610) 926-3136; www.portal .state.pa.us/portal/server.pt?open=514&objl D=562957&mode=2

Finding the trailhead: From Allentown, drive west on I-78 for about 17 miles to exit 35. Drive north on PA 143 for 0.9 mile to Mountain Road. Turn left onto Mountain Road and drive 2.4 miles to Reservoir Road. Turn right onto Reservoir Road and drive to the parking area. *DeLorme: Pennsylvania Atlas & Gazetteer.* Page 66 D3. GPS: N40 35.012' / W75 56.517'

The Hike

Many Appalachian Trail (AT) thru-hikers contend that Pennsylvania is one of the rockiest sections on the entire trail. Climbing up to The Pinnacle will give you an idea of just what they're talking about. It's also said that the deep forests of Pennsylvania make hikers feel as though they are out in the boonies, miles from the nearest town, when all along they're only a few miles from civilization. You'll get a taste of that here as well. Actually, you're just a few miles from I-78 and all the fast food, gasoline, and glory that comes with the average interstate outpost.

This trek along the AT affords some outstanding views of Hawk Mountain, the Lehigh Valley, and Blue Rocks, as well as opportunities to view hawks riding the wind currents along Kittatinny Ridge. The views from The Pinnacle are said to be among the best of those found along the Pennsylvania stretch of the AT. The climb up the rocky path to the top is strenuous, but the descent along the wide dirt road will give you time to recoup. Be mindful that mountain bikers are allowed on the dirt road section of the hike (the AT is hiker-only).

Many experienced hikers see this view from Blue Mountain ridge as the best in the state.

There's an optional side trip you can take before or after this hike that you won't want to miss—even if you have to stay overnight. The Hawk Mountain Sanctuary, just a few miles north of The Pinnacle, is one of the most popular sites in the country for viewing raptor migration. And, as is often the case with other natural phenomena in Pennsylvania, the mountains play a major role.

Raptors (also known as birds of prey) are easy to spot because they don't flap their wings like smaller birds. They soar, and to do that they need to catch rising air currents. In the Ridge and Valley Province of central Pennsylvania, the prevailing wind is from the northwest. When that wind hits the parallel ridges that run southwest to northeast, it's deflected upward, creating considerable updrafts. Hawk Mountain is located on Kittatinny Ridge, the southernmost ridge of the Ridge and Valley Province. The ridge is located just before the Great Valley, a broad flatland to the south. Raptors gather above Kittatinny Ridge to catch an updraft that will send them on their way, soaring south across the valley.

The sanctuary was founded in 1934 when Rosalie Edge, an environmental activist from New York State, happened to see a photo of hundreds of dead raptors killed by hunters at Hawk Mountain. In those days raptors were not protected by federal law; in fact, many hunters who came to Hawk Mountain thought they were performing a

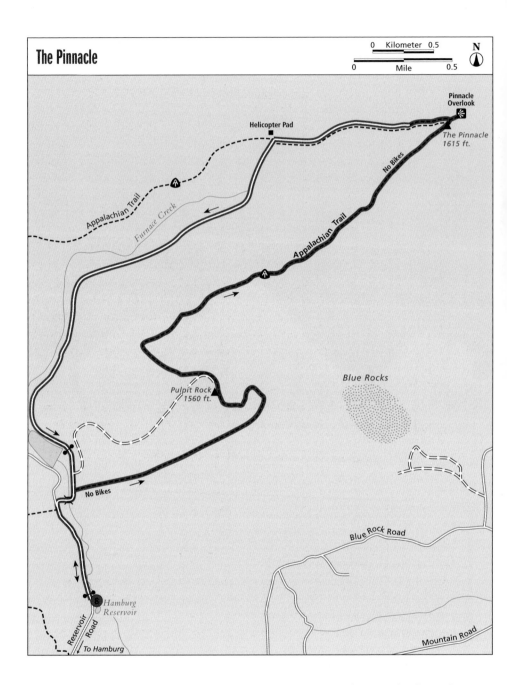

worthy service. Edge got involved, and Hawk Mountain soon became the first refuge in the world to protect birds of prey.

Since its inception, Hawk Mountain Sanctuary has kept a census of migrating raptors—the longest-running raptor census in the world. The season begins August 15 and continues for four months because migrating periods vary by species. Bald eagles and ospreys migrate early, in August and September, while golden eagles and goshawks cross the ridge in November. Visitors can spot an endless variety of hawks, including the northern goshawk, Cooper's hawk, sharp-shinned hawk, rough-legged hawk, and red-shouldered hawk. There are also plenty of ospreys, peregrine falcons, merlins, and American kestrels to be seen.

The official raptor migration count is conducted from the North Lookout, which is at an elevation of 1,521 feet. Aside from the birds, you'll discover a breathtaking view from North Lookout stretching 70 miles across the Ridge and Valley Province. During peak migration season, the trail leading to North Lookout can be crowded. On the busiest days it may be best to try the South Lookout—less popular and less crowded. The trail to the South Lookout is only 300 yards long and is wheelchair accessible.

Hawk Mountain Sanctuary receives 80,000 visitors a year from all over the world. Look for the impressive visitor center that contains a raptor museum, a gift shop with a variety of natural history books, and an art gallery. A network of hiking trails and paths lead visitors to the same outcroppings where hunters once stood and slaughtered these birds as they soared by. Today these ledges are filled with birders, amateur naturalists, and professional ornithologists from all over the world. In fact, this gathering of raptor fans has earned the sanctuary the nickname the Crossroads of Naturalists.

Miles and Directions

0.0 Start at the Hamburg Reservoir parking area. Walk through the gate to the map board and pick up the blue blazes. Continue on the gravel road, which for a while is also the white-blazed Appalachian Trail.

0.4 Turn right and cross the bridge over Furnace Creek. On the other side bear right, following the white blazes.

0.8 Come to a trail intersection and turn right onto an abandoned road.

1.9 Pass the blue-blazed side trail to the Blue Rocks Campground.

2.2 The trail turns right onto a rocky trail with stone steps.

2.4 Arrive at Pulpit Rock.

4.2 Pass a yellow-blazed side trail.

4.5 Arrive at the blue-blazed trail to the right that leads about 150 yards to the Pinnacle Overlook. Retrace your steps back to the Appalachian Trail and keep to the right.

5.0 Pick up an abandoned road.

6.4 Arrive at the helicopter pad. Continue across the grassy area and turn left onto the dirt road, following the blue blazes.

7.8 Pass the Hamburg Reservoir, on your right.

8.0 Pass a service road, on your left.

8.3 Arrive at an intersection with the Appalachian Trail. Turn right, crossing Furnace Creek; retrace your steps on the gravel road.

8.7 Arrive back at the parking area.

Local Information

Berks County Visitors Bureau, 2525 N. 12th St., Reading 19605; (610) 375-4085; www.gogreaterreading.com

Local Events/Attractions

Hawk Mountain Sanctuary, 1700 Hawk Mountain Rd., Kempton; (610) 756-6000; www.hawkmountain.org

To get to Hawk Mountain Sanctuary from the Pinnacle Trailhead, return to I-78. Drive 6 miles west on I-78 to exit 29B. Take PA 61 and drive north 4 miles to the town of Molino. In Molino turn right onto PA 895 and drive east 2 miles to the village of Drehersville and the Hawk Mountain Sanctuary sign. Turn right onto Hawk Mountain Road and drive 2 miles up the mountain to the sanctuary parking lot, on your right.

Accommodations

Hawk Mountain Bed & Breakfast, 221 Stony Run Valley Rd., Kempton; (610) 756-4224; hawkmountainbb.com

Campgrounds

Mountain Springs Camping Resort, 3450 Mountain Rd., Hamburg; (610) 488-6859; www.mountainspringscampground.com

9 Swatara State Park

Set this hike aside to do after it rains and all your favorite trails are muddy. Except for a 0.1-mile stretch on a shale road, the trail surfaces here are paved. This hike is suitable for all ages. And, although it is almost a 4-mile loop, you could walk, say, to the historic Waterville Bridge and never be farther than a mile or so from your vehicle. Other highlights include the stone ruins of a flooded-out nineteenth-century dam and the abandoned canal system that was connected to the dam.

Start: Intersection of PA 443 and Moonshine Road
Distance: 3.9-mile loop
Hiking time: About 2 hours
Difficulty: Easy, due to the flat terrain
Schedule: Open year-round
Season: Spring, summer, fall
Trail surface: Mostly paved roads and an abandoned railroad grade
Elevation gain: 529 feet

Land status: State park
Nearest town: Pine Grove
Fees and permits: No fees or permits required
Other trail users: Backpackers, cyclists
Canine compatibility: Leashed dogs permitted
Maps: USGS Indiantown Gap, PA
Trail contacts: Swatara State Park, c/o Memorial Lake State Park, Grantville 17028; (717) 865-6470; www.dcnr.state.pa.us/stateparks/findapark/swatara/

Finding the trailhead: From Harrisburg, take I-81 North for 19 miles to the junction with I-78. Bear left at the junction with I-78 and continue on I-81 North for about 9 miles to exit 100. Drive west on PA 443 exactly 8.2 miles to the intersection with Moonshine Road and the abandoned section of Old State Road, on your left. Park on your left by the access gate across abandoned Old State Road. *DeLorme: Pennsylvania Atlas & Gazetteer:* Page 79 A5. GPS: N40 28.940' / W76 33.001'
Note: There's an optional hike (described below), bicycle ride, or car ride to a popular fossil pit within the park.

The Hike

The highlight of this hike is the historic cast-iron Waterville Bridge, originally built across Little Pine Creek in Lycoming County in 1890. In the 1980s the Pennsylvania Department of Transportation determined that the bridge was too narrow for safe automobile travel. It was dismantled, repaired, and reconstructed at its present site so that day hikers and Appalachian Trail thru-hikers could cross Swatara Creek without having to use an automobile bridge.

The modern history of this region began in the early 1800s, when anthracite coal was discovered. The coal needed to be exported, so the Union Canal was built to connect the Schuylkill and Susquehanna Rivers. (A branch of the Union Canal was built to run from Lebanon to Pine Grove, through what is now Swatara State Park.) In 1830 a dam and 672-acre reservoir were built where the Waterville Bridge stands

Remains of the Union Canal that once connected the Schuylkill and Susquehanna Rivers

today. The dam was washed away in the Flood of 1862 and has never been rebuilt; you can check out the remnants of the dam and canal locks on the bank of Swatara Creek. The stone ruins under I-81 are remains of the canal.

After the canal came the railroad, which ran through what's now the park on the north side of Swatara Creek. After the railroad's heyday, the state acquired the land, created the park, and built the multiuse trail on the abandoned railroad bed. To complete the park, the Department of Conservation and Natural Resources (DCNR)—the agency that runs the state parks—has plans to build a new dam near the location of the original dam. However, DCNR is getting pressure from environmental groups concerned that the land below the dam could flood, so the project is

THE GEOLOGIC CALENDAR

There are four distinct intervals used to establish the Earth's age. The longest intervals are eons, which are subdivided into eras. Each era can be divided into periods, and each period is divided into epochs.

on hold. A compromise is expected, most likely in the form of a considerably smaller dam.

Despite the fact that Swatara State Park is classified as "undeveloped," there's still plenty to do here. Swatara Creek is a big, brawny creek with hemlocks and deciduous trees growing right up to its banks. There are a number of put-in spots along the way, making the creek an excellent spot to canoe through the picturesque setting. Best of all, because the park is not well known, there's little chance of the creek being crowded. Canoeists can paddle in virtual solitude.

Anglers can fish Swatara Creek for warm-water species like smallmouth bass and panfish. Trout Run is a (stocked) cold-water trout stream that empties into Swatara Creek. There are also a few smaller streams with populations of native brook trout. Non-powered boats are permitted on the creek as long as they have one of the following permits: a state park launching permit, state park mooring permit, or current Pennsylvania boat registration. (**Note:** There's no park office on-site. The park office is located at Memorial Lake State Park. To get there, take exit 85 off I-81 and drive north on PA 934 for about 1 mile, following the signs.)

The multiuse trail runs 10 miles, from Lickdale at exit 90 off I-81 to exit 100 at Pine Grove. Swatara State Park ends before the trail goes under I-81, but the trail continues.

As for the future of the park, the new dam was to be built about 700 feet upstream from the Waterville Bridge. In preparation for that dam, the roads used on this hike are closed to traffic. If and when the dam is built, the abandoned roads on the north side of Swatara Creek will be underwater. In the meantime, all the roads along this hike (within the park) are closed to traffic except for DCNR vehicles.

Option:

Here's a popular loop ride within the park: Start at the Waterville Bridge and ride east on the trail for about 5 miles to Swopes Valley Road; return on the abandoned Old State Road. This route gives riders (or hikers) a chance to visit the Suedberg Fossil Pit, a terrific side trip. (To get to the fossil pit by car, drive east about 4 miles on PA 443 to Swopes Valley Road. Turn right on Swopes Valley Road and cross over Swatara Creek; then turn right on Old State Road, which is a dirt road at this point, and drive about 0.25 mile to the pit on your left.)

The fossil pit provides evidence that 375 million years ago—during the Middle Devonian period of the Paleozoic era—a shallow ocean covered this area. The fossils found here are casts and molds of marine animals with names like asteroids, trilobites, brachiopods, gastropods, cephalopods, and pelecypods. While a typical fossil is the remains of a prehistoric plant or an animal buried and preserved in sedimentary rock, here at the Suedberg site the organisms' original shells were buried and dissolved by groundwater, leaving only impressions or molds. Some impressions were filled with new deposits, creating a replica of the shell, or what are called casts. Fossils range in age from the 3.5-billion-year-old blue-green algae cyanobacteria to 10,000-year-old animals from the last ice age.

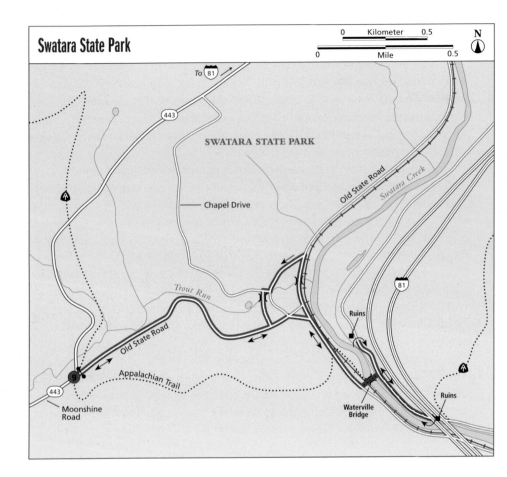

Swatara State Park

0 — Kilometer — 0.5
0 — Mile — 0.5
N

SWATARA STATE PARK

To 81

443

Old State Road

Swatara Creek

Chapel Drive

Trout Run

81

Ruins

Old State Road

Appalachian Trail

9

443

Waterville
Bridge

Ruins

Moonshine
Road

Miles and Directions

0.0 Start from the access gate on PA 443 at the intersection with Moonshine Road and abandoned Old State Road.

0.6 The trail turns left.

0.8 Stay to the right at a fork in the trail.

1.1 Turn right onto the paved road.

1.3 Turn left onto the Waterville Bridge and cross over Swatara Creek. On the other side, turn left onto the trail walkway.

1.4 Turn left onto the paved road and walk past the bulletin board. Note the stone ruins on your left. Turn left into an open area alongside Swatara Creek; you'll find more stone ruins on your left.

1.5 Leave the open area and turn left onto the paved road. Note the second ruins on your left. Turn around and walk back toward Waterville Bridge.

1.6 Pass Waterville Bridge on your right.

1.9 Arrive at the stone ruins under I-81. Turn around and retrace your steps back to the Waterville Bridge.

2.1 Cross Waterville Bridge and turn right onto the trail.

2.3 Stay to the right at the fork in the trail.

2.4 Pass a woods trail on your right. Pass an intersection with abandoned Old State Road.

2.6 Cross Trout Run on an old concrete bridge.

2.7 Arrive at open area on your right (this is where Greenpoint Station was located). Turn left at the intersection.

3.0 Turn left onto a shale road and cross Trout Run a second time on an old concrete bridge.

3.1 Pass under a power line and turn right onto abandoned Old State Road.

3.9 Arrive back at the access gate.

Local Information

Schuylkill County Visitors Bureau, Union Station Building, One Progress Circle, Ste. 100, Pottsville 17901; (570) 622-7700 or (800) 765-7282; www.schuylkill.org

Local Events/Attractions

Bloomsburg Fair, last week in September, Bloomsburg; (570) 784-4949; www.bloomsburgfair.com

Campgrounds

Echo Valley Campground, 52 Camp Rd., Tremont; (570) 695-3659; www.echovalleycamp.com

Honorable Mentions

Southeast Pennsylvania

Here are five great hikes in the Southeast region that didn't make the A-list this time around but deserve recognition. Check them out and let us know what you think. You may decide that one or more of these hikes deserves higher status in future editions, or you may have a hike of your own that merits some attention.

A John Heinz National Wildlife Refuge: Lagoon Loop

Part of 1,200-acre Tinicum Marsh, the John Heinz National Wildlife Refuge is the largest remaining freshwater tidal wetland in Pennsylvania. The refuge seems wild and remote, yet it's less than a mile from the Philadelphia International Airport and just a few miles from downtown. The hike is an 8.9-mile loop on a wide gravel path that circles the Impound Area. Allow 3 to 4 hours or more; there's plenty of wildlife viewing here. (See Hike 1.)

From Philadelphia, drive south on I-95 to the Bartram Avenue exit. Drive west on Bartram Avenue to 84th Street. Turn right onto 84th Street and drive to Lindbergh Boulevard. Turn left onto Lindbergh Boulevard and follow the signs to the John Heinz Visitor Contact Station; park in the lot just beyond the visitor center. For more information call the visitor contact station at (215) 365-3118. *DeLorme: Pennsylvania Atlas & Gazetteer*: Page 96 A1

B Wissahickon Gorge South Loop

Wissahickon Gorge is located in Fairmount Park in Northwest Philadelphia. (See Hike 2.) There are two hike options: You can hike a 5.5-mile loop by following Forbidden Drive downstream and returning on the trail closest to Wissahickon Creek; or you can do a 9.0-mile loop that also begins downstream but follows a network of connecting trails that take you farther away from Wissahickon Creek. Either way, you'll see plenty of natural and American history.

From Philadelphia, drive west on I-76 to I-476. Drive north on I-476 to the Germantown Avenue exit. Drive east on Germantown Avenue for 6.1 miles to Springfield Avenue. Turn right onto Springfield Avenue and travel 0.7 mile. Bear right on Valley Green Road and drive 0.4 mile to the parking area, on your right. For more information call the Fairmount Park Rangers at (215) 685-2172. *DeLorme: Pennsylvania Atlas & Gazetteer*: Page 82 D2

C Delaware Canal State Park

This park, in Upper Black Eddy (Bucks County), is one of scores of access points to the 60-mile-long Delaware Canal. Design your own hike and walk alongside the last remaining intact canal system of the great towpath-building era of the early and mid-nineteenth century. Examine twenty-three locks, ten aqueducts, four river islands, locktenders' houses, spillways, and historical houses. Learn how barges carried 33 million tons of anthracite coal on the canal.

From Easton, drive south on PA 611 into Bucks County. Continue on PA 611 for about 5 miles past the county line to PA 32. Turn left onto PA 32 and drive about 8 miles to Upper Black Eddy and the park office, which is right at the canal. For more information call the Delaware Canal State Park at (610) 982-5560. *DeLorme: Pennsylvania Atlas & Gazetteer.* Page 68 D3

D Jacobsburg Environmental Education Center

Jacobsburg is a state park situated on the eastern fringes of the Lehigh Valley. There are more than 12 miles of hiking trails in the park; loop hikes can be designed to run from 4.0 to about 8.5 miles, depending on how energetic you feel that day. There are two highlights: a highly rated environmental center (one of only four) run by the Department of Conservation and Natural Resources and the Jacobsburg Historical District, which showcases the weapons manufactured here by the Henry family and used in the Revolutionary and Civil Wars.

From Allentown, follow US 22 to PA 33. Drive north on PA 33 to the Belfast exit. Turn left on Henry Road and drive 1.1 miles to Jacobsburg Road, then another 1.2 miles to Belfast Road. Turn left onto Belfast Road and continue for 0.7 mile to the parking area on the right. For more information call the Jacobsburg Environmental Education Center, Wind Gap, at (610) 746-2801. *DeLorme: Pennsylvania Atlas & Gazetteer.* Page 68 B1

E Middle Creek Wildlife Management Area

Middle Creek Wildlife Area is 6,000 acres of state game lands in Lancaster and Lebanon Counties, north of Lititz. The area is a great spot for viewing wildlife in its natural habitat: More than 250 bird species have been noted here. There is a network of trails, a lake, picnic area, visitor center, and theater. A map of the trails and a brochure is available at the visitor center. Suggestion: Visit the MCWMA from January to March and you'll see 50,000 or more greater snow geese on their winter migration. These geese are unusually large, weighing up to 30 pounds, with a 4- to 5-foot wingspan.

From Reading, drive south on US 222 to the US 322 exit near Ephrata. Drive west on US 322 through Ephrata and continue west on US 322 for 4.3 miles to the village of Clay. In Clay turn right on North Clay Road at the sign for the Middle Creek Wildlife Management Area. Drive 1.1 miles on North Clay Road and turn right onto Hopeland Road; continue 0.6 mile and turn left onto Kleinfeltersville Road. Drive 2.3 miles on Kleinfeltersville Road to Museum Road and the MCWMA. MCWMA is closed Monday. For more information call the Middle Creek Wildlife Management Area at (717) 733-1512. *DeLorme: Pennsylvania Atlas & Gazetteer.* Page 79 C7

Northeast Pennsylvania

Look at a road map of northeastern Pennsylvania and it looks like any other. Look at topographic maps of the area, however, and you'll see that northeastern Pennsylvania is made up of three different mountain systems. From the south, the first of these is the Pocono Plateau. There's not a city or town on the Pocono Plateau with a population over 15,000. The name of the game in this part of the state is tourism—specifically outdoor vacation and recreation sites. The terrain here is mostly rolling hills with lakes, wetlands, and bogs. The Hickory Run Boulder Field—a must-see natural phenomenon (see Hike 13)—is here, part of the sprawling 15,000-acre Hickory Run State Park.

The second mountain system is the Glaciated Low Plateau. It derives its name from the geologic phenomenon glaciation, which occurs when a glacier melts, or retreats, and changes the topography by creating lakes, bogs, and ravines and, in some cases, reversing the flow of water as a result of moraines created by the debris left behind. Like the Pocono Plateau, this area is not heavily developed. The largest town is Sayre, with a population of less than 10,000. There are plenty of wooded areas, fishing streams, lakes, and creeks—what more could you want?

The third mountain system is the Ridge and Valley Province, which passes through northeastern Pennsylvania as it makes its way northeast to the border. This system runs north and south of the Pocono Plateau; on a map it looks like a thumb and a forefinger holding the Pocono Plateau in its grip.

If all this sounds confusing, it is; Pennsylvania's mountains are difficult to get a grip on. The Ridge and Valley Province covers 25 percent of the state, covering all or part of twenty-seven counties, and provides some of the most dramatic views, waterfalls, and plunging ravines around.

The most dramatic of these plunging ravines is in Ricketts Glen State Park, where a raging stream sends water 1,000 feet down the Allegheny Front, creating dozens of waterfalls. The biggest thing going in northeastern Pennsylvania, however, is the Delaware Gap National Recreation Area—a 67,000-acre recreation paradise that runs for 40 miles on both the Pennsylvania and the New Jersey sides of the Delaware River. It hosts more than 5 million visitors a year, and there's everything here from canoe-camping to rock climbing to bicycling alongside the river and of course—our favorite—hiking.

10 Dingmans Falls

This is a fun hike and a great place to be on a hot summer day. Wooden walkways, steps, and a series of wooden footbridges lead through the bottom of a deep hemlock ravine to two dramatic and distinctly different waterfalls, where the mist and the shade from the hemlocks cool the air. Follow a trail that parallels Dingmans Creek to another spot with three more dramatic waterfalls, old factory ruins, and a picnic area.

Start: Dingmans Falls Visitors Center parking lot
Distance: 5.0 miles out and back
Hiking time: About 3 hours
Difficulty: Easy; mostly level trail with a short climb out of a ravine
Schedule: Open year-round
Season: Best spring to fall (*Note:* During winter the Dingmans Falls access road, which runs from Johnny Bee Road to the visitor center, is closed to vehicles. If you want to visit the falls then, you must walk in and out from that intersection, a distance of approximately 0.5 mile each way.)

Trail surface: A combination of wooden walkways, wooden steps, and pine needle paths
Elevation gain: 558 feet
Land status: National recreation area
Nearest town: Milford
Fees and permits: No fees or permits required
Other trail users: Tourists
Canine compatibility: Leashed dogs permitted
Maps: USGS Lake Maskenozha, PA
Trail contacts: Delaware Water Gap National Recreation Area, 1978 River Rd., Bushkill Falls 18324; (570) 828-2253; www.nps.gov/dewa

Finding the trailhead: From Wilkes-Barre, drive south on I-476 and get on I-80 heading east toward Stroudsburg. From I-80 take exit 309 in Stroudsburg and drive north on US 209 for 4 miles to the intersection of Business US 209 and US 209. Turn right at the stoplight to stay on US 209. Drive north on US 209 for 20 miles and turn left onto Johnny Bee Road; then turn right at the sign for Dingmans Falls. *DeLorme: Pennsylvania Atlas & Gazetteer:* Page 55 C5. GPS: N41 13.763' / W74 53.234'

The Hike

This hike is located within the Delaware Water Gap National Recreation Area—a 67,000-acre watershed atop the Pocono Plateau that stretches for 40 miles on both the Pennsylvania and New Jersey sides of the Delaware River. The trail begins on a wooden walkway that takes you to the foot of Silver Thread Falls, where water from a tributary to Dingmans Creek drops 80 feet through a narrow shale crevasse, cascading over a series of ledges.

At Dingmans Falls, rushing waters leap from one shale ledge to the next, creating a dramatic 130-foot drop. The walkway leads to a viewing platform at the base of the falls. From the viewing platform, steps take you to a higher viewing ledge, then on to a rock outcrop above the falls. For the non-hikers, this is the end of the tour.

Dingmans Falls drops 130 feet, making it one of the tallest waterfalls in the state.

There are three more falls to visit; non-hikers can return to their cars and drive to the upper falls area.

Our hike continues with a short climb into the forest on a well-worn, root-covered path beside the rock outcrop above Dingmans Falls. From this point the trail essentially follows the creek side through a hemlock ravine for 2.0 miles to our destination, the George Childs Recreation Area.

As you walk through the ravine, it's easy to see why the eastern hemlock is Pennsylvania's state tree. With its shallow root system, the hemlock can grow just about anywhere. In fact, it thrives in damp ravines. (And as experienced hikers know, you can't walk a mile in any direction in Pennsylvania's mountains without running into a ravine.) Native Americans and early settlers ground hemlock bark into a powder that was used to stop bleeding. They made tea from hemlock bark and used it as a remedy for sore gums and other ailments. Tannin from the hemlock bark was used in tanning leather.

Check out the hemlocks for round or oblong holes; this is the work of the pileated woodpecker. At 1.5 feet long, it's the largest woodpecker in North America and easy to spot: It has black and white neck stripes and a flaming red crest on its head. And although hikers may not see one, naturalists have observed the short-tailed shrew in the ravine. These gray, mole-like rodents tend to be about 4 inches long with a 1-inch-long tail. Their diet consists of worms, insects, snails, amphibians, and mice.

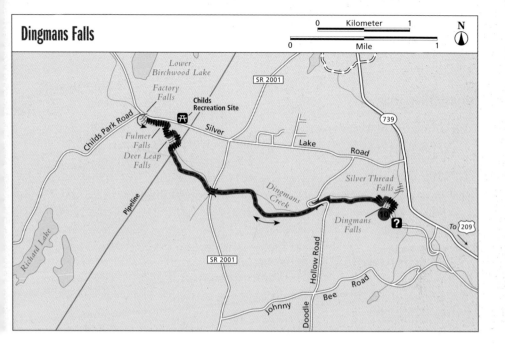

Dingmans Falls

0   Kilometer   1

0   Mile   1

N

Lower Birchwood Lake

SR 2001

Factory Falls

Childs Recreation Site

Childs Park Road

Silver

739

Fulmer Falls

Deer Leap Falls

Lake

Road

Silver Thread Falls

Dingmans Creek

Pipeline

Richard Lake

Dingmans Falls

10

To 209

SR 2001

Hollow Road

Road

Johnny

Doodle

Bee

Hikers may not see a black bear either. Many lifelong outdoorsmen have never seen one in the wild, but they're alive and well in the Delaware Water Gap National Recreation Area. These opportunistic feeders—who are primarily nocturnal—tend to raid campers' and picnickers' food stashes and garbage. They walk in a shuffling, flat-footed manner; and while most are black with a tan muzzle and a white mark on their chests, a few are cinnamon-colored.

Adult black bears in Pennsylvania are anywhere from 50 to 85 inches long and stand about 30 inches at the shoulder. Weights for adults range from 140 to 400 pounds, with rare individuals weighing as much as 800 pounds. Here in Pike County, a record-setting adult male weighing 864 pounds was taken in 2003.

Statewide, the black bear population has risen steadily. In 1970 there were approximately 4,000; in 2007 the population was estimated to be between 14,000 and 15,000, and as of January 2015 the population is estimated at 18,000. To control the population there's a three-day hunting season monitored by the Pennsylvania Game Commission in late November.

This section of the trail is a pleasant stroll through open woods. At times you'll have to climb out of the ravine, away from the stream, but these jaunts are short. Most of the time you walk beside the creek until you reach the Childs Recreation Area, where once again you'll find yourself in a somewhat touristy area. A network of walkways and wooden steps complete with viewing platforms lead from the parking lot to the picnic area and to the falls.

There are three falls here: Deer Leap, Fulmer, and Factory—one right above the other—and each is uniquely different from the others. There's also a stone ruin, a reminder that the waters from Dingmans Creek have run a number of mills throughout the years.

Miles and Directions

0.0 Start on the gravel path from the parking lot and walk past the information booth. Cross Dingmans Creek on a wooden footbridge and continue on the wooden walkway to Silver Thread Falls.

0.2 Stay on the walkway. Cross Dingmans Creek on a second bridge.

0.3 Arrive at Dingmans Falls and walk to the viewing platform. Retrace your steps and turn right onto the wooden steps.

0.5 Cross Dingmans Creek on a wooden bridge.

0.6 Arrive above Dingmans Falls at the fenced viewing area and educational plaque. This is the end of the walkway at this section. Turn left onto a worn path and climb uphill over the roots. Enter a forest of hemlock and rhododendron.

0.7 Cross Doodle Hollow Road. Note the blocked bridge on your right. Continue on the south side of the creek.

1.4 An abandoned railroad grade comes in from your left and merges with the trail. The trail turns right.

1.6 Cross the paved SR 2001.

1.7 The trail becomes an abandoned logging road. Turn right onto an earthen mound and walk to the creek. Turn left at the creek.

2.0 Cross a pipeline swath.

2.1 Cross a wooden bridge over Dingmans Creek and arrive at Deer Leap Falls. Walk through the picnic area and turn left onto the wooden steps.

2.2 Pass a set of steps on your right. Turn left onto a bridge above Deer Leap Falls.

2.3 Turn right onto the wooden walkway.

2.4 Cross the creek on a wooden bridge at Fulmer Falls. Turn left and walk through the picnic area to Factory Falls.

2.5 Arrive at Factory Falls. View the falls and retrace your steps to the parking lot.

5.0 Arrive back at the parking lot.

Local Information

Pocono Mountains Visitors Bureau, 1004 W. Main St., Stroudsburg 18360; (800) 762-6667; www.800poconos.com

Local Events/Attractions

Bushkill Falls, Bushkill Falls Road, Bushkill; (570) 588-6682 or (888) 628-7454; www.visitbushkillfalls.com

Campgrounds

Timothy Lake North RV Resort, 6837 Timothy Lake Rd., East Stroudsburg; (570) 588-6631; www.rvonthego.com/pennsylvania/timothy-lake-north-rv/

11 Mount Minsi

This bold hike uses a stretch of the Appalachian Trail as it weaves along the ridge of the Delaware Water Gap, at one point taking hikers to an overlook 1,000 feet above the Delaware River. This is one of the most—if not the most—rugged sections of the AT in Pennsylvania. There are heart-stopping views of the Delaware Water Gap, the Delaware River, and the I-80 bridge across the Delaware. From the summit, look across the Gap to Mount Tammany and Kittatinny Ridge in neighboring New Jersey.

Start: Parking lot for Lake Lenape
Distance: 4.9-mile loop
Hiking time: About 3 hours
Difficulty: Moderate, due to plenty of climbing over boulders and a rocky trail
Schedule: Open year-round
Season: Spring, summer, fall
Trail surface: Typical mountain footpath over rocks and through outcroppings
Elevation gain: 1,221 feet

Land status: National recreation area
Nearest town: Stroudsburg
Fees and permits: No fees or permits required
Other trail users: Backpackers
Canine compatibility: Leashed dogs permitted
Maps: USGS Stroudsburg, PA
Trail contacts: Delaware Gap National Recreation Area, 1978 River Rd., Bushkill 18324; (570) 426-2452; www.nps.gov/dewa

Finding the trailhead: From Scranton, drive south on I-380 and connect with I-80, heading east toward Stroudsburg. Take exit 310 and drive south on PA 611 for 0.6 mile to the stoplight in the town of Delaware Water Gap. At the stoplight, turn left onto PA 611 South. Drive 0.3 mile and turn right onto Mountain Road. Drive 0.1 mile, turn left at the fork in the road, and drive to the Lake Lenape parking lot. *DeLorme: Pennsylvania Atlas & Gazetteer*: Page 68 A2. GPS: N40 58.75' / W75 08.596'

The Hike

The town of Delaware Water Gap has the air of an alpine skiing village. The town is small, and its outskirts look like any other small Pennsylvania town; but as soon as you reach the downtown area, you get the feeling something outdoorsy is happening around the place.

Something is happening: The Appalachian Trail passes through town. You get the feeling that residents are used to seeing weary hikers plodding into their town for a little R&R. The town of Delaware Water Gap is also the southern terminus of the Delaware Water Gap National Recreation Area—a 67,000-acre recreation paradise that runs for 40 miles on both the Pennsylvania and the New Jersey sides of the Delaware River and hosts more than 5 million visitors a year.

At the center of all this activity is the Delaware River. Even though it's just the twenty-fifth largest river in the country, its importance cannot be overstated. Despite its relative size, the Delaware provides 10 percent of the nation's population with

A once-in-a-lifetime view of the Delaware River as it winds its way between Pennsylvania and New Jersey

water. Even more remarkable, its water is clean, and it is one of the few remaining free-flowing rivers in the country. To recognize this small miracle, this section of the Delaware has been designated a Middle Delaware Scenic and Recreation River and a National Scenic River.

One of the popular activities here is river camping, which, for those unfamiliar with it, involves canoeing a stretch of the river and stopping for the night at one of the many riverside campsites along the way. Within the park boundaries the river is a series of shallow riffles and quiet pools, with no difficult rapids. There are access points every 8 to 10 miles, allowing for easy day trips; or boaters can camp (for one night only) in one of the primitive campsites along the river. Tubing and rafting are allowed as well. There are a number of local liveries that rent tubes, rafts, and canoes and have a launch and pickup service.

Whether it's a leisurely sightseeing tour along the Delaware or a more aggressive ride on a mountain bike, there are a number of bicycle trails inside and outside the park. The longest touring route is the Old Mine Road, which is on the New Jersey side and runs the length of the park. Mountain bike riders can check out the

Zion Church Road for a ride past Hidden Lake and the historic Zion Church and cemetery.

There are more than 20 ice climbs and 200 rock-climbing sites in the park, ranging in level from novice to advanced. Climbers don't have to register with the park, but park officials recommend that climbers tell a friend where they intend to climb and leave them the park's 24-four-hour emergency number: (800) 543-4295.

This hike starts at the trailhead for the Appalachian Trail, just a few blocks south of town at the parking lot of tiny Lake Lenape. This is a popular spot for both tourists and locals, so when you start out, you get the feeling that the trail will be crowded. But as soon as you begin the first serious climb, you realize that your fellow hikers have opted to stay low. It's just you and the boulders, proving once again what all serious hikers have always known: When the air gets thin, so does the crowd.

Just 0.5 mile into the hike, you'll get your first vista. Standing on an outcrop, you can see the cars and eighteen-wheelers whizzing along I-80. Interestingly, while you can see the traffic, you won't hear it. Not only are there no crowds this high up, but there is no traffic noise either. As you climb higher and higher up the rocky cliff edge of Mount Minsi, each time you stop for a view, the trucks and cars get smaller and smaller; when you reach the summit, the vehicles are indistinguishable from the roadway.

After hugging the cliff edge for 1.0 mile, you turn onto the View Trail. From this point the trail cuts away from the rim and into the forest for your last, short climb to the summit of Mount Minsi—a flat open area where a fire tower once stood. All that remains of the tower is a set of stone steps and the concrete pylons where the tower legs were anchored into the earth. When you feel the force of the wind as it whips up out of the gap, you get an idea of what it must have been like in that tower. But like all the other fire towers in the state, this one was shut down when the USDA Forest Service began using small airplanes to monitor forest fires.

It's lonely at the top. There's not much else up here but the wind and a fenced-in microwave tower, hanging on the edge of the cliff. There's a grove of table mountain pine trees; in one of them there's a sign that reads "Mount Minsi."

Miles and Directions

0.0 Start at the parking lot. Walk to the iron access gate across the Mount Minsi Fire Road and the trailhead bulletin board. Turn left onto a paved path and follow the white blazes of the Appalachian Trail.

0.1 Cross the breast of Lake Lenape. Start an uphill climb.

0.3 Turn left at the double white blazes (the blazes are on a tree on your right). Stay to the left at the fork in the trail.

0.4 Arrive at the first outcropping for a view of I-80.

0.5 Come to an outcropping with a sign that reads "Council Rock."

1.1 Cross a stream with a sign that reads "Eureka Creek."

1.2 Turn right at the View Trail sign.

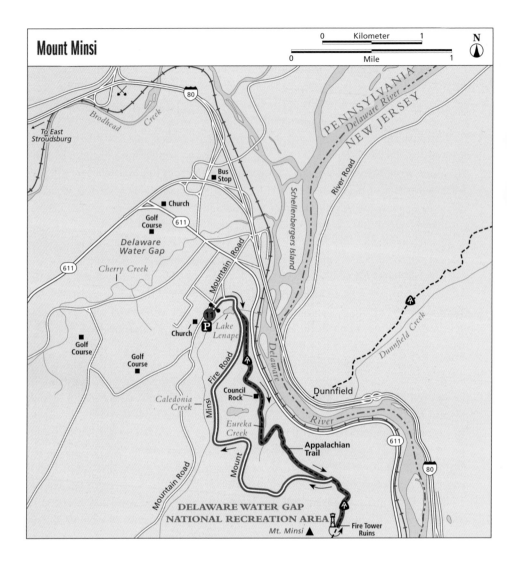

Mount Minsi

1.9 Reach a flat area. Turn left onto the Mount Minsi Fire Road for 50 feet, then turn right onto the white-blazed Appalachian Trail.

2.2 Reach the summit of Mount Minsi. Retrace your steps back to the Mount Minsi Fire Road.

2.5 Turn right onto the Mount Minsi Fire Road. Begin descent.

2.6 Pass the Appalachian Trail on your left, then again on your right. Continue straight on the fire road.

4.6 Pass the Appalachian Trail on your right.

4.8 Arrive at Lake Lenape.

4.9 Arrive back at the parking lot.

Local Information

Pocono Mountains Visitors Bureau, 1004 W. Main St., Stroudsburg 18360; (570) 421-5791; www.800poconos.com

Local Events/Attractions

Water Gap Trolley, Route 611 South, Delaware Water Gap; (570) 476-9766; http://watergaptrolley.com. Tour points of interest on an antique-style trolley.

Campgrounds

Mountain Vista Campground, 415 Taylor Dr., Stroudsburg; (570) 223-0111; www.mtnvistacampground.com

Restaurants

Sycamore Grille, 92 Main St., Delaware Water Gap; (570) 426-1200; www.sycamoregrille.com

Local Outdoor Retailers

Dunkelberger's Sports Outfitters, 585 Main St., Stroudsburg; (570) 421-7950; www.dunkelbergers.com

12 Hawk Falls

The highlight of this hike is the spectacular and unusual Hawk Falls. The falls occur when Hawk Run, which is 40 feet above Mud Run, empties into the lower creek at a three-sided canyon. The water cascades down the center of the canyon, ever widening, from one ledge to the next and empties into a deep pool of crystal-clear water.

The trail passes through a huge rhododendron tunnel to the magnificent Mud Run Natural Area in the bottom of Mud Run Gorge. It then turns downstream and runs alongside Mud Run, one of the top trout streams in the state. There are plenty of streamside boulders and smaller waterfalls along the way.

Start: Hawk Falls Trail trailhead parking lot on the south side of PA 534 just east of I-476
Distance: 3.1-mile loop
Hiking time: About 2.5 hours
Difficulty: Easy, due to mostly level trail with one short switchback climb
Schedule: Open year-round
Season: Spring, summer, fall
Trail surface: Paved and forest roads
Elevation gain: 424 feet

Land status: State park
Nearest town: Wilkes-Barre
Fees and permits: No fees or permits required
Other trail users: Tourists, campers, anglers
Canine compatibility: Leashed dogs permitted
Maps: USGS Blakeslee, PA; Hickory Run, PA
Trail contacts: Hickory Run State Park, RR 1 Box 81, White Haven 18661; (570) 443-0400; www.dcnr.state.pa.us/stateparks/findapark/hickoryrun/

Finding the trailhead: From Wilkes-Barre, drive south on I-476 and take exit 95. Go west on I-80 to exit 274 (one exit). Drive south on PA 534 for 1.8 miles to the town of Lehigh Tannery. Turn left at the stop sign in town and drive east on PA 534 into Hickory Run State Park. Drive past the park office and continue about 4 miles until you pass under I-476. Park on the right, immediately after passing under I-476. *DeLorme: Pennsylvania Atlas & Gazetteer:* Page 53 D5. GPS: N41 0.574' / W75 38.163'

The Hike

There are two misnomers on this hike. First off, the waters of Mud Run are astonishingly clear. Second, you won't see any hawks or other raptors diving for fish at Hawk Falls. The creek and the falls are named for the Hawk family that once owned the property on which the eponymous creek and falls are located.

Of the twenty-two hikes in the 15,500-acre Hickory Run State Park, Hawk Falls is the most popular with both locals and tourists. The majority of these hikers take the direct route from the parking lot, across Hawk Run, and on to the falls. Some may wander upstream along Mud Run for a ways and then return the way they came. Anglers generally drive through the campground and park at the parking lot just before the closed access gate. (This way they only have to carry their gear about 0.5 mile.)

Hawk Falls rushes water on its way to the Lehigh River.

But anglers and tourists miss the pine forest and thriving rhododendron tunnels. Rhododendrons, some as tall as 15 feet, line both sides of the forest road that leads into a pristine forest of pines, beech, maple, and oak to Mud Run. Mud Run is popular with fly fishers angling for a chance to hook a native or brook trout. If you do this hike in fishing season, you'll almost certainly be able to watch a fly fisherman in waist-high boots wading into the stream and flicking his line about. He's aiming toward one of the deep, shaded pools where he's convinced an enormous, cagey old trout is just waiting to take his bait.

There is one short switchback climb out of the steepest section of the ravine. Once you make the summit, the yellow-blazed trail divides. One branch continues across the plateau; the other turns left. You must take the branch that turns left to descend the ravine and make your way back to Mud Run. Look for a sheared-off stump, taller than you, with a yellow blaze. Back at the creek, it's a short side trek to Hawk Falls—at the juncture where Hawk Run empties into Mud Run, which continues west until it empties into the Lehigh River.

Aside from the wonders of nature, hikers on this trail can marvel at the wonders of man's ingenuity. When you're at Hawk Falls, you are almost directly under the I-476 bridge that spans this gorge. From this vantage point you have a clear view of

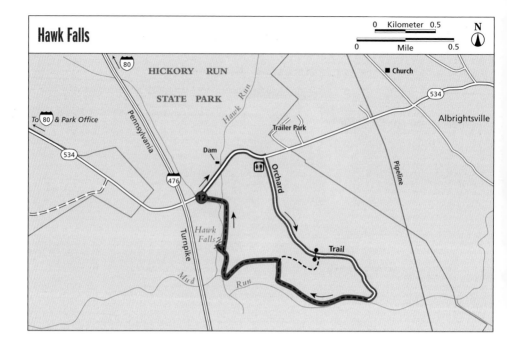

Hawk Falls

0   Kilometer   0.5

0   Mile   0.5

N

HICKORY RUN

STATE PARK

■ Church

534

To 80 & Park Office

Albrightsville

Pennsylvania

Hawk Run

Trailer Park

534

Dam

Orchard

Pipeline

476

Turnpike

Hawk Falls

Trail

Mud Run

the underside of the bridge, which is high enough and far enough away that there is no traffic noise in the gorge.

After the falls the trail takes you out of the ravine bottom and on to a very short side trail, where you can view Hawk Falls from above. From there the trail continues, crossing over Hawk Run and then taking you back to PA 534, where you turn right to return to your vehicle.

Miles and Directions

0.0   Start at the trailhead parking lot on PA 534. Walk east alongside PA 534.

0.1   Hawk Run passes under PA 534. Note the small dam on your left.

0.4   Turn right at the Organized Group Camping sign onto the forest road. Follow the yellow blazes.

0.5   Pass restrooms on your right.

0.7   Pass another restroom on your right.

1.0   Come to an access gate across the road.

1.4   Pass an unmarked footpath on your right.

1.5   Turn right into a rhododendron tunnel.

1.6   Arrive at Mud Run; turn right.

2.0   The trail turns right to climb out of the ravine.

2.2   Trail turns left at the edge of the plateau. Turn left and begin your descent back down the ravine to Mud Run. Look for the yellow blaze on a large stump. (***Note:*** Another set of yellow blazes for the Orchard Trail continues across the plateau.)

2.5 Arrive at a trail intersection. Turn left and follow Mud Run to Hawk Falls.

2.6 Reach Hawk Falls. Retrace your steps to the trail intersection.

2.7 Arrive at the trail intersection. Continue straight.

2.8 Turn left on a short side trail to an overlook above Hawk Falls. Retrace your steps to the trail and turn left.

2.9 Cross over Hawk Run.

3.1 Arrive at PA 534 and turn right to the parking lot.

Local Information

Pocono Mountains Visitors Bureau, 1004 W. Main St., Stroudsburg 18360; (570) 421-5791; www.800poconos.com

Campgrounds

Hickory Run State Park Campground, Route 534, White Haven; (570) 443-0400; (888) 727-2757 (camping information and reservations); www.dcnr.state.pa.us/stateparks/findapark/hickoryrun/

13 Hickory Run Boulder Field

This hike is designed to give hikers a chance to explore the Hickory Run Boulder Field Natural Area—a 16-acre, 12-foot-deep phenomenon created during the last ice age. The Boulder Field—the only geological formation of this type in the East—has been studied by scientists for more than one hundred years; the core of their studies is displayed on bulletin boards in the on-site educational area.

Start: Boulder Field Trailhead parking lot on the north side of PA 534 just east of I-476
Distance: 7.0 miles out and back
Hiking time: About 3 hours
Difficulty: Easy, due to a level trail
Schedule: Open year-round
Season: Spring, summer, fall
Trail surface: Meadow path and abandoned forest roads
Elevation gain: 550 feet

Land status: State park
Nearest town: Wilkes-Barre
Fees and permits: No fees or permits required
Other trail users: Tourists, hunters (in season)
Canine compatibility: Leashed dogs permitted
Maps: USGS Blakeslee, PA; Hickory Run, PA
Trail contacts: Hickory Run State Park, RR 1 Box 81, White Haven 18661; (570) 443-0400; www.dcnr.state.pa.us/stateparks/findapark/hickoryrun/

Finding the trailhead: From Wilkes-Barre, drive south on I-476 and take exit 95. Go west on I-80 to exit 274 (one exit). Drive south on PA 534 for 1.8 miles to the town of Lehigh Tannery. Turn left at the stop sign in town and drive east on PA 534 into Hickory Run State Park. Drive past the park office and continue about 4 miles until you pass under I-476. Park on the left, immediately after passing under I-476. *DeLorme: Pennsylvania Atlas & Gazetteer:* Page 53 D5. GPS: N41 0.574' / W75 38.163'

The Hike

At 15,500 acres, Hickory Run State Park is one of Pennsylvania's largest state parks. It's also one of the most picturesque. Its forests are a mixture of second-growth white pine and hemlock, mixed oaks, and northern hardwoods. Sand Spring Lake, the largest of the four dams impoundments, has a swimming beach. Two clear mountain streams, Sand Spring Run and Hickory Run, intersect in the center of the park, at the site where a booming nineteenth-century logging mill and village once stood. A few of the village buildings remain and are used by the park service; one is the park office. From March to November, park environmental education specialists can help you fully appreciate the natural beauty of the park through their hands-on activities, guided walks, and presentations on natural and historical resources.

For hikers there's a 40-mile network of well-maintained trails leading through dense mountain laurel and rhododendron patches, along the pristine streams to dams and rustic spillways, and through to scenic areas like the Shades of Death Trail. (Early settlers named the trail because the dense forests of virgin white pine and hemlock

Hickory Run Boulder Field Natural Area is a 16-acre, 12-foot-deep phenomenon created during the last ice age.

were so thick they blocked the sun from reaching the forest floor.) But for many the major attraction in Hickory Run State Park is the Hickory Run Boulder Field, a geological formation of boulders created during the Pleistocene epoch or, as it's commonly referred to, the last ice age.

Scientists who have studied the Boulder Field believe it was created 15,000 years ago as a result of the same glacial activity that created the Great Lakes in North America. During the Pleistocene huge ice sheets covered most of the earth. (Referring to the most recent ice age, the term "Pleistocene" is, quite logically, derived from the Greek words *pleistos* [most] and *kainos* [recent]. That "recent" thing is a relative term, though: The Pleistocene lasted from about 1.6 million to 10,000 BC.) In North America the latest ice sheet—the Wisconsin—stretched across most of the northern United States, creating a climate similar to that of modern-day Greenland. This ice sheet reached its southernmost point in northeastern Pennsylvania, about 1 mile north and 1 mile east of the Boulder Field.

When the sheet retreated (melted), it left behind a moraine—an accumulation of boulders, stones, and debris. Meltwater from the glacier produced a freeze-thaw cycle that heaved the earth and split the cap rocks. This action, repeated over thousands of years, carried the rocks and boulders farther and farther downslope, until the cycle stopped 15,000 years ago. The boulders' rough edges were rounded as they shifted. The resulting fine gravel, clay, and sand deposited around the boulders were washed away by glacial meltwater. Because there is no soil around the boulders, the field is

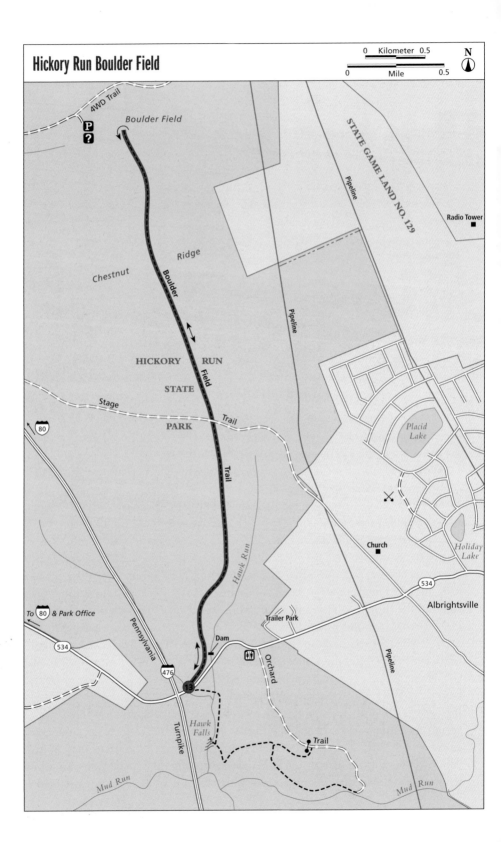

Hickory Run Boulder Field

0 Kilometer 0.5

0 Mile 0.5

N

4WD Trail

Boulder Field

P

?

STATE GAME LAND NO. 129

Pipeline

Radio Tower

Ridge

Boulder

Chestnut

Pipeline

HICKORY   RUN

Field

STATE

Stage

Trail

80

PARK

Placid
Lake

Trail

Church

Holiday
Lake

Hawk Run

534

Albrightsville

To 80 & Park Office

Pennsylvania

Trailer Park

534

Dam

Orchard

Pipeline

476

13

Hawk
Falls

Trail

Turnpike

Mud Run

Mud Run

more or less devoid of vegetation. But with every passing year, the red maple, alder, hemlock, and spruce that surround the field drop their foliage and contribute to humus eventually capable of supporting small plants and trees.

The boulders, which are red sandstone at the north end and red conglomerate with white quartz pebbles in the south end, vary in size from 4 to 25 feet in length. The field is 400 feet wide on an east–west axis and 1,800 feet long north to south. It's remarkably level and at least 12 feet deep. There are holes—what geologists call reliefs—that look as though someone had fashioned them around giant bowls.

The hike to and from the field is a pleasant walk through a pine forest. At a little over 1.5 miles, you'll cross the Stage Trail, originally the stagecoach route that ran from Bethlehem to Wilkes-Barre and stopped at the once-bustling sawmill town of Saylorsville, just north of the park's center.

Miles and Directions

0.0   Start at the trailhead parking lot on the north side of PA 534. Walk to the trail sign and a set of wooden steps, then onto a path through an open field.

0.1   Come to the Boulder Field Trail sign. Follow the yellow blazes.

0.8   Cross a washout stream.

1.7   Cross the Stage Trail.

3.4   Arrive at the Boulder Field. Walk across the field to the educational bulletin boards.

3.5   Arrive at the bulletin boards. Retrace your steps back to the trailhead.

5.3   Cross the Stage Trail.

7.0   Arrive back at the parking lot.

Local Information

Pocono Mountains Visitors Bureau, 1004 W. Main St., Stroudsburg 18360; (570) 421-5791; www.800poconos.com

Local Events/Attractions

Lehigh Gorge Scenic Railway, 1 Susquehanna St., Jim Thorpe; (570) 325-8485; www.lgsry.com

Jim Thorpe River Adventures, 1 Adventure Ln., Jim Thorpe; (800) 424-7238; www.jtraft.com

Accommodations

The Inn at Jim Thorpe, 24 Broadway, Jim Thorpe; (800) 329-2599; www.innjt.com

Campgrounds

Jim Thorpe Camping Resort, 129 Lenz Trail, Jim Thorpe; (570) 325-2644; www.jimthorpecamping.com

14 Ricketts Glen State Park

Here's the bottom line: Ricketts Glen is the best hike in Pennsylvania. It may also be one of the top hikes in the East. There are twenty-two named waterfalls; the tallest, Ganoga Falls, is 94 feet. The other twenty-one falls range from 15 to 49 feet, plus there are a dozen or more waterfalls that are unnamed. At the center of the hike is Kitchen Creek, a torrential mountain stream that drops 1,000 feet down the face of the Allegheny Front.

Starting at the bottom of the ravine, the trail runs a short ways; then it's up one branch of Kitchen Creek, a mile across the top, and down the other. The man-made pathway is stone steps, ledges, and wooden bridges made of timbers the size of telephone poles. On your way through the bottom of the ravine, you pass through Glens Natural Area, where exotic flora grows beneath 500-year-old hemlocks, pines, and oaks.

Start: Ricketts Glen Natural Area parking lot on PA 118
Distance: 7.1-mile lollipop
Hiking time: About 5 hours
Difficulty: Moderate, due to the extensive, steep climb and stone steps
Schedule: Open year-round
Season: Spring, summer, fall; Falls Trail closed to visitors during winter
Trail surface: Well-worn forest path, shale walkways, and dirt roads
Elevation gain: 1,081 feet
Land status: State park
Nearest town: Williamsport
Fees and permits: No fees or permits required
Other trail users: Tourists
Canine compatibility: Leashed dogs permitted

Maps: USGS Red Rock, PA
Trail contacts: Ricketts Glen State Park, 695 Route 487, Benton 17814; (570) 477-5675; www.dcnr.state.pa.us/stateparks/findapark/rickettsglen
Special considerations: Regardless of the season, the stone steps can be wet and slippery. Hiking boots with good tread are strongly advised. The weather in the ravine can change abruptly—usually to a cold rain—so foul-weather gear is also recommended. On the plus side, take your swimming suit: There are shallow pools where hikers can walk under the falls. Because of the heights, slippery stones, and (sometimes) muddy and slippery walkways, this hike is not recommended for those who are not physically fit.

Finding the trailhead: From Williamsport, drive east on I-180/US 220 approximately 15 miles and take the US 220 exit. Continue on US 220 about 10 miles to Beech Glen and the intersection with PA 42. Turn right onto PA 42 South and drive 4.5 miles to PA 239. Continue on PA 239 for 5.1 miles to PA 118 East. Continue on PA 118 for 12 miles, past the village of Red Rock and past the (first) Ricketts Glen State Park sign. Continue 2.3 miles on PA 118 to the Ricketts Glen State Park sign and parking lot, on your right. *DeLorme: Pennsylvania Atlas & Gazetteer:* Page 51 B7. GPS: N41 17.943' / W76 16.469'

The Hike

At Ricketts Glen State Park history meets geology; the result is a truly unique hike. This is not only the most magnificent hike in the state, but it also ranks up there with the top hikes in the East.

This hike has everything: It is a National Natural Landmark, with trees estimated to be up to 900 years old. There are breathtaking waterfalls, pristine settings boasting unique flora and fauna, and mammoth trees strewn along the trail and across the creeks. Here at Ricketts Glen, even the drainage streams that pour into Kitchen Creek produce picture-postcard waterfalls.

Ricketts Glen State Park encompasses 13,050 acres along the Allegheny Front in Sullivan, Columbia, and Luzerne Counties. It's named for Colonel Robert Bruce Ricketts, a Civil War veteran who enlisted in the Union Army as a private and, after leading a battery of men at Gettysburg, was awarded the rank of colonel upon his discharge. But Ricketts's greatest impact on this area was as a businessman, not a colonel. When the railroad reached the area, Ricketts began a major logging industry, at one point employing more than 1,000 men. To more easily move the massive logs, two lakes were built on the plateau above the glen; Lake Jean and Mountain Stream Lake still exist today. The 245-acre Lake Jean is used for recreation and fishing. The Pennsylvania Fish & Boat Commission owns Mountain Stream Lake and the land around it. It too is open for fishing.

Kitchen Creek drains Lake Jean and drops 1,000 feet down the ravine. A little more than halfway down, it's joined by its eastern branch, which drains the other side of the ravine. Together they form the Y around which the hike is formed. You'll hike uphill along one branch and then downhill along the other.

The Glens Natural Area is remote and is believed to be just as it was when Europeans first came to America; this remoteness has yielded an ecosystem free of introduced species. The glen is home to a wide variety of mosses and lichens, false nettle (also called bog hemp), ferns, and wild sarsaparilla—a member of the ginseng family. Throughout this forest there are 100-foot-tall hemlocks and oaks boasting 5-foot diameters, as well as birch, ash, and striped maple. The trail itself is more than one hundred years old; workers employed by Ricketts built it to make a path along the falls. The trail is mostly placed stone steps, which, because of the spray of the falls, can be wet and muddy even on a sunny day.

The forces of nature are hard at work in the glen. Huge fallen trees crisscross Kitchen Creek at every turn. A heavy rain sometimes obliterates steps, and walkways are frequently washed away. But the repair work is ongoing. There are a number of newly built bridges, and the entire walkway to Onondaga Falls, washed out during a storm, has been rebuilt.

Ricketts Glen State Park is a haven for hikers, photographers, botanists, outdoor lovers, and tourists; it is not, however, suitable for small children. For those who can't manage this hike, there is an excellent waterfall south of PA 118, adjacent to the

With 22 breathtaking waterfalls, Rickett's Glen is one of the most photographed sites in the state. DEBRA YOUNG

parking lot. Adams Falls cascades 36 feet into a deep bowl formed by the shale bottom. The trail to it passes through a stand of picturesque pines, where there are picnic tables and benches.

Miles and Directions

0.0 Start at the parking area. Cross PA 118 at the crosswalk and walk to the trailhead and Glens Natural Area Falls Trail sign.

0.1 Arrive at the Falls Trail map and bulletin board.

0.2 Turn right onto a footbridge across Kitchen Creek.

0.3 Turn left onto a dirt road.

0.5 Cross a tributary on a footbridge. Arrive at a trail sign and turn right.

0.8 Turn left onto a footbridge and cross Kitchen Creek.

0.9 The trail veers left, away from the creek. Look for the yellow arrow signpost.

1.3 Arrive at Murray Reynolds Falls.

1.5 Arrive at Sheldon Reynolds Falls.

1.6 Arrive at Harrison Wright Falls.

1.8 Turn right on Waters Meet Bridge and onto the Glen Leigh Trail.

1.9 Arrive at Wyandot Falls. Turn right onto the footbridge.

2.1 Arrive at B. Reynolds Falls. Turn left onto the footbridge and arrive at B. Ricketts Falls.

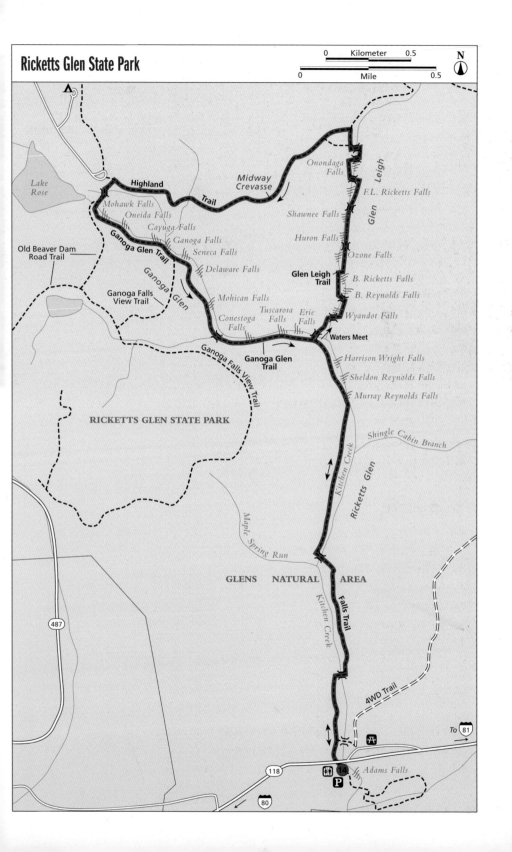

Ricketts Glen State Park

Lake Rose

Highland Mohawk Falls Oneida Falls Cayuga Falls **Ganoga Glen Trail** Ganoga Falls Seneca Falls Delaware Falls

Old Beaver Dam Road Trail

Ganoga Falls View Trail

Ganoga Glen

Mohican Falls

Conestoga Falls Tuscarora Falls Erie Falls

Ganoga Glen Trail

Ganoga Falls View Trail

RICKETTS GLEN STATE PARK

Midway Crevasse

Onondaga Falls

F.L. Ricketts Falls

Glen Leigh

Shawnee Falls

Huron Falls

Ozone Falls

Glen Leigh Trail

B. Ricketts Falls

B. Reynolds Falls

Wyandot Falls

Waters Meet

Harrison Wright Falls

Sheldon Reynolds Falls

Murray Reynolds Falls

Shingle Cabin Branch

Ricketts Glen

Kitchen Creek

Maple Spring Run

GLENS   NATURAL   AREA

Kitchen Creek

Falls Trail

4WD Trail

To 81

487

118

14

Adams Falls

80

N

Kilometer

Mile

0   0.5

0   0.5

2.2 Arrive at Ozone Falls.

2.3 Turn right onto the footbridge and arrive at Huron Falls.

2.4 Arrive at Shawnee Falls.

2.6 Turn left onto the footbridge and arrive at F. L. Ricketts Falls. Climb the wooden steps.

2.7 Turn right onto the footbridge and arrive at Onondaga Falls.

2.8 Turn left onto a wooden bridge.

2.9 Cross a feeder stream.

3.0 Turn left onto the Highland Trail. At the trail fork, stay to the right.

3.4 Pass through Midway Crevasse.

4.0 Turn left onto the Ganoga Glen Trail.

4.2 Cross the West Branch Kitchen Creek on a large wooden bridge. Pass the intersection with the Old Beaver Dam Road Trail. Turn left at the sign for Falls Trail and arrive at Mohawk Falls.

4.4 Arrive at Oneida Falls.

4.5 Arrive at Cayuga Falls.

4.6 Arrive at Ganoga Falls. Pass the Ganoga Falls View Trail on your right.

4.8 Arrive at Seneca Falls and Delaware Falls.

4.9 Arrive at Mohican Falls.

5.0 Arrive at Conestoga Falls.

5.2 Arrive at Tuscarora Falls and Erie Falls.

5.3 Arrive at the Waters Meet Bridge. Turn right and retrace your steps toward PA 118.

7.1 Cross PA 118 and arrive back at the parking lot.

Local Information

Luzerne County Convention and Visitors Bureau, 56 Public Sq., Wilkes-Barre 18701; (888) 905-2872; www.tournepa.com

Local Events/Attractions

Lycoming County Fair, second week in July, Hughesville; (570) 584-2196; www .lycomingfair.net

Accommodations

Ricketts Glen Hotel, 221 Route 118, Benton; (570) 477-3656; www.rickettsglen hotel.net

Campgrounds

Ricketts Glen State Park, Route 118, Benton; (570) 477-5675; (888) 727-2757 (camping information and reservations); www.dcnr.state.pa.us/stateparks/findapark/ rickettsglen. Camping, cabins, groups.

Restaurants

Ricketts Glen Hotel, 221 Route 118, Benton; (570) 477-3656; www.rickettsglen hotel.net

15 Canyon Vista

This hike provides one of the premier vistas in the state, but you do have to work for it—the climb to the summit is more than 1.0 mile. The Rock Garden is a rock climber's delight, as you make your way over and around the huge sandstone boulders.

Start: Worlds End State Park Family Campground parking lot on PA 154
Distance: 4.2-mile loop
Hiking time: About 3 hours
Difficulty: Moderate, due to an extensive uphill climb
Schedule: Open year-round
Season: Spring, summer, fall
Trail surface: Typical forest footpath and shale roads
Elevation gain: 744 feet

Land status: State park
Nearest town: Laporte
Fees and permits: No fees or permits required
Other trail users: Tourists
Canine compatibility: Leashed dogs permitted
Maps: USGS Eagles Mere, PA
Trail contacts: Worlds End State Park, 82 Cabin Bridge Rd., Forksville 18616; (570) 924-3287; www.dcnr.state.pa.us/stateparks/findapark/worldsend

Finding the trailhead: From Williamsport, drive east on US 220/I-180 for 12 miles to the US 220 exit. Take the US 220 exit and continue on US 220 for 24 miles to Laporte. Drive through Laporte for less than 1 mile to the intersection with PA 154. Turn left onto PA 154, drive 6.5 miles, and turn left into the family campground. *DeLorme: Pennsylvania Atlas & Gazetteer:* Page 51 A5. GPS: N41 28.097' / W76 34.304'

The Hike

If you want to do some hiking in the Worlds End region, you should know that hiking here means climbing. Canyon Vista is a good example of a typical out-of-the-gorge trek. The summit is 1,750 feet above sea level, but because of the switchbacks and lengthy circumnavigation, you'll end up walking more than 1.0 mile to reach the top.

But the top is where the views are—some of the best in the state. It's difficult to describe a vista. It's like trying to describe a song, or a hole-in-one. Canyon Vista is one of those things you have to experience to appreciate. The view seems to stretch forever—one deep hollow and ridge after another, all the way to the seemingly endless horizon. Try to keep this appreciation and peace of mind when you leave the vista and head for the Rock Garden. It's here you'll discover that while you were huffing and puffing and sweating your way to the top, most of the people milling around the summit drove up in their air-conditioned cars.

Next visit the Rock Garden. Here, enormous boxy boulders of coarse-grained sandstone and conglomerate litter the landscape and serve as a playground for visitors. So take advantage of them. Frost action in the vertical rock joints has created deep,

Canyon Vista in World's End State Park is one of the top vistas in the state.

narrow crevices known as fissures. These fissures are interconnected and create passageways so that children and (thin) adults can walk through the maze.

Visitors with an interest in plant life can examine the mosses, lichens, and liverworts that live on the rocks. In late spring and early summer, birders can sit quietly and listen for the songs of the breeding warbler or walk into the forest in hopes of encountering a wood thrush, hermit thrush, or veery—also a thrush.

Although the trail on the way up is steep, it's hiker-friendly; the trail back down is another story. It's rocky, and in sections bristles with thorny blackberry and cat briar. And in some sections the canopy is so dense the path is actually dark, even at midday. There are numerous patches of striped maple, as well as plenty of hemlock, pines, oaks, beech, and birch.

You eventually leave the bushes behind and concentrate on making your way down an extremely steep gorge. There are switchbacks to make it easier going, and every so often you get lucky and find a sturdy sapling just when you need something to hold on to. Once on the floor of the gorge, the trail becomes an access road through the campgrounds on back to the trailhead.

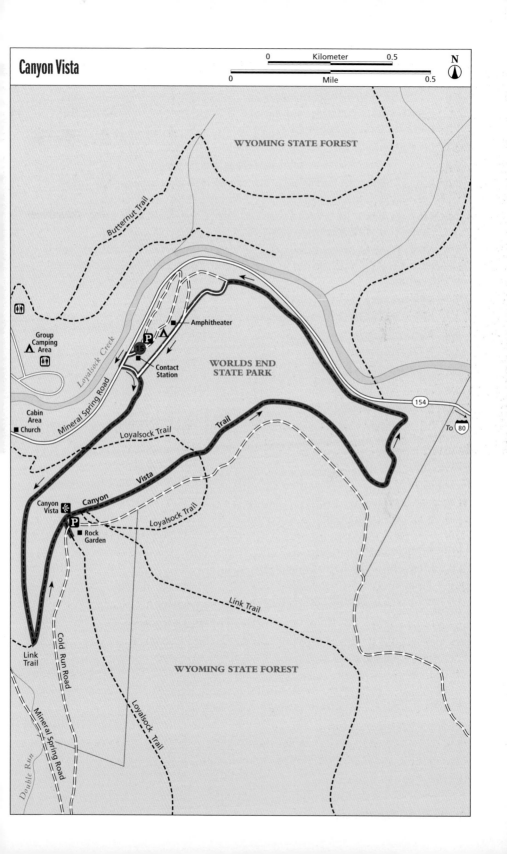

Canyon Vista

0   Kilometer   0.5

0   Mile   0.5

N

WYOMING STATE FOREST

Butternut Trail

Loyalsock Creek

Group
Camping
Area

Amphitheater

Mineral Spring Road

Contact
Station

WORLDS END
STATE PARK

Cabin
Area

Church

Loyalsock Trail

Trail

154

To 80

Vista

Canyon

Canyon
Vista

Loyalsock Trail

Rock
Garden

Cold Run Road

Link Trail

Link
Trail

Mineral Spring Road

Loyalsock Trail

Double Run

WYOMING STATE FOREST

Miles and Directions

0.0 Start at the family campground parking area and turn right on the campground access road. Pass the contact station and turn left onto Mineral Spring Road. Walk across the road to the Canyon Vista Trailhead.

0.1 The trail cuts uphill away from the road. Follow the blue blazes.

0.4 Come to an intersection with the Loyalsock Trail. Continue straight.

1.0 Begin a serious climb. The trail makes a switchback to the left and merges with the Link Trail.

1.4 Reach the summit and arrive at Canyon Vista. Walk up the wooden steps, through the parking area, to the Rock Garden sign.

1.6 Arrive at the Rock Garden. Retrace your steps back to Canyon Vista and turn right. Come to a sign for the Loyalsock and Link Trails, which merge into the Canyon Vista Trail. Follow the blue blazes.

1.7 Arrive at a fork in the trail. Bear left, following the blue blazes.

2.1 Pass an intersection with the Loyalsock Trail. Continue straight.

2.8 The trail turns right through a boulder outcropping. Begin your descent.

3.2 The trail turns left.

3.7 Enter the campground.

3.8 Turn left onto the shale road.

4.0 Pass the amphitheater.

4.1 Pass the Canyon Vista Trailhead on your left. Turn right onto Mineral Spring Road and then right again on the access road.

4.2 Arrive back at the parking lot.

Local Information
Endless Mountains Visitors Bureau, 5405 US 6, Tunkhannock 18657; (570) 836-5431; www.endlessmountains.org

Local Events/Attractions
Eagles Mere Historic Village, Eagles Mere; (570) 525-3697; http://visithistoriceagles mere.com

Campgrounds
Worlds End State Park Campgrounds, Route 154, Forksville; (570) 924-3287; (888) 727-2757 (camping information and reservations); www.dcnr.state.pa.us/stateparks/findapark/worldsend/

16 Worlds End State Park

This trail runs alongside Loyalsock Creek, where hikers will need to step lively from one creekside boulder to the next. From there it's a challenging climb up out of the gorge, through a boulder field to a 30-foot waterfall, followed by a steep hand-over-hand climb across a talus slope. The next section is a short—but precarious—walk along the edge of the ridge to an impressive overlook.

Start: Double Run Nature Trail trailhead in Worlds End State Park
Distance: 3.6-mile circuit
Hiking time: About 3 hours
Difficulty: Difficult, due to a rocky climb out of the gorge (*Note:* The High Rock Trail portion of this hike is not for children.)
Schedule: Open year-round
Season: Spring, summer, fall
Trail surface: Pine-needle nature trail and park roads; boulder outcroppings and steep gorge
Elevation gain: 1,133 feet
Land status: State park
Nearest town: Laporte
Fees and permits: No fees or permits required

Other trail users: Backpackers, tourists, anglers
Canine compatibility: Leashed dogs permitted
Maps: USGS Eagles Mere, PA
Trail contacts: Worlds End State Park, 82 Cabin Bridge Rd., Forksville 18616; (570) 924-3287; www.dcnr.state.pa.us/stateparks/findapark/worldsend
Special considerations: Signs along the High Rock Trail advise hikers to stay on the trail. If you're new to hiking or afraid of heights, you may want to skip this trail. If you want to get to High Rock Vista without the rocky climb, enter the trail below the swimming beach on PA 154.

Finding the trailhead: From Williamsport, drive east on US 220/I-180 for 12 miles to the US 220 exit. Take the US 220 exit and continue on US 220 for 24 miles to Laporte. Drive through Laporte for less than 1 mile to the intersection with PA 154. Turn left onto PA 154 and drive 6.7 miles to the Double Run Nature Trail parking lot, on your left. *DeLorme: Pennsylvania Atlas & Gazetteer:* Page 51 A5. GPS: N41 27.960' / W76 34.729'

The Hike

Hikers, intent on their agendas, sometimes miss the highlights of an area. Fortunately, that won't happen here. This hike was designed to incorporate Worlds End highlights, such as Loyalsock Creek and High Rock Vista, with a vigorous workout.

As soon as you enter Worlds End State Park, you hear it—the never-ending rush of the waters of Loyalsock Creek. These are the waters that have created (over the past 200 million years or so) the 1,600-foot-deep gash known as Loyalsock Gorge. This hike provides the opportunity to see Loyalsock Creek up close, and if you do this hike

World's End offers many features, including a chapel in the woods.

in early spring or late fall, you may see kayakers maneuvering through the whitewater rapids. The abundant boulders in the creek create some appreciable rapids, as well as a few treacherously deep spots. For this reason swimming is permitted only at the swimming beach area. If you need further deterrent, summer water temperatures range from the low 50s to the mid-60s.

After the creek you'll arrive at the High Rock Trailhead; here you'll find signs warning that the trail is not suitable for children. The first stop up the gorge is at High Rock Run and Falls, a drainage stream that cascades over an outcrop. There is evidence that hikers have climbed down alongside the falls, but the payoff isn't worth the danger. In fact, signs at the trailhead warn hikers to stay on the trail.

It's less than 0.5 mile from the falls to High Rock Overlook, but there's a short stretch along the edge of the gorge subject to washouts. Use extra caution along this section.

High Rock Vista provides a striking view of the gorge, the serpentine creek, and the surrounding mountains. After the vista life gets easy again. The trail is a typical hardwood forest trail through a dense canopy of shade, and it's all downhill. When you reach PA 154 and turn left, look on your left for a jungle of blackberry bushes, loaded with dark, juicy fruit in season.

As you walk along PA 154, you can see that the creek has been dammed and a sand beach created for a swimming area. The dam spillway is a favorite photo opportunity. The trail winds through the park and passes the park office and park store along the way. The park office has outdoor exhibits, maps, trail updates, and a bulletin board–size map of the entire Loyalsock Trail.

The trail leads you through a picnic area and back to the paved park road where you came out earlier after you walked alongside Loyalsock Creek. Once you're at this juncture, retrace your steps until you get to PA 154, where you can turn left and walk back to your vehicle.

Miles and Directions

0.0 Start at the Double Run Nature Trail parking lot and walk under the arch into the forest. Look for a white rectangular blaze with a green crossmember.

0.1 Go up the wooden steps.

0.2 The stream branches come together. Meet the Loyalsock Trail, marked by a yellow rectangular blaze with a red crossmember. Turn right onto the plank footbridge and cross the stream. Turn left onto the Double Run Trail. The stream is on your left.

0.4 Arrive at Cottonwood Falls. Walk beyond the falls and easily ford the stream on the exposed rocks.

0.5 Turn left onto the Link Trail. Look for yellow blazes with a red "X."

0.7 Arrive at a trail intersection. The trail turns left toward the stream at the double-X blazes. Turn left at the stream and then turn right; retrace your steps across the stream on the same plank footbridge, going in the same direction you crossed it the first time. This time, on the other side of the stream, turn right at the yellow arrow and follow the Link Trail. (**Note:** Three trails merge for about 30 feet.)

0.8 Cross a stream branch on a wooden footbridge and turn right onto the Link Trail, following the yellow blaze with a red "X."

0.9 The trail divides. The Loyalsock Trail (red blaze with yellow "LT") goes off to the left. Continue straight on the Link Trail.

1.0 Cross PA 154.

1.1 Arrive at Loyalsock Creek. Turn left and walk along the streambank.

1.4 Turn right onto the paved park road. Cross over Loyalsock Creek on an auto bridge. Look for a yellow arrow to the High Rock and Butternut Trails. Turn left and walk across the parking lot to the trailhead. Continue on the High Rock Trail.

1.8 Pass through a boulder outcropping and arrive at High Rock Falls.

2.0 The Loyalsock Trail veers off to the right. Continue straight on the High Rock Trail, following the yellow blazes.

2.2 Arrive at High Rock Vista.

2.3 Come to a trail intersection sign for the Loyalsock Trail. Continue on the High Rock Trail.

2.7 Turn right at a trail fork. Turn left onto PA 154.

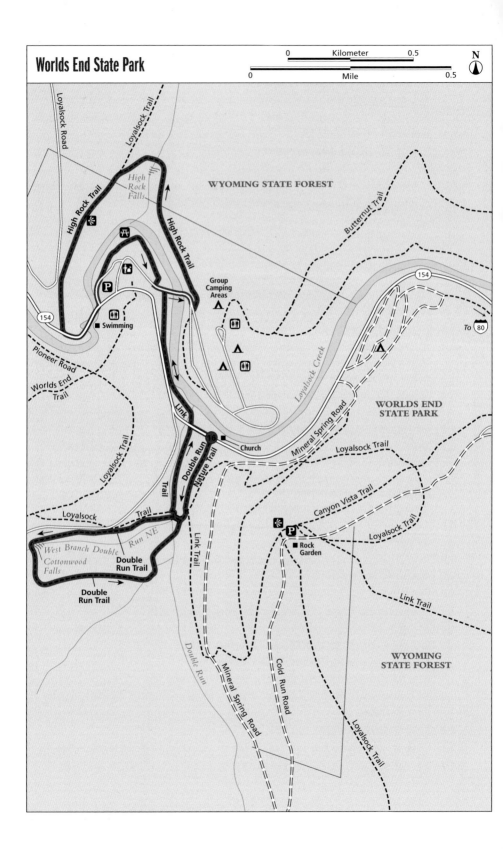

Worlds End State Park

0   Kilometer   0.5

0   Mile   0.5

N

Loyalsock Road

Loyalsock Trail

High Rock Trail

High Rock Falls

High Rock Trail

WYOMING STATE FOREST

Butternut Trail

154

To 80

P

Group Camping Areas

Swimming

154

Pioneer Road

Worlds End Trail

Loyalsock Trail

Loyalsock Creek

Mineral Spring Road

WORLDS END STATE PARK

Loyalsock Trail

Link Trail

Double Run Trail

Nature Trail

Church

Canyon Vista Trail

Loyalsock Trail

Loyalsock   Trail

Run NE

West Branch Double

Cottonwood Falls

Double Run Trail

Double Run Trail

P

Rock Garden

Link Trail

WYOMING STATE FOREST

Double Run

Mineral Spring Road

Cold Run Road

Loyalsock Trail

2.8 Cross the bridge over Loyalsock Creek. Turn left into the parking lot and walk to the picnic area. Stay on the road nearest Loyalsock Creek.

3.0 Walk past the park store. Reach the Loyalsock Trail sign beside the store. Turn left and head down the steps. Turn right at the bottom of the steps and walk through the picnic area.

3.1 Turn left onto the paved park road.

3.2 Turn right onto the Link Trail and retrace your steps. Look for yellow blazes with a red "X."

3.6 Cross PA 154. Turn left and arrive back at the Double Run Nature Trail parking area.

Local Information

Endless Mountains Visitors Bureau, 5405 US 6, Tunkhannock 18657; (570) 836-5431; www.endlessmountains.org

Local Events/Attractions

Flaming Foliage Show and Sale, first weekend in October; Forksville Fairgrounds, Forksville; www.pa-vendors.com/events/sullivan-county/forksville-pa-october-flaming -foliage-festival/

Campgrounds

Worlds End State Park Campgrounds, Route 154, Forksville; (570) 924-3287; (888) 727-2757 (camping information and reservations); www.dcnr.state.pa.us/stateparks/findapark/worldsend/

17 Haystacks

This is an easy, pleasant hike along Loyalsock Creek to the Haystacks boulders area and Dutchman Run Falls. At the falls you can explore the site where the falls empties into the creek. With its deep, hemlock-shaded valleys and plenty of pine needles covering the ground, this area could justly be described as picturesque.

Start: Loyalsock Trail trailhead parking lot on US 220

Distance: 4.5-mile loop

Hiking time: About 3 hours

Difficulty: Easy, with short steep ascents

Schedule: Open year-round

Season: Spring, summer, fall

Trail surface: Cinder railroad grade, shale roads, and pine-needle paths

Elevation gain: 648 feet

Land status: State forest

Nearest town: Laporte

Fees and permits: No fees or permits are required

Other trail users: Backpackers

Canine compatibility: Leashed dogs permitted

Maps: USGS Laporte, PA

Trail contacts: Loyalsock State Forest, Pennsylvania Department of Conservation, 6735 US 220, Dushore 18614; (570) 946-4049; www.dcnr.state.pa.us/forestry/stateforests/loyalsock/index.htm

Hillsgrove Ranger Station, 4 Dry Run Rd., Hillsgrove; (570) 924-3501

Finding the trailhead: From Williamsport, drive east on US 220/I-180 for 12 miles to the US 220 exit. Take the US 220 exit and continue on US 220 for 24 miles to Laporte. Drive through Laporte for approximately 3.5 miles and turn left onto Mead Road. Drive 0.25 mile and turn right into the parking lot. *DeLorme: Pennsylvania Atlas & Gazetteer:* Page 51 A6. GPS: N41 26.759' / W76 27.140'

The Hike

This hike got its name from a section of Loyalsock Creek where sandstone boulders—which are said to look like haystacks—create a series of rapids in an otherwise calm creek. The best time to see these rapids is when the water level is high—in spring after the winter melt-off or late fall after the area's rainy season.

The Haystacks lie at the eastern terminus of the 59.3-mile-long Loyalsock Trail. The name Loyalsock is derived from the Native American term *lawi-saquick*, meaning "middle creek." In this case, Loyalsock Creek runs between Muncy and Lycoming Creeks on its way to the Susquehanna River at Montoursville. The trail, which is described as a wilderness footpath, runs alongside Loyalsock Creek through Worlds End State Park and ends on PA 87 a few miles north of Montoursville. The trail is broken up into eight sections, each with road access at both ends.

The beginning of this hike is a 1.0-mile-long section of abandoned railroad grade. Here during summer, you'll pass families with children rolling tubes they've brought from home, heading for the Haystacks rapids. This section of the hike is popular and

The rock formations in this stream are known locally as haystacks.

very easy; you may even see parents pushing strollers. Of course these walkers go in and come out on the railroad grade and the improved shale road.

At the Haystacks area the trail follows the creek upstream. Walking the gorge bottom is easy and relaxing. Eastern hemlocks provide plenty of shade, the trail is covered with pine needles, and the rushing waters of Loyalsock Creek create a hypnotic spell that makes you forget you're just a few miles from civilization. Along this section you can see where visitors have built fire rings and spent some time enjoying the tranquility. (**Note:** There are seasonal and conditional bans on fires in Loyalsock State Forest. For more information call the Hillsgrove Ranger Station at 570-924-3501.)

Before the parking lot was built, hikers parked on US 220, walked in on the railroad grade to Dutchman Run Falls, and then continued their trek. If you park in the parking lot off Mead Road, you are west of the falls. That's why, when the hike is almost completed, you have to walk a short distance past your starting point on the railroad grade and turn left to see the falls.

In order to appreciate Dutchman Run Falls, it's necessary to climb down the gorge to the streambed, where the water from the falls empties into Loyalsock Creek. You can go down either side of the waterfalls, making your way from one flat boulder to the next.

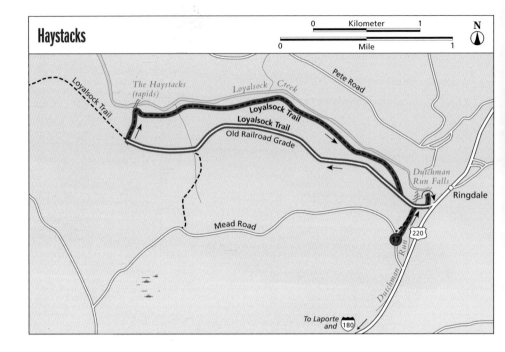

Miles and Directions

0.0 Start from the trailhead parking lot. There are two paths to get to the trailhead, one at each end of the parking lot. Take the one nearest to Mead Road. Walk to the "Alternative Hiking and Biking Trail to Loyalsock Trail & Haystacks" sign and walk between the two boulders.

0.4 Turn left onto the abandoned railroad grade. Look for the round red blazes with a yellow "LT."

1.6 Turn right at the "Haystacks ½ Mile" sign. Follow the round yellow blaze with a red "X."

2.0 Arrive at Loyalsock Creek and the Haystacks area. Turn right and follow the yellow rectangular blaze with red crossmember and the red round blaze with a yellow "LT."

2.7 Pass mile marker 58.

3.4 Begin a climb up the gorge.

3.6 Turn left onto the railroad grade and retrace your steps.

3.9 Pass mile marker 59 and walk past the Parking Lot sign. Walk past the trail blazed with "XX" and turn left onto the trail blazed with a single "X." Look for the Dutchman Falls sign.

4.0 Arrive at Loyalsock Creek. Retrace your steps out of the gorge.

4.1 Turn right onto the railroad grade. Turn left onto the alternative path to the parking lot where you started out and retrace your steps.

4.5 Arrive back at the parking lot.

Local Information

Endless Mountains Visitors Bureau, 5405 US 6, Tunkhannock 18657; (570) 836-5431 or (800) 769-8999; www.endlessmountains.org

Local Events/Attractions

Visit two covered bridges that span Loyalsock Creek. The Forksville covered bridge can be accessed from PA 154 in Forksville (GPS: N41 29.309' / W76 35.991'). The Hillsgrove covered bridge can be accessed just north of Hillsgrove off PA 87 (GPS: N41 27.642' / W76 40.242').

Campgrounds

Worlds End State Park Campgrounds, Route 154, Forksville; (570) 924-3287; (888) 727-2757 (camping information and reservations); www.dcnr.state.pa.us/stateparks/findapark/worldsend/

18 Mount Pisgah State Park

If you do this hike in summer, be sure to take your camera and plenty of water. There are plenty of steep, Ironman–type ascents, the last of which lands you at the top of Mount Pisgah for an impressive view of the surrounding valley. As for photo ops, the trail passes through a number of wildflower meadows bursting with vibrant colors. These meadows are not only breathtakingly beautiful but also provide an excuse for a much–needed rest after the climb.

Start: Fishing area parking lot on Stephen Foster Lake (in Mount Pisgah State Park)
Distance: 7.9-mile loop
Hiking time: About 4 hours
Difficulty: Moderate, with steep, strenuous climbs
Schedule: Open year-round, day use only
Season: Best in spring for wildflowers
Trail surface: Pine-needle trail and boardwalk; very steep dirt road
Elevation gain: 1,732 feet

Land status: State and county parks
Nearest town: Troy
Fees and permits: No fees or permits required
Other trail users: Picnickers, anglers
Canine compatibility: Leashed dogs permitted
Maps: USGS East Troy, PA
Trail contacts: Mount Pisgah State Park, 28 Entrance Rd., Troy 16947; (570) 297-2734; www.dcnr.state.pa.us/stateparks/findapark/mountpisgah

Finding the trailhead: From Williamsport, drive north on US 15 for 47 miles to US 6 in Mansfield. Turn right onto US 6 and drive east for 17 miles through Troy and East Troy to the Mount Pisgah State Park sign at SR 3019. Turn left on SR 3019 and drive 2 miles to the park and Stephen Foster Lake. *DeLorme: Pennsylvania Atlas & Gazetteer:* Page 37 B4. GPS: N41 48.082' / W76 40.107'

The Hike

Mount Pisgah State Park is a 1,302-acre day-use park. There's no overnight camping, and the park isn't near anything. Some might say Mount Pisgah is remote and inconvenient. It is. But this kind of isolation ensures a pristine park, and for many hikers and outdoorspeople, Mount Pisgah is a favorite.

The centerpiece of the park is 75-acre Stephen Foster Lake, created in 1979 when Mill Creek was dammed. There's a large swimming pool in the park, so the lake is used primarily by recreational boaters and anglers. There's a boat rental shed on the north side of the lake for pedal boats, V-bottom aluminum boats, and canoes. There's also a single-lane boat-launching ramp, seasonal mooring area, and a courtesy dock for loading and unloading.

Because powerboats aren't allowed on the lake, anglers—especially bass anglers—use electric trolling motors on their boats to get to their favorite spots (the shallow and weedy areas where bass hang out). In addition to the bass, perch, bluegill, and

Another view from the top

crappies are sometimes planted in the lake. There are plenty of spots for shoreline fishing, making this a popular spot for children to learn to fish.

The lake is named for Stephen Foster (1826–1864), a Pittsburgh native and former resident of this region. He was the composer of such popular nineteenth-century songs as "Oh! Susanna" (his first hit) and "De Camptown Races," which immortalized the horse races run from nearby Camptown to Wyalusing. Foster composed 285 songs, hymns, arrangements, and instrumental works; some of these, such as "Old Folks at Home," "Jeanie with the Light Brown Hair," and "Old Black Joe," are considered the most popular songs ever written. Unfortunately for Foster, nineteenth-century copyright laws offered little protection, and he received minimal income from his work. The last three years of his life, he lived alone in New York City, where he died of a fever in the charity ward of Bellevue Hospital.

The trail begins across the street from the fishing area parking lot and makes its way along Mill Creek. You're in a pine plantation as you walk along the inlet. There is an abundance of vegetation, such as cattails and Queen Anne's lace, throughout the marshy area. As the trail enters the forest canopy, you can see the ruins of stone fences, boundary lines when this area was first settled. This type of fence accomplished two

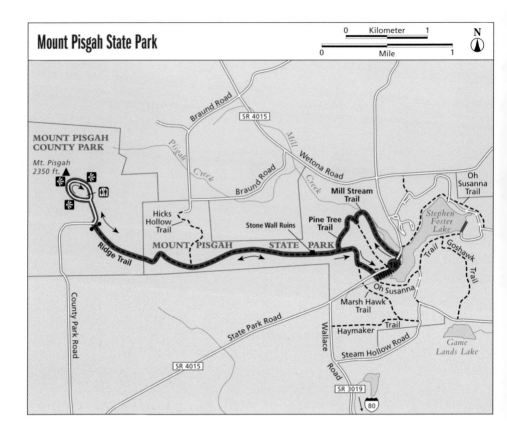

Mount Pisgah State Park

MOUNT PISGAH COUNTY PARK

Mt. Pisgah 2350 ft.

Braund Road

SR 4015

Pisgah Creek

Braund Road

Mill Creek

Wetona Road

Mill Stream Trail

Oh Susanna Trail

Hicks Hollow Trail

Stone Wall Ruins

Pine Tree Trail

Stephen Foster Lake

Ridge Trail

MOUNT PISGAH STATE PARK

Trail

Goshawk Trail

County Park Road

State Park Road

Oh Susanna Trail

Marsh Hawk Trail

Haymaker Trail

Wallace Road

Steam Hollow Road

Game Lands Lake

SR 4015

SR 3019

80

things: It set the boundary between farms, and it was a convenient way for farmers to get rid of the stones from their fields.

The trail is not blazed in the state park, but it is well maintained. Along the way you pass from the state to the county park; you can tell when you begin the county park section because you'll notice the faded red blazes. After you make your first serious climb in the forest, you enter into a meadow on a mowed path. Continue on this trail to a larger meadow filled with black-eyed Susans, Queen Anne's lace, common goldenrod, and wild bergamot in summer.

Enjoy the leisurely stroll through the meadows for as long as you can; the climb to the summit is next on your agenda. It's more than 1.0 mile to the top, and the trail varies between steep and very steep. Once at the summit, though, you can eat your lunch and take in one of the many vistas of the Bradford County farmlands and valleys. For your convenience there are restrooms and a number of strategically placed picnic tables set alongside natural overlooks.

If you're smart and plan ahead, you'll have a cold chicken dinner, a thermos of coffee, and your fishing rod waiting for you in your vehicle. You'll have rented a boat with a trolling motor and have it waiting for you so you can slip into the lake and let the cool afternoon breeze and gentle rocking of the boat lull you into a much-needed rest.

Miles and Directions

0.0 Start from the fishing area parking lot on Stephen Foster Lake. Turn right onto the park road and walk to a split-rail fence on the left side of the road. Turn left onto the Mill Stream Trail then veer right.

0.6 Turn right onto the Pine Tree Trail. Pass through the stone wall ruins.

0.8 Turn right onto the Ridge Trail. Pass through a meadow and join an abandoned jeep road.

0.9 Pass ruins of a second stone wall on your right.

1.8 The Hicks Hollow Trail goes off to your right. Continue straight past the Ridge Trail sign.

3.0 Come to an access gate.

3.5 Come to a cable gate across the trail. Turn right onto the paved road.

3.7 Turn left onto a dirt road and pass a red concrete building on your left.

3.8 Pass through a small picnic area on your right.

3.9 Turn left to an overlook; retrace your steps and turn left onto the road.

4.0 Turn left and walk uphill through a children's wooden playground.

4.3 Walk to two viewing areas on your left. Walk the loop around the tower.

4.7 Arrive at a viewing area on your left; continue downhill on the paved road.

4.8 Come to the cable gate across the trail. Turn left onto Ridge Trail and retrace your steps.

7.3 Arrive at an intersection with the Pine Tree Trail on your left. Continue straight.

7.5 Pass through a small meadow and turn right at a sign for snowmobiles and the Ridge Trail.

7.7 Cross the park road and turn left onto the Oh Susanna Trail.

7.9 Follow the boardwalk parallel to the lake and arrive back at the parking area.

Local Information

Endless Mountains Visitors Bureau, 5405 US 6, Tunkhannock 18657; (570) 836-5431 or (800) 769-8999; www.endlessmountains.org

Campgrounds

Worlds End State Park Campgrounds, Route 154, Forksville; (570) 924-3287; (888) 727-2757 (camping information and reservations); www.dcnr.state.pa.us/stateparks/findapark/worldsend/

Honorable Mentions

Northeast Pennsylvania

Here are three great hikes in the Northeast region that didn't make the A-list this time around but deserve recognition. Check them out and let us know what you think. You may decide that one or more of these hikes deserves higher status in future editions, or you may have a hike of your own that merits some attention.

F Lehigh Gorge State Park

Lehigh Gorge State Park is a lineal park that parallels the Lehigh River in Carbon and Luzerne Counties. The trail is an abandoned railroad grade that stretches 25 miles from White Haven in the north to Jim Thorpe in the south. There are a number of access points along the way in this stunning gorge, so you can plan your hike accordingly. Expect to see plenty of bicyclists and whitewater rafters: The Lehigh River is one of the top whitewater rivers in the country, and the bike trail is considered by *Outside* magazine to be Pennsylvania's best.

From Allentown, drive north on I-476. Take exit 74 and drive west on PA 209 into the village of Jim Thorpe. In Jim Thorpe turn right on PA 903 and cross the Lehigh River. At the stop sign turn left onto Front Street, which becomes Coalport Road, and continue for 0.4 mile to the park entrance. For more information call Lehigh Gorge/Hickory Run State Park at (570) 443-0400. *DeLorme: Pennsylvania Atlas & Gazetteer*: Page 67 A5

G Promised Land State Park

The park is located just south of I-84 halfway between Scranton and Milford. Take exit 26 off I-84 and drive south a few miles on PA 390. The 3,000-acre park is surrounded by the Delaware State Forest and is recognized as one of the most spectacular areas for mountain laurel and rhododendron blooms in early summer and for its breathtaking fall foliage. There are more than 50 miles of hiking trails, and with a name like Promised Land, who can resist stopping at the park office for a brochure that tells all about the Quakers who settled the area.

From Milford, drive west on I-84, take exit 26 and drive south on PA 390 for 4 miles and turn right onto Lower Lake Road to enter the park. For more information call Promised Land State Park, Greentown; (570) 676-3428; www.visit PAparks.com. De Lorme: Pennsylvania Atlas & Gazetter: Page 54 B2

H Big Pocono State Park

The park is located just south of I-80 and just east of the intersection of I-80 and I-380 in Monroe County. There are 10 miles of trails here; two of these, the Indian and North Trails, are not for inexperienced hikers. Climb famous Camelback Mountain for a visit to the fire tower, which has been declared a historical structure, and for world-class views. For those who want to see the views without hiking, a 1.4-mile paved auto road girdles the mountaintop, providing views in all directions.

From Scranton, drive south on I-380 and connect with I-80 East. Take exit 298 and follow signs to the park. For more information call the Big Pocono State Park c/o Tobyhanna State Park at (570) 894-8336. *DeLorme: Pennsylvania Atlas & Gazetteer.* Page 54 D1

Plan to hike in early June if you want to see plenty of Mountain Laurel in bloom.
DEBRA YOUNG

North Central Pennsylvania

Northorth Central Pennsylvania is big country. It's sparsely populated and remote. One local legend says that in Potter County there are more deer than people. That could be: There are 1.5 million deer in Pennsylvania; and as any weekday hiker will tell you, you'll see more deer on the trail than people. You'll also see huge ravines, some so steep you'll wish you had climbing gear in your pack instead of that mushed peanut butter and jelly sandwich.

Nature has been busy on the Allegheny High Plateau. The plateau, which includes the highest point in Pennsylvania's Appalachian Plateau range, borders the Ridge and Valley Province to the south along the escarpment known as the Allegheny Front. Want to see the Allegheny Front up close and personal? Take the Loyalsock Trail and you can walk right to the edge. Many hikers say the top hike in this region is the majestic Pine Creek Gorge—better known as Pennsylvania's Grand Canyon. At more than 5,000 feet wide, 800 feet deep, and 47 miles long, it's the most spectacular gorge in the state. In fact, *Outdoor* magazine named one of the gorge hikes "one of the best trails in Pennsylvania." (See Hike 22: Bohen Run Falls and West Rim Trail.)

With its deep ravines, snakelike creeks, cliffs, and boulder outcrops, it's difficult to think of the North Central region as a plateau—but it is. It started out as somewhat level terrain, but what with tectonic shifts, erosion, and water running everywhere, it got to be, well, inhospitable to foot travel. If you like big challenges and big rewards, this region is for you.

19 R. B. Winter State Park

This hike uses a challenging, little-known cross-country skiing trail to take you across the ridgetops and in and out of the 500-foot-deep hemlock valleys. It connects with an abandoned narrow-gauge railroad bed that runs for 2.0 miles over extremely rocky terrain. From there it runs up another ridge to an overlook 300 feet above the valley and then down the ridge to a nature trail through a second-growth pine and hemlock forest.

Start: R. B. Winter State Park parking lot on PA 192
Distance: 7.5-mile loop
Hiking time: About 4 hours
Difficulty: Moderate, due to uphill climbs and rocky footpaths
Schedule: Open year-round
Season: Spring, summer, fall
Trail surface: Rocky footpath, cross-country skiing trails, a power line service road, improved roads, and a nature trail
Elevation gain: 898 feet

Land status: State park
Nearest town: Lewisburg
Fees and permits: No fees or permits required
Other trail users: Hikers, cross-country skiers, hunters (in season)
Canine compatibility: Leashed dogs permitted
Maps: USGS Carroll, PA; Hartleton, PA
Trail contacts: R. B. Winter State Park, 17215 Buffalo Rd., Mifflinburg 17844; (570) 966-1455; www.dcnr.state.pa.us/stateparks/findapark/raymondbwinter

Finding the trailhead: From Williamsport, drive south on US 15 for 33 miles to Lewisburg. In Lewisburg turn right onto PA 192 and drive 17 miles west to R. B. Winter State Park. Park in the parking lot on your right, next to Halfway Lake. *DeLorme: Pennsylvania Atlas & Gazetteer:* Page 63 A7. GPS: N40 59.427' / W77 11.440'

The Hike

The 695-acre R. B. Winter State Park lies within the Bald Eagle State Forest—195,000 acres of some of the most rugged and remote land in the state. The park sits in a narrow valley between two ridges, part of the Ridge and Valley Province—a series of parallel ridges that arc from Maryland to the New Jersey border. The ridges were created by an upheaval that folded, or faulted, the earth. As a result, the ridges and valleys produce two distinctly different environments: dry, rocky ridges and slopes with an abundance of deciduous hardwoods; and lush, marshy valleys carpeted with immense pines. You'll have an opportunity to sample a bit of each—or at least what's left of the original habitat—along this trail.

In earlier times the best way to traverse this region was to travel in the valleys. In the 1700s a wagon road was built through the narrow valley to haul produce from the agricultural region of Centre County to the Susquehanna River, where it was loaded onto barges. The road—now PA 192—was called, appropriately, Narrows Road.

The dam at Halfway Lake is a favorite tourist attraction.

Logging began here in the late 1800s and ended in 1910, when there were no more trees to cut. A sawmill was set up and a log dam was built across Rapid Run, the site of today's Halfway Lake. The forest was once so thick with white pine and hemlock—some more than 6 feet in diameter and reaching heights of 200 feet—that it was referred to as the shrouded forest because the forest canopy virtually blocked the sun, keeping the forest in semidarkness.

Starting at Halfway Lake, this hike begins with a brisk uphill warm-up. In less than 0.5 mile, the trail levels out and you begin to see cross-country skiing signs. There are a few stretches so thickly strewn with rocks that you wonder how anyone could ski over this terrain. Needless to say, in order to ski over such a trail, there needs to be at least 10 inches of snow.

At a little more than 1.0 mile, you cross under a power line. Here, in the clearing that runs under the power line, there's a clear view across the valley to Naked Mountain. In a little more than 5.5 miles you'll be standing on that site, under the power line that looks impossibly far away.

The next section, the Tram Road Trail, runs for a little more than 2.0 miles—and a good portion of the trail surface is rocky, rocky, rocky. As you walk this section, you've got to wonder who would build a railroad over such rocky, rough terrain. Indeed, there are reports of rides so bumpy that cargo bounced off the train. Such was the case when a cracker barrel bounced off and rolled down the mountainside at a site now called Cracker Bridge.

After the overlook, the trail leads down to the 34-acre natural area, a pristine second-growth pine-hemlock forest in the Rapid Run Valley. The area was set aside to give visitors an idea of what the forest looked like before it was clear-cut. And although it may not be quite as good as the original, it's not a bad substitute.

Miles and Directions

0.0 Start at the steps in the Halfway Lake parking lot on PA 192 near the breast of the dam. Walk east alongside PA 192 and cross the bridge.

0.1 Turn left at the end of the guardrails and walk toward the dam spillway. Look for the orange blaze on a large hemlock tree near the spillway.

0.2 Turn right at the double orange blazes near the spillway and begin an uphill climb. Cross Boyer Gap Road and arrive at the trailhead for the Bake Oven Trail. The trail sign reads "Mid State Trail & Sand Mountain Tower." Continue straight.

0.8 Pass the Old Boundary Trail on your left.

1.2 Pass under the power line.

2.3 Arrive at a trail intersection. Cross Boyer Gap Road and continue straight on the Mid State Trail.

2.8 Arrive at a trail intersection. Turn left onto the blue-blazed Buffalo Path Trail. (The Mid State Trail continues straight toward the [now closed] Sand Mountain Fire Tower.)

3.0 Turn right onto Boyer Gap Road.

3.2 Cross Sand Mountain Road. Continue straight onto the red-blazed Cracker Bridge Trail.

3.3 The cross-country skiing trail goes off to your left. Continue straight up a rocky knoll.

3.6 Arrive at a trail intersection. Turn left onto the Tram Road Trail.

3.7 Cross Spruce Run on a series of wooden footbridges.

5.4 Come to a sign that reads "Old Tram Trail." Pass Boiling Spring Trail on your left; continue straight.

5.8 Turn left onto a jeep road and make an immediate right turn to get under the power line. Make an immediate left onto the power line service road and walk along the road under the power line.

5.9 Look for the red blaze and blue cross-country sign on a power line pole.

6.0 Turn right at a power stanchion with double red blazes and a white arrow.

6.6 Turn left onto McCall Dam Road and arrive at the McCall Dam Overlook. Turn left on the viewing platform to the man-made steps and begin your descent on a series of switchbacks.

7.0 Cross Sand Mountain Road and turn left at the sign for the nature trail.

7.1 Come to the Nature Trail & Beach sign. Follow the yellow arrow. Pass through a hemlock stand and come to a trail intersection. Continue straight, following the white blaze. (The Rapid Run Nature Trail goes off to your right.)

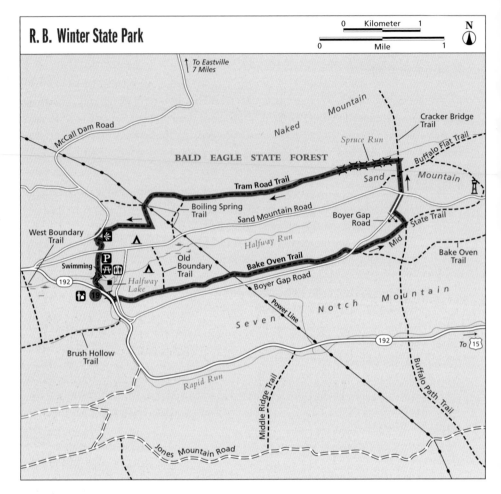

R. B. Winter State Park

0   Kilometer   1

0   Mile   1

N

To Eastville
7 Miles

McCall Dam Road

Naked   Mountain

Spruce Run

Cracker Bridge
Trail

Buffalo Flat Trail

BALD EAGLE STATE FOREST

Tram Road Trail

Sand   Mountain

Boiling Spring
Trail

Sand Mountain Road

Boyer Gap
Road

State Trail

West Boundary
Trail

Halfway Run

Mid

Bake Oven
Trail

Swimming

Old
Boundary
Trail

Bake Oven Trail

P

192

Halfway
Lake

Boyer Gap Road

Power Line

Seven   Notch   Mountain

192

To 15

Brush Hollow
Trail

Rapid Run

Middle Ridge Trail

Buffalo Path Trail

Jones Mountain Road

7.2   Pass under a power line.

7.3   Turn right onto a shale road. Cross the bridge over Rapid Run; turn left and walk along the edge of Halfway Lake.

7.5   Arrive back at the parking lot steps.

Local Information

Susquehanna River Valley Visitors Bureau, 81 Hafer Rd., Lewisburg 17837; (570) 524-7234; www.visitcentralpa.org

Local Events/Attractions

Mifflinburg Buggy Museum, 598 Green St., Mifflinburg; (570) 966-1355; www.buggymuseum.org

Campgrounds

R. B. Winter State Park, Route 192, Mifflinburg; (570) 966-1455; (888) 727-2757 (camping information and reservations); www.dcnr.state.pa.us/stateparks/findapark/raymondbwinter

20 Loyalsock Trail

This hike begins with a difficult, steep climb up the side of a gorge. It's a challenging climb with short switchbacks and rock and root handholds. Once on top you cross a plateau with huckleberry bushes and pine plantations. From the plateau's edge there are spectacular views and a cool breeze that sweeps up the gorge.

Start: Loyalsock Trail trailhead on PA 87
Distance: 6.9-mile loop
Hiking time: About 5 hours
Difficulty: Difficult, with very steep ascents and rugged descents
Schedule: Open year-round
Season: Spring, summer, fall
Trail surface: Rocky switchback footpath, open plateau trail, very rugged and rocky washout, and a shale road
Elevation gain: 1,430 feet
Land status: State forest
Nearest town: Montoursville
Fees and permits: No fees or permits required for hikers. There is a no-charge permit required for thru-hikers who plan to primitive camp along the trail. Call the Tiadaghton State Forest

at (570) 753-5409 or Hillsgrove Ranger Station, for the Loyalsock State Forest section of the trail, at (570) 924-3501. Overnight hikers within Worlds End State Park must register at the park office; call (570) 924-3287.
Other trail users: Backpackers
Canine compatibility: Leashed dogs permitted
Maps: USGS Montoursville North, PA; Huntersville, PA
Trail contacts: Tiadaghton State Forest, 10 Lower Pine Bottom Rd., Waterville 17776; (570) 327-3450; www.dcnr.state.pa.us/forestry/stateforests/tiadaghton
Loyalsock State Forest, 6735 US 220, Dushore 18614; (570) 946-4059; www.dcnr.state.pa.us/forestry/stateforests/loyalsock/index.htm

Finding the trailhead: From Williamsport, drive approximately 7 miles east on US 220 and take the Montoursville exit. Get on PA 87 and drive north for 8.8 miles to the Loyalsock Trailhead and parking area, on your right. *DeLorme: Pennsylvania Atlas & Gazetteer:* Page 50 A2. GPS: N41 21.692' / W076 52.607'

The Hike

This hike is the western terminus of the 59.3–mile Loyalsock Trail, which parallels Loyalsock Creek, passes through Worlds End State Park, and eventually ends at the Susquehanna River. The name is taken from the Native American *lawi-saquick,* or "middle creek," because it flows between Muncy and Lycoming Creeks. The trail is well marked and well cared for, with convenient access trailheads every 4 to 10 miles dividing the hike into eight sections. In fact, as you leave the forest on this hike, you pass the access point of the next section of the trail, which leads to Smiths Knob.

There is no warm-up period on this hike; it's an assault from the very first step. As soon as you sign in at the trail register, you begin a 0.7-mile climb up the side of

Once you climb the steps, there is a one-mile climb to the top.

Loyalsock Gorge. The climb is steep—if it were any steeper, you'd need to trade in your hiking boots for mountain climbing gear.

At the summit you'll come out onto a plateau. Interestingly, you're on top of the Allegheny High Plateau, which comprises the northern and western regions of the Appalachian Plateau. The plateau, which is also called Allegheny Mountain, stretches north to the New York border and south to meet the Ridge and Valley Province—creating an escarpment called the Allegheny Front. It's difficult to think of any area with such deep gorges as a plateau. But as you listen to the never-ending rush of Loyalsock Creek, you begin to understand that waters have been draining this area and cutting streambeds into the rock for more than 200 million years.

This hike is your chance to walk right to the edge of the Allegheny Front and take in the vistas of the valley below and the ridgetops off in the distance. A cool wind sweeps up from the ravine, cooling you as you walk through huckleberry bushes to rock outcroppings where you can rest, take in the scenery, and eat your lunch.

Once you leave the ridgetop, you're on your way down into Pete's Hollow. This trail back to civilization may challenge most hikers' belief that going down is always easier than going up. Calling the steep, rocky washout into the hollow a trail is being

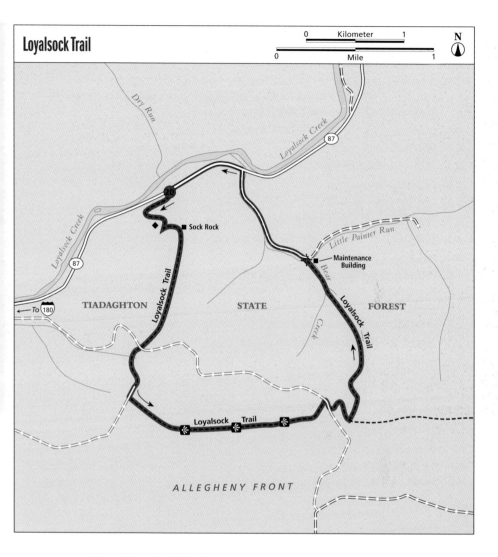

Loyalsock Trail

0   Kilometer   1

0   Mile   1

N

Dry Run

Loyalsock Creek

87

Sock Rock

Loyalsock Creek

Little Painter Run

Maintenance Building

87

Bear Creek

To 180

TIADAGHTON

STATE

FOREST

Loyalsock Trail

Loyalsock Trail

Loyalsock   Trail

ALLEGHENY FRONT

generous. It's well marked like the rest of the trail, but for more than a mile, you're tracking slow and easy from one slippery boulder to the next.

The trail levels out in a hemlock valley beside Bear Creek. There's a dam just below the bridge where you can splash water on your face or take off your boots and give your feet a dip. From there it's a level walk on a forest road beside Bear Creek. Along the way you pass rustic cabins, set in deep shade on both sides of the road.

Miles and Directions

0.0   Start from the trailhead on PA 87. Walk to the Loyalsock Trail trailhead sign and trail register and begin an uphill climb. Turn right at the yellow arrow.

0.2   The trail turns left.

0.6 Come to a round blue sign that reads "Sock Rock" above a sandstone boulder that supposedly looks like a sock. Follow the yellow arrow to the right.

0.7 Arrive at the top. The trail levels out on a plateau.

1.5 Arrive at an intersection with an abandoned jeep road. Continue straight and then veer right. Cross a small stream. Look for red "LT" blazes and yellow rectangular blazes with red crossmembers. Cross a second stream. The trail becomes a jeep road.

1.8 Turn left at the yellow arrow and then left again.

2.0 Pass the 2.0-mile marker.

2.1 Arrive at the Allegheny Front.

3.0 Pass the 3.0-mile marker.

3.5 Turn right onto a jeep road.

3.7 The trail turns left, then left again.

4.1 Enter the forest canopy. Look for the yellow and red blazes.

5.3 Ford a small washout stream.

5.6 Pass through the Tiadaghton State Forest maintenance parking lot and cross a bridge over Bear Creek. On the other side turn left onto the shale road. Look for the blazes along the road.

5.7 Pass the Loyalsock Trail sign on your right. Continue straight on the shale road.

6.3 Turn left at PA 87 and walk alongside the road.

6.9 Arrive back at the trailhead.

Local Information

Lycoming County Visitor Center, 210 William St., Williamsport 17701; (570) 327-7700 or (800) 358-9900; www.vacationpa.com/

Local Events/Attractions

Hiawatha Paddlewheel Riverboat, on the Susquehanna River at Susquehanna State Park, 2205 Hiawatha Blvd., Williamsport; (570) 326-2500 or (800) 248-9287; www.ridehiawatha.com

Campgrounds

Sheshequin Campground, 389 Marsh Hill Rd., Trout Run; (570) 995-9230; www.sheshequincampground.com

Restaurants

Le Jeune Chef, Pennsylvania College of Technology, One College Ave., 17701 Williamsport 17701; (570) 327-4776; www.pct.edu/lejeunechef

21 Gillespie Point

This hike asks only one question: Would you climb a little more than a mile up the side of a gorge to take in a once-in-a-lifetime view? Begin on an improved forest road, climb to the viewing area, and then loop back to this same forest road for an easy walk back to the starting point.

Start: Blackwell Boaters Access Area parking lot on PA 414
Distance: 4.9-mile loop
Hiking time: About 3 hours
Difficulty: Moderate, due to a short, steep climb
Schedule: Open year-round
Season: Spring, summer, fall
Trail surface: Shale road, forest footpath, and rock outcroppings
Elevation gain: 1,159 feet

Land status: State forest
Nearest town: Wellsboro
Fees and permits: No fees or permits required
Other trail users: Hikers
Canine compatibility: Leashed dogs permitted
Maps: USGS Cedar Run, PA; Morris, PA
Trail contacts: Tioga State Forest, One Nessmuk Ln., Wellsboro 16901; (570) 724-2868; www.dcnr.state.pa.us/forestry/stateforests/tioga

Finding the trailhead: From Williamsport, drive north on US 15 for 26 miles to the village of Liberty and look for the PA 414 sign. Turn left onto PA 414 and drive west 15 miles to the village of Blackwell and the Blackwell Boaters Access Area parking lot, on your left. *DeLorme: Pennsylvania Atlas & Gazetteer.* Page 35 D5. GPS: N41 33.364' / W77 22.925'

The Hike

Tioga State Forest consists of 160,000 acres of mountains and valleys, with a range in elevation from 780 feet to more than 2,500 feet. Unlike the state's Ridge and Valley Province, faulting (folding of the earth) didn't create this area. It was formed during the last ice age when a glacier blocked the northerly flowing water, creating a glacial pond. When the glacier retreated, glaciations occurred, leaving behind a moraine of gravel, clay, and sand that reversed the flow of the water. Over the next 10 million years, this stream, now known as Pine Creek, carved out the gorge. From Gillespie Point you can have a commanding view of this project, eons in the making.

The 12,163-acre Pine Creek Gorge, more than 5,000 feet across at its widest point, is commonly referred to as the Grand Canyon of Pennsylvania. Because of its beauty and distinct natural characteristics, the gorge was declared a National Natural Landmark in 1968. Two state parks, Colton Point and Leonard Harrison, claim the northern end of the gorge, but this hike doesn't include them. These parks are more touristy—with more than 300,000 annual visitors, wooden steps, guardrails, and viewing platforms on the trails—and neither offers anything near the views you'll experience at Gillespie Point.

This view from Gillespie Point shows Pine Creek flowing through the Grand Canyon of Pennsylvania.

Because of its conical shape, the apex of Gillespie Point is not very big—no bigger, say, than a full-size car. The viewpoint is nothing more than an outcropping that hangs over the cliff edge like a shelf. When you walk out onto it, snug down your hat—the wind whips up out of the gorge and whistles through the trees with appreciable force, just as it has for millions of years. This is the vista you've come for, but a second view to the south of Big Run Valley and Oregon Hill is also impressive.

Before this area was settled and seriously logged, the forests were predominately white pine, red maple, chestnut, and hemlock. Today the forest is made up of two communities: One is dominated by hardwoods, such as yellow birch, sugar maple, beech, and black cherry; the other, by white pine.

For the wildflower enthusiast spring is the best time to visit. More than fifty species of wildflowers bloom in April and May. Among them are columbine, jack-in-the-pulpit, wild ginger, false Solomon's seal, and Canada mayflower. In summer look for helleborine (a wild orchid), white snakeroot, hairy beardtongue, and red bee balm.

For birders spring is also the best time to see ospreys (also called fish hawks) migrating north. This large raptor, with a wingspan of 5 to 6 feet, was once almost wiped out by DDT but has rebounded well since the pesticide was banned.

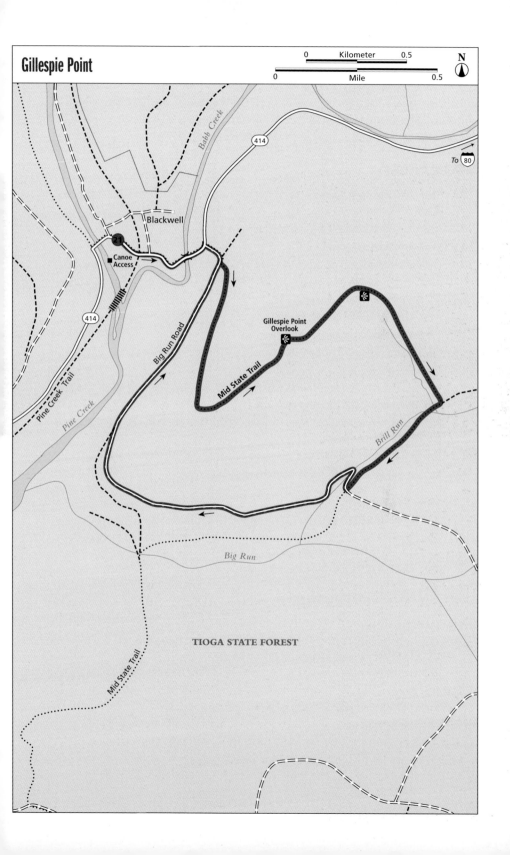

Gillespie Point

0   Kilometer   0.5

0   Mile   0.5

N

To 80

Babb Creek

414

Blackwell

21

Canoe
Access

414

Big Run Road

Pine Creek Trail

Pine Creek

Mid State Trail

Gillespie Point
Overlook

Brill Run

Mid State Trail

Big Run

TIOGA STATE FOREST

In addition to wildlife viewing from the trails, some birders go a step farther—heading out on the water in canoes for a chance to view the bald eagles that nest around the tiny village of Blackwell. If you're interested, you too can launch your canoe from the Blackwell Boater Access Area and comb the river, possibly witnessing one of these raptors diving into the waters to pluck a fish.

Miles and Directions

0.0 Start at the Blackwell Boaters Access Area. Turn right onto PA 414 and walk through the village of Blackwell.

0.2 Cross over Babb Creek on the one-lane traffic bridge.

0.3 Turn right onto Big Run Road.

0.4 Arrive at the Mid State Trail sign and a sign for Gillespie Point and Little Pine State Park. Begin an uphill climb, following the orange blazes.

1.0 The trail turns left at the double orange blazes.

1.3 Arrive at Gillespie Point Overlook.

1.7 The trail turns right and passes through an open area.

1.9 Cross a washout stream and an abandoned logging road.

2.3 The trail turns right.

2.8 Turn right onto Big Run Road. Arrive at the Mid State Trail and a sign that reads "Mid State Trail," "Brill Hollow," and "Gillespie Point."

4.5 Pass a sign marking the Tioga State Forest boundary. Pass the Mid State Trailhead, where you first left Big Run Road.

4.6 Turn left onto PA 414 and retrace your steps across the traffic bridge.

4.9 Turn left and arrive back at the Blackwell Boater Access Area.

Local Information
Tioga County Visitors Bureau, 2053 Route 660, Wellsboro 16901; (570) 724-0635; www.visittiogapa.com

Local Events/Attractions
Pine Creek Outfitters, 5142 US 6, Wellsboro; (570) 724-3003; www.pinecrk.com—whitewater rafting, canoe and bicycle rentals, guided tours

Accommodations
Cedar Run Inn, 281 Beulah Land Rd., Cedar Run; (570) 353-6241; www.pavisnet.com/cedarruninn

Campgrounds
Pettecote Junction Campground, 400 Beach Rd., Cedar Run; (570) 353-7183; www.pettecotejunction.com

Restaurants
Wellsboro Diner, 19 Main St., Wellsboro; (570) 724-3992

22 Bohen Run Falls and West Rim Trail

There is one world-class view of Pennsylvania's Pine Creek Gorge on this section of the West Rim Trail—and legions of hikers consider the climb out of the gorge worth it. Along the way to the top, there are views of Pine Creek and sparkling mountain waterfalls. The final leg is on the Pine Creek Rail Trail.

Start: Blackwell Boaters Access Area parking lot on PA 414
Distance: 8.5-mile loop
Hiking time: About 5 hours
Difficulty: Moderate, due to the extensive uphill climbs
Schedule: Open year-round
Season: Spring, summer, fall
Trail surface: Abandoned logging roads, mountain footpaths, wheatgrass meadow, and shale bicycle path
Elevation gain: 859 feet
Land status: State forest
Nearest town: Wellsboro

Fees and permits: No fees or permits required for hikers. Camping/backpacking on state forest land in the Pine Creek Corridor requires a permit. Call the Tioga State Forest (570-724-2868) or the Tiadaghton State Forest (570-753-5409)
Other trail users: None
Canine compatibility: Leashed dogs permitted
Maps: USGS Cedar Run, PA
Trail contacts: Tioga State Forest, One Nessmuk Ln., Wellsboro 16901; (570) 724-2868; www.dcnr.state.pa.us/forestry/stateforests/tioga

Finding the trailhead: From Williamsport, drive north on US 15 for 26 miles to the village of Liberty and look for the PA 414 sign. Turn left onto PA 414 and drive west 15 miles to the village of Blackwell and the Blackwell Boaters Access Area lot, on your left. *DeLorme: Pennsylvania Atlas & Gazetteer:* Page 35 D5. GPS: N41 33.364' / W77 22.925'

The Hike

This hike comprises sections of two of the state's most popular backpacking trails: the West Rim and the Mid State Trails. The West Rim Trail stretches 30 miles along the western rim of Pine Creek Gorge—Pennsylvania's Grand Canyon. The Mid State Trail runs from the Pennsylvania-Maryland border south of Everett to its connection with the West Rim Trail near Bohen Run in the north. Regardless of where you enter this gorge, you'll be struck by the sheer strength of the force that turned a mountain plateau into a corrugated landscape that, seen from an adjoining mountain peak, looks like a giant green washboard.

On this hike you achieve not only the northern terminus of the Mid State Trail but also walk the final leg of the West Rim Trail to its southern terminus on PA 414. If you are new to this area, these hikes will afford you a quality Pine Creek Gorge experience, far from the tourist-friendly Leonard Harrison and Colton Point State Parks in the northern end of the gorge.

A different look at the Bohen Run Trailhead

Hikers are not the only ones who sing the praises of this rugged wilderness. In 1968 Congress declared an 18-mile stretch of the gorge—from Ansonia south to Blackwell—a National Natural Landmark. Our hike takes you into the southern tip of this 12,163-acre natural wonderland.

You begin at Pine Creek, the lowest point in the gorge. Keep your eyes open for bald eagles as you walk along the creek. Sightings are common along Pine Creek, especially around Blackwell. You may also see a bald eagle diving into the water and emerging with its dinner between its talons.

Runoff waters from the mountaintops cut gashes in the hollow bottoms as they make their way to the bottom of the gorge. Once you have climbed up the face of Pine Creek Gorge, you encounter your first runoff streams: Jerry and Bohen Runs.

If you do this hike in early spring, the waterfalls will be dancing and the trails will be slippery. If you come later in the year or during a dry spell, you're unlikely to find waterfalls—and if it has been an extended dry season, there may be no water at all. This is important to note if you're one of the many hikers who use waterfalls and streams as reference points.

The Mid State Trail ends at its junction with the West Rim Trail. From there it's a short climb to the West Rim Overlook—a great place to eat your lunch, stretch out on the grassy flat area for a snooze, or just sit on a rock and listen to the wind.

The Rattlesnake Rock Access Area to the Pine Creek Rail Trail is directly across PA 414. Restrooms and seasonal water are available here. The trail, which has a

Pine Creek runs through Pennsylvania's Grand Canyon.

crushed limestone base, runs from Ansonia in the northern end of the gorge to Jersey Shore in the southern end, for a total of 62 miles. Lucky for you, the weary hiker, you only have to walk a scant 1.5 miles to your car.

Miles and Directions

0.0 Start at the Blackwell Boaters Access Area parking lot. Turn left onto PA 414 and cross the traffic bridge over Pine Creek.

0.1 Turn right at the double orange blazes painted on the back side of a street sign. You must step over the guardrail.

0.2 Arrive at stone steps and a trail sign for the Mid State Trail, Jerry Run Falls, Bohen Run Falls, and the West Rim Trail.

1.0 Arrive at a rock outcropping and a view area.

1.2 Arrive at a natural overlook and Jerry Run Falls.

1.3 The trail turns right onto an old logging road at the double orange blazes.

1.5 Pass a trail that goes off to the right, down the gorge to campsites. Continue straight.

1.6 Arrive at double orange blazes. Trail turns uphill onto an old logging road.

2.3 Arrive at Bohen Run.

2.8 Arrive at the intersection with the West Rim Trail and trail register. Make a severe left turn and begin climbing on the West Rim Trail.

3.6 Arrive at the West Rim Trail Overlook.

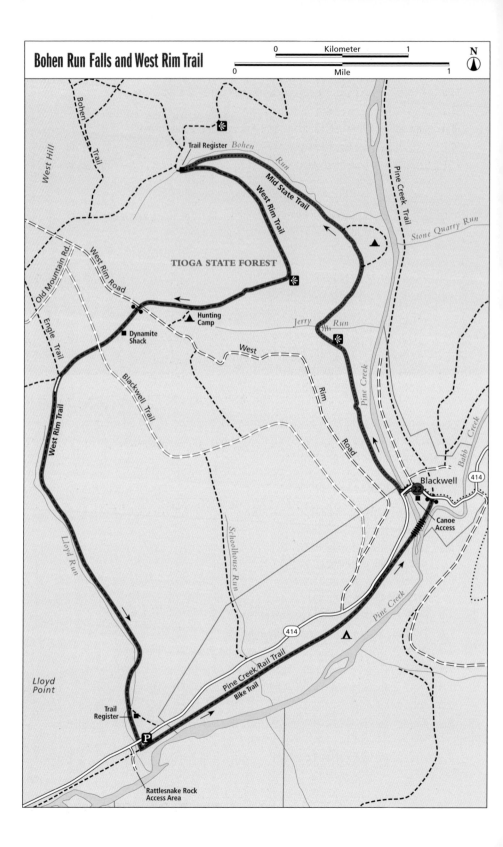

Bohen Run Falls and West Rim Trail

N

Bohen Run

West Hill

Bohen Trail

Trail Register

Mid State Trail

West Rim Trail

TIOGA STATE FOREST

Old Mountain Rd.

West Rim Road

Engle Trail

Hunting Camp

Dynamite Shack

West Rim Trail

Blackwell Trail

West

Rim

Road

Jerry Run

Pine Creek

Stone Quarry Run

Pine Creek Trail

Lloyd Run

Schoolhouse Run

Blackwell

414

Canoe Access

Babb Creek

Lloyd Point

Trail Register

P

414

Pine Creek Rail Trail
Bike Trail

Pine Creek

Rattlesnake Rock
Access Area

4.4 Cross West Rim Road and arrive at a sign that reads "West Rim Trail to Route 414–2.3 Miles."

4.9 The trail turns left onto a dirt road and then becomes a rocky footpath.

5.1 The trail turns left at Lloyd Run stream.

6.4 Arrive at fork in the trail. Go to the right, following the orange blazes.

6.6 Arrive at the West Rim Trail register.

6.9 Cross PA 414 to Rattlesnake Rock Access Area parking lot. Walk on the path past the restrooms and turn left onto the Pine Creek Bicycle Trail.

8.4 Cross Pine Creek on the wooden rail trail bridge.

8.5 Pass the auto access gate and turn left onto PA 414. Shortly afterward, turn left and arrive back at the Blackwell Boaters Access Area parking lot.

Local Information

Tioga County Visitors Bureau, 2053 Route 660, Wellsboro 16901; (570) 724-0635; www.visittiogapa.com

Local Events/Attractions

Tioga County Fair, August, Tioga County Fair, 2258 Charleston Rd., Wellsboro; (570) 724-3196; tiogacountyfair.com

Accommodations

Penn Wells Hotel and Lodge, 62 Main St., Wellsboro; (570) 724-2111; pennwells.com

Campgrounds

Stony Fork Creek Campground, 658 Stony Fork Creek Rd., Wellsboro; (570) 724-3096; www.stonyforkcamp.com

Restaurants

The Mary Wells Dining Room at the Penn Wells Hotel and Lodge, 62 Main St., Wellsboro; (570) 724-2111; pennwells.com

23 Pine Trail and Hemlock Mountain

This hike begins with an easy walk alongside crystal-clear Pine Creek, followed by a trek out of the gorge. Near the top of the gorge, the footpath narrows as it passes through an outcropping of boulders that forces hikers to bend over at points. Although it's not a dangerous spot, you may have to hold onto the boulders to keep your balance. There is a rough 0.75-mile climb through a steep, rocky washout to the mountaintop, where an unused forest road leads from one spectacular view of Pine Creek Gorge to the next. Because of the enormity of the gorge and the high visibility, many hikers contend these are the best views in the state.

Start: Pine Trail trailhead at the end of Naval Run Road in the Tiadaghton State Forest
Distance: 8.3-mile loop
Hiking time: About 6 hours
Difficulty: Difficult, due to a steep 0.75-mile climb out of a hollow on a rocky washout
Schedule: Open year-round
Season: Spring, summer, fall
Trail surface: Abandoned logging roads, typical mountain footpath, narrow cliff-side path, rocky washouts, and outcroppings

Elevation gain: 2,006 feet
Land status: State forest
Nearest town: Wellsboro
Fees and permits: No fees or permits required
Other trail users: Hikers only
Canine compatibility: Leashed dogs permitted
Maps: USGS Slate Run, PA
Trail contacts: Tiadaghton State Forest, 10 Lower Pine Bottom Rd. Waterville 17776; (570) 327-3450; www.dcnr.state.pa.us/ forestry/stateforests/tiadaghton

Finding the trailhead: From Williamsport, drive west on US 220 to exit 24. Take exit 24 and drive north on PA 44 about 12 miles through the village of Waterville to the intersection of PA 44 and PA 414. (Here PA 44 becomes PA 414.) Drive north on PA 414 for approximately 15 miles to the village of Slate Run. Just 0.1 mile before Wolfe's General Store, turn left onto Slate Run Road and cross over Pine Creek. You'll know you've gone too far if you wind up in downtown Slate Run (which consists of the Wolfe's General Store & Gas Station). Once across Pine Creek, turn left onto Naval Run Road and drive 1.3 miles to the picnic area and cul-de-sac at the end of Naval Run Road. *DeLorme: Pennsylvania Atlas & Gazetteer:* Page 49 A4. GPS: N41 27.489' / W77 30.948'

The Hike

Pine Creek Gorge, Pennsylvania's Grand Canyon, runs 47 miles alongside Pine Creek—from Ansonia in the north to Jersey Shore (that's Pennsylvania, not the New Jersey Shore) in the south. The gorge is a result of a glacial melt that left behind a natural dam of gravel, sand, and clay. The dam, which geologists call a moraine, not only stopped the northerly flow of water but also reversed the flow from north to south. That mass of water, raging southward for millions of years, formed the gorge, which is at some points 1,000 feet deep and 1 mile wide. Today it's Pine Creek that flows through the bottom of the gorge.

Entering the forest on Pine Trail

Pine Trail is one of the best ways to appreciate Pine Creek Gorge, though it will involve a bit of pain and suffering. When you've climbed 200 feet up the face of the gorge, the trail guides you past an outcropping of giant boulders, where, if you let your imagination take over, you might think you're exploring the Anasazi cliff dwellings of the American Southwest. The man-made trail consists of a well-maintained red-clay base with sideboards in the spots that are prone to washout. Despite the construction effort, you'll find yourself holding onto the boulders and doing a little ducking and weaving as you traverse the face of this steep ravine.

Once you've completed your first climb, you enter the canopy of the Black Forest. When the first Europeans settled the area, the stands of pine and hemlock were so dense within these 750,000 acres that they essentially blocked all sunlight from the forest floor.

Calling the section of trail that leads you out of Riffle Run Valley a trail is generous. It's well marked, but rough going. It's obvious that this 0.75-mile section is subject to perennial washouts. When you see mountain laurel, you can relax; you're out of Riffle Valley. Soon you turn onto a wide, flat road that leads across the top of Hemlock Mountain. Along this road you'll pass four vistas. This stretch of the hike is the easiest, but the best is yet to come.

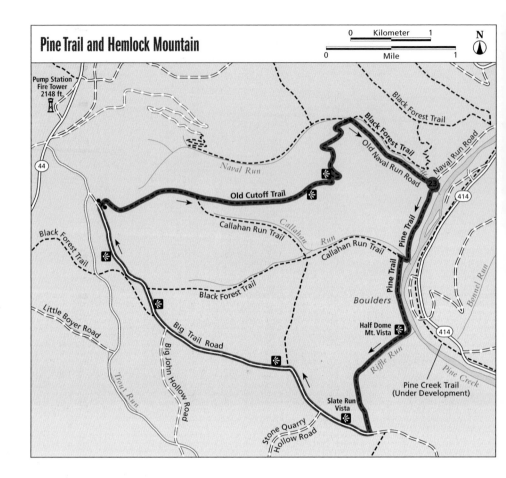

Pump Station
Fire Tower
2148 ft.

44

Naval Run

Old Cutoff Trail

Black Forest Trail

Old Naval Run Road

Black Forest Trail

Naval Run Road

25

414

Black Forest Trail

Callahan Run Trail

Callahan Run

Callahan Run Trail

Pine Trail

Pine Trail

Bonnel Run

Black Forest Trail

Little Boyer Road

Big Trail Road

Big John Hollow Road

Trout Run

Boulders

Half Dome
Mt. Vista

414

Riffle Run

Pine Creek

Slate Run
Vista

Stone Quarry
Hollow Road

Pine Creek Trail
(Under Development)

When you turn right onto the Old Cutoff Trail, it's pretty much like any other mountain trail. But hold on. Just before you begin your descent back to civilization, you come to one of the top views in the state. Looking north from this natural overlook, you take in Pine Creek as it winds its way through the endless series of ridges and valleys within the gorge. At the bottom of the mountain, along Old Naval Run Road, keep an eye out for a waterfall.

At a little more than 8.0 miles, the trail crosses Naval Run at the same point where you crossed the stream when you first started out. There was once a culvert here so that Old Naval Run Road used to connect with Naval Run Road. But Hurricane Agnes washed it out in 1972. Today Naval Run Road dead-ends, and there's no visible attempt to reconnect the two roads. Once you cross the stream, you merely retrace your beginning steps up a small incline to the trailhead and your vehicle.

Miles and Directions

0.0 Start at the picnic area at the dead end of Naval Run Road. Walk to the Pine Trail trailhead and follow the sign that points you toward Callahan, Riffle, and Big Trail Runs. Follow the blue blazes.

0.1 Cross Naval Run and turn left on the other side for a short uphill climb.

0.9 Come to Callahan Run. Cross the stream and turn right for a short jog then turn left at the double blue blazes and stay on the Pine Trail. (Callahan Run Trail continues straight.)

1.6 Arrive at Half Dome Mountain Vista. The trail turns right and parallels Riffle Run.

1.8 The trail becomes a rocky washout. Look for the blue blazes on the rocks.

2.5 Turn right onto Big Trail Road.

2.6 Arrive at Riffle Run Valley and Slate Run Vista, on your right.

4.2 Pass the orange-blazed Black Forest Trail intersection on your left. Arrive at the viewing area of Hemlock Mountain on your right. Pass an intersection with Black Forest Trail on your right.

4.9 Turn right at the log gate onto the Old Cutoff Trail.

5.4 Connect with the Black Forest Trail. The trail turns right; follow the orange blazes.

6.3 Reach the top of an outcropping and a vista.

6.5 Arrive at the vista to the north.

6.6 Trail begins a descent and makes a series of switchbacks.

7.0 Enter a hemlock grove. The trail turns right at the double blue blazes and begins another series of switchbacks.

7.6 Arrive at an intersection. (The Black Forest Trail turns to the left.) Continue straight as the trail becomes the Naval Run Trail Horse Path.

7.7 Turn right onto Old Naval Run Road.

8.0 Pass a waterfall.

8.2 Turn left and cross Naval Run. This is where you crossed Naval Run at the beginning of the hike.

8.3 Arrive back at the trailhead.

Local Information

Tioga County Visitors Bureau, 2053 Route 660, Wellsboro 16901; (570) 724-0635; www.visittiogapa.com

Local Outdoor Retailers

Wolfe's General Store & Slate Run Tackle Shop, Route 414, Slate Run; (570) 753-8551; slaterun.com

24 Splash Dam Hollow

This hike gives you a taste of a popular 85-mile backpacking trail. It starts out on the Susquehannock Trail System but soon connects with lesser-used trails as it descends one hollow and meets Splash Dam Stream, whose banks are now overgrown and whose already marshy areas are aggravated by beaver dams. The trail leads up out of a second hollow to the ridgeline, where you reconnect with the main trail.

Start: Susquehannock State Forest District Office parking area
Distance: 7.8-mile loop
Hiking time: 4 to 4.5 hours
Difficulty: Moderate, due to the steep climb out of a hollow
Schedule: Open year-round
Season: Spring, summer, fall
Trail surface: Old fire trails, abandoned logging roads, cross-country ski trails, a paved road, overgrown marshes, and hollow bottoms
Elevation gain: 1,124 feet

Land status: State forest
Nearest town: Coudersport
Fees and permits: No fees or permits required
Other trail users: Hikers, cross-country skiers, hunters (in season)
Canine compatibility: Leashed dogs permitted
Maps: USGS Brookland, PA; Cherry Springs, PA
Trail contacts: Susquehannock State Forest, 3150 E. Second St. (PO Box 673), Coudersport 16915; (814) 274-3600; dcnr.state.pa .us/forestry/stateforests/susquehannock/ index.htm

Finding the trailhead: From Dubois, drive north on US 219 for 48 miles to the intersection with US 6. Turn right onto US 6 and drive 53 miles to the Susquehannock State Forest Office and parking lot, on your right. *DeLorme: Pennsylvania Atlas & Gazetteer:* Page 34 B2. GPS: N41 46.145' / W77 52.224'

The Hike

The Susquehannock Trail System (STS) is a popular 85-mile backpacking trail that runs through the Susquehannock State Forest—262,000 acres of deeply cut ravines and plateaus. The trail passes through Lyman Sun, Patterson, Cherry Springs, and Ole Bull State Parks, with Ole Bull being the southern gateway. The STS is well maintained and well marked with orange blazes. In order to do a loop, our hike encompasses three lesser-used trails that are, at some points, a little overgrown. When you begin on the STS, you can sign in at the logbook station and then start out on the White Line Trail.

Follow the STS across a high plateau and into a deep ravine. This forest was logged extensively in the late 1800s and early 1900s, and from the trail you can see evidence of the clear-cutting. The recovering areas are mostly second-growth hardwoods, such as black cherry, beech, and maple. Second-growth pine and hemlock can be seen mostly in the lower wetlands. Scattered throughout are black, pin, northern red, chestnut, and white oaks; however, the bulk of the oak population has been destroyed by a caterpillar known as the oak leaf roller.

One of the nicest trail registers in the state

The trail descends along the slope of a ravine and onto the bottom of Splash Dam Hollow and an intersection with Splash Dam Stream. The deep pools in the stream (or splash dams, for which this hollow was named) were built by loggers to temporarily store their logs. When full, the dams were smashed open and logs were floated downstream to be milled into lumber in places like Williamsport. The term "splash dam" comes from the enormous splash that occurred when logs were rolled down the hollow into the dam.

THE OAK LEAF ROLLER

This mottled-brown, 0.5-inch-long caterpillar seems to thrive on oak leaves. In satisfying this urge, it severely reduces the trees' ability to perform photosynthesis. This defoliates and weakens the trees, so when the rollers return year after year, the trees stand little chance of survival. The oak leaf roller began appearing in the state's forests in the 1960s and 1970s. There have been periodic outbreaks since, most recently in Cambria, Cameron, Clearfield, Clinton, and Warren Counties.

The trail cuts away from the stream and intersects an all-terrain vehicle (ATV) road for a short 0.1 mile. (There is a 43-mile network of ATV and snowmobile trails. These roads are not marked on the state forest hiking maps, but ATV maps are available at the state forest office.) The trail leaves the road at a wooden post. The trail here can sometimes be overgrown. Shortly after, you begin a marshy section and then cross Lyman Run and connect with Lyman Run Road.

The trail continues on Lyman Run Road, passing dozens of quaking aspens on the right. Even the slightest breeze causes the aspens' almost circular leaves to tremble, hence the name. Many of the forest animals graze on its twigs, and although its inner bark is bitter, it's a staple in the beaver diet. Aspen, which sprout quickly from a widespread root system, have the widest range geographically and ecologically of any species in North America. The aspen is also an important pioneer species—the first tree to invade an area that has recently been burned or cut.

From Lyman Run Road you connect with the Township Trail on your right. The Township Trail takes you alongside a deep hollow and leads you up the steep climb out of the hollow, across an unpaved ATV road, and through a plateau until you reconnect with the STS and turn left.

The National Register of Historic Places lists downtown Coudersport, Pennsylvania, as a well-preserved example of a nineteenth-century small town.

Miles and Directions

0.0 Start at the Susquehannock State Forest District Office parking area. Walk past the maintenance building on your left to the black-and-yellow access gate and follow the orange blazes.

0.1 Cross over a small run and arrive at a blue trail sign with a black arrow. Turn right and climb a short hill that once had man-made steps.

0.4 Come to the trail register. After you sign in, take the White Line Trail.

0.7 Cross an unpaved ATV/maintenance road.

1.3 Cross Lyman Run Road.

1.4 Come to a hand-carved orange sign that reads "STS."

2.7 Come to the signpost at Splash Dam Creek. The STS turns right; you turn left.

3.8 Turn right onto an unpaved ATV road.

3.9 Leave the road and walk straight toward a wooden post.

4.3 Cross over Lyman Run. (There may be two branches.)

4.4 Turn left onto Lyman Run Road.

5.5 Lyman Run Road makes a sweeping curve. Turn right onto the Township Trail.

6.3 Cross an unpaved ATV road.

6.5 Come to the Susquehannock Trail and turn left.

7.4 Arrive back at the trail register. At the fork, follow the blue blazes to the right and retrace your steps.

7.8 Arrive back at the access gate and parking area.

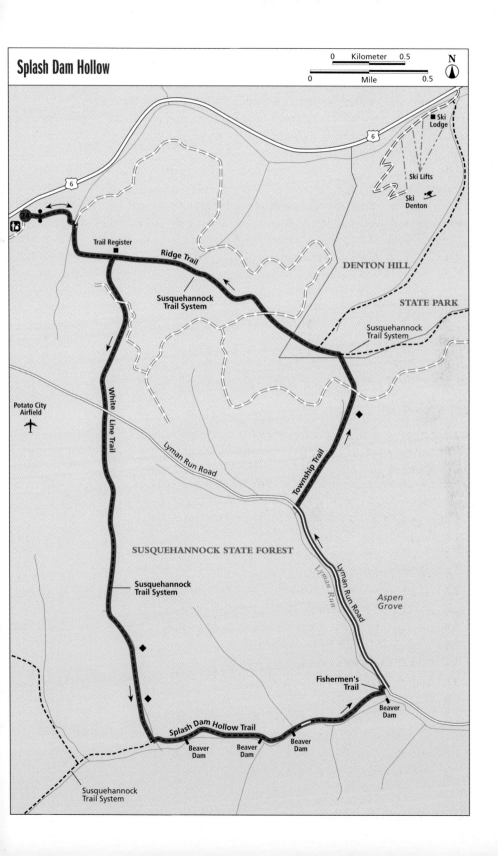

Splash Dam Hollow

0   Kilometer   0.5

0   Mile   0.5

N

Ski Lodge

6

Ski Lifts

Ski Denton

Trail Register

Ridge Trail

DENTON HILL

Susquehannock Trail System

STATE PARK

Susquehannock Trail System

6

Potato City Airfield

White Line Trail

Lyman Run Road

Township Trail

SUSQUEHANNOCK STATE FOREST

Susquehannock Trail System

Lyman Run

Lyman Run Road

Aspen Grove

Fishermen's Trail

Beaver Dam

Splash Dam Hollow Trail

Beaver Dam

Beaver Dam

Beaver Dam

Susquehannock Trail System

Local Information
Potter County Visitors Association, 227 N. Main St., Coudersport 16915; (814) 274-3365; www.visitpottercounty.com

Local Events/Attractions
God's Country Marathon, June, Galeton; (814) 274-3365; www.godscountrymarathon .com

Campgrounds
Lyman Run State Park, 454 Lyman Run Rd., Galeton; (814) 435-5010; (888) 727-2757 (camping information and reservations); www.dcnr.state.pa.us/stateparks/finda park/lymanrun/

25 Wykoff Run Natural Area

This is an easy hike through stands of white birch, mountain laurel, and meadows teeming with blueberry bushes. You're at an elevation of 2,000 feet—not the highest point in the state, but high enough to sense you're on top of a mountain. As you hike through a meadow to the trees, at times it feels surprisingly like an alpine forest.

Start: Wykoff Run Natural Area trailhead on Quehanna Highway

Distance: 4.8-mile loop

Hiking time: About 2.5 hours

Difficulty: Easy, due to the level terrain

Schedule: Open year-round

Season: Spring, summer, fall

Trail surface: Abandoned jeep roads, cross-country ski trails, and footpaths

Elevation gain: 342 feet

Land status: State forest and natural area

Nearest town: Clearfield

Fees and permits: No fees or permits required

Other trail users: Cross-country skiers, hunters (in season)

Canine compatibility: Leashed dogs permitted

Maps: USGS Devil's Elbow, PA; Driftwood, PA

Trail contacts: Elk State Forest, 258 Sizerville Rd., Emporium 15834; (814) 486-3353; www .dcnr.state.pa.us/forestry/stateforests/elk/
Quehanna Trail and Wild Area, Moshannon State Forest, 3372 State Park Rd., Clearfield 15849; (814) 765-0821; www.dcnr.state.pa .us/forestry/stateforests/moshannon/index .htm

Finding the trailhead: From Dubois, drive east on I-80 and take exit 120 at Clearfield. Drive north on PA 879 for about 17 miles to Karthaus. In the village of Karthaus, take the Quehanna Highway and drive north 8.7 miles to the trailhead and parking lot, on the right at the intersection with Wykoff Run Road. *DeLorme: Pennsylvania Atlas & Gazetteer:* Page 47 C6. GPS: N41 13.795' / W78 11.510'

The Hike

Wykoff Run Natural Area is a 1,252-acre segment of the Elk State Forest section of the 48,000-acre Quehanna Wild Area. This massive network of natural areas, wilderness, and state forest along the Allegheny High Plateau was once the site of oil and gas well drilling, as well as extensive logging. When the loggers pulled out, they left behind the limbs and waste wood, which fueled the wildfires that left this area treeless and devoid of vegetation.

In the years after World War II, Clearfield and Cameron Counties suffered recession-level unemployment. In an effort to attract businesses and create jobs, the government promoted this barren land as an industrial site. In 1955 the Curtiss-Wright Corporation opened a testing and manufacturing site on 50,000 acres, which they had either purchased or leased from the state. On this lonely site they built and operated a four-megawatt nuclear reactor, developed and tested jet engines, and experimented with nuclear engines for aircraft.

The original wooden bridge lasted a long time, but had to be replaced.

Curtiss-Wright felt that it would be advantageous to operate these types of projects in a remote area, far from any neighbors, and the Wykoff Run area provided just that. Curtiss-Wright also needed a pool of workers to staff its plant; the depressed local economy could provide that too. But nuclear-powered jet engines never came to be, and area coal miners and loggers didn't fit into the manufacturer's high-tech environment. Ultimately, the endeavor failed; the plant closed in 1963.

Evidence of the company's aborted projects can be found along the trail. Just 0.75 mile in from the trailhead, you'll pass a concrete bunker-type building with slits for windows. The structure was built to test jet engines, but after the tests were discontinued, the company used the building to store hazardous and explosive material. Today the building is covered in graffiti and looks like an apocalyptic-movie relic. Just past that, at about mile 1.0, there's an open area to the left. This is the site where the company buried beryllium oxide, an aluminum-like material widely used in the aircraft industry because of its rigid, lightweight, and heat-resistant properties.

Industry didn't end with Curtiss-Wright's collapse. After Curtiss-Wright left, the Piper Aircraft Company moved in and used some of the buildings. But by the mid-1980s, they too had moved out. Today these buildings are part of the 100-acre Quehanna Industrial Complex, located alongside Quehanna Highway.

Despite its past, this area is popular with hikers; it's also a favorite trailhead for backpackers, who use this hike to connect with the Quehanna Trail—a 73-mile loop that covers some of the roughest, most remote terrain in the state. For the most part, this section of the mountains is like any other—except that you encounter

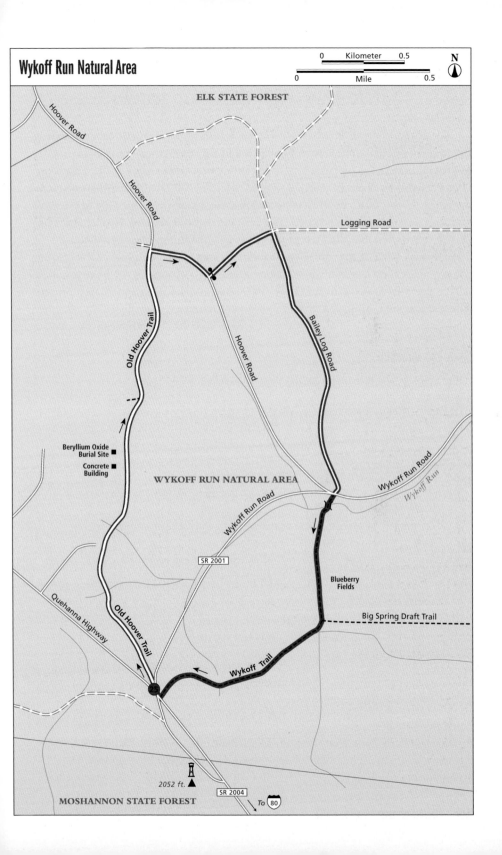

Wykoff Run Natural Area

0   Kilometer   0.5

0   Mile   0.5

N

ELK STATE FOREST

Hoover Road

Hoover Road

Logging Road

Old Hoover Trail

Hoover Road

Bailey Log Road

Beryllium Oxide
Burial Site ■

Concrete
Building ■

WYKOFF RUN NATURAL AREA

Wykoff Run Road

Wykoff Run Road

Wykoff Run

Wykoff Run Road

SR 2001

Blueberry
Fields

Quehanna Highway

Old Hoover Trail

Big Spring Draft Trail

Wykoff Trail

2052 ft. ▲

SR 2004

To 80

MOSHANNON STATE FOREST

magnificent stands of white birch trees, surrounded by typical northern hardwoods as well as hemlocks and other conifers. One of the reasons the area was set aside was to protect the birch trees, a species that thrives in upland forests and burned-out or clear-cut areas.

Since the area has reverted to its natural state, wildlife here is once again abundant. If you spent enough time here, you might catch a glimpse of the elusive wild turkey or a black bear at the blueberry patches—you almost surely will see the ubiquitous white-tailed deer. *Note:* Hunting is permitted in the natural area and the surrounding forest. Always be aware of hunting season dates before going into the forest. (You may be relieved to know, however, that hunting amphibians and reptiles, including snakes—permitted in some parts of the state—is forbidden in the natural area.)

The hike itself is pleasant. The abandoned jeep roads are groomed for cross-country skiing; and along the footpaths, especially if you come in mid-June, you'll see endless patches of mountain laurel. Wykoff Run is a typical Allegheny Plateau stream: The water is clear and cold, and the gorge it has created is evidence that Mother Nature, regardless of how she was abused, is alive and well . . . and busy.

Miles and Directions

0.0 Start at the trailhead on Quehanna Highway and follow the red blazes.

0.7 Come to an abandoned concrete building on your left. Cross a wide meadow.

1.7 Turn right onto the Hoover Road. A sign reads "Old Wykoff Road."

1.9 Turn left onto a logging road.

2.0 Come to an access gate.

2.2 Turn right at the sign that reads "Wykoff Road 1 Mile."

3.2 Cross Wykoff Run Road and come to the sign that reads "Ski Trails." Cross a wooden footbridge over Wykoff Run.

3.9 Arrive at a trail intersection with multiple signposts. Turn right and follow the sign that reads "Quehanna Highway 1 Mile."

4.8 Turn right at the Quehanna Highway and walk about 300 feet back to the trailhead parking area.

Local Information
Clearfield County Recreation and Tourism Authority, 511 Spruce St., Ste. 8, Clearfield 16830; (814) 765-5734; www.visitclearfieldcounty.org

Local Events/Attractions
Elk County Visitor Center, 134 Homestead Dr., Benezette; (814) 787-5167; www
.elkcountryvisitorcenter.com. Observe wild elk in their natural habitat.

Campgrounds
Parker Dam State Park, Mud Run Road, Penfield; (814) 765-0630; (888) 727-2757 (camping information and reservations); www.dcnr.state.pa.us/stateparks/findapark/parkerdam/

26 Black Moshannon State Park

This easy hike provides a tour of popular Black Moshannon State Park. It starts on the bridge across Black Moshannon Lake and continues along the lakeside and past the dam spillway; it then follows Black Moshannon Creek as it meanders through the forest at the north end of the park. The trail leaves the stream and loops back to the bridge across the lake. Here you cross the lake a second time and head toward the south end of the park, where you can explore the bog and its wildlife and exotic flora from an elevated boardwalk.

Start: Boat launch area No. 1 parking lot
Distance: 7.3-mile lollipop
Hiking time: About 3 hours
Difficulty: Easy, due to the level terrain
Schedule: Open year-round
Season: Spring, summer, fall
Trail surface: Paved road, lakeside path, forest footpath, shale road, and elevated boardwalk; park road, elevated boardwalk leading into a bog and a wildlife-viewing platform
Elevation gain: 581 feet

Land status: State park
Nearest town: Philipsburg
Fees and permits: No fees or permits required
Other trail users: Anglers, swimmers, birders
Canine compatibility: Leashed dogs permitted
Maps: USGS Black Moshannon, PA
Trail contacts: Black Moshannon State Park, 4216 Beaver Rd., Philipsburg 16866; (814) 342-5960; www.dcnr.state.pa.us/stateparks/findapark/blackmoshannon

Finding the trailhead: From Dubois, drive east on I-80 and take exit 133 (PA 53). Drive south on PA 53 for 8 miles to Philipsburg. In the city of Philipsburg, turn left onto US 322 and drive south 1 mile to South Philipsburg and the intersection with PA 504. Turn left onto PA 504 and drive 8.5 miles to the entrance of Black Moshannon State Park. Once in the park, drive over the bridge across Black Moshannon Lake and immediately turn right into the boat launch area No. 1 parking lot. *DeLorme: Pennsylvania Atlas & Gazetteer.* Page 61 A7. GPS: N40 54.888' / W78 3.497'

The Hike

Pennsylvania has a number of interesting geological sites, but one thing it will never have is its own alpine lake—since, by definition, an alpine lake must be at least 10,000 feet above sea level. However, at the center of Black Moshannon State Park you'll find the next best thing: Black Moshannon Lake, a 250-acre lake situated in a basin-shaped area high atop the Allegheny Front. The basin, at 1,900 feet above sea level, traps the cooler, heavier air, creating mild summers and longer winters. More than 350,000 people come to observe and indulge in this phenomenon each year.

Because of these cooler temperatures, the area is home to an array of plants and animals usually observed much farther north. The bog is also home to some peculiar vegetation, such as the insect-eating pitcher plant and the sundew. Carnivorous plants

Walk along the shoreline to the Bog Trail where you will find an elevated wildlife viewing area.

usually grow in nutrient-poor soil; they've evolved to supplement their diets by trapping insects. The pitcher plant has a 20-inch stalk with purplish-red, vaselike leaves that contain water (hence pitcher plant). Its color attracts insects into its curled leaves, where tiny hairs hold the insects until they drown. The sundew is quite a bit smaller. It has an 8-inch stalk that supports a curved cluster of white- to pink-tinged flowers and sticky hairs that it uses to trap insects and digest them. Both are fascinating and unusual. Take the time to find a few and appreciate nature's adaptive abilities.

Black Moshannon State Park comprises 3,394 acres of forests and wetlands, surrounded by another 43,000 acres of the Moshannon State Forest. In 1994 the state designated 1,592 acres of swamps, bogs, marshes, and forests in the southern end of the park as the Black Moshannon Bog Natural Area.

Our hike begins with a walk alongside the dark waters of Black Moshannon Lake. The water appears almost black—hence the park's name. The waters here are darker than usual because of the abundance of sphagnum moss, which is just about everywhere you look. Acres of sphagnum moss absorb tannin from decaying plant life and hold onto it; then, like a giant teabag, it releases the tannin into the water, making it the color of strong tea.

As for the park's unusual name: According to local legend, "moshannon" is derived from the Seneca Indian phrase *moss-hanne*, which means "moose stream." However, since moose aren't native to Pennsylvania, what they called moose were most likely elk, which at one time were present throughout the state.

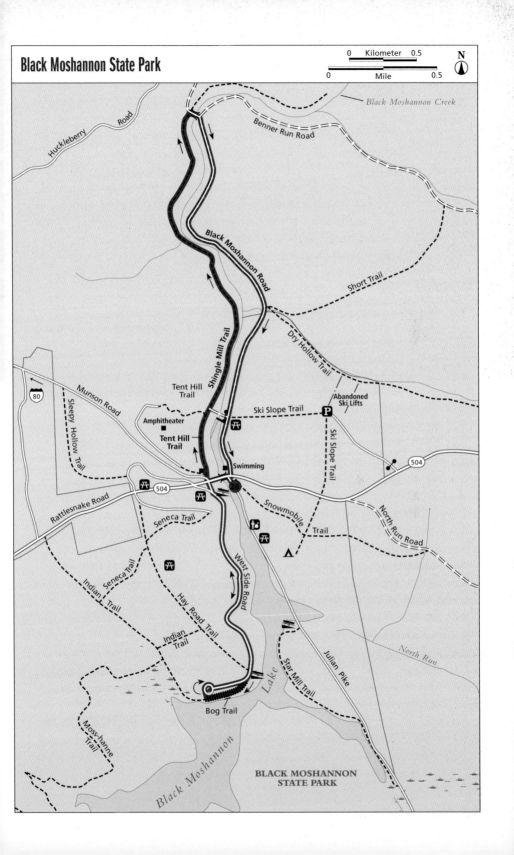

Black Moshannon State Park

0 Kilometer 0.5
0 Mile 0.5

N

Black Moshannon Creek

Huckleberry Road

Benner Run Road

Black Moshannon Road

Short Trail

Shingle Mill Trail

Dry Hollow Trail

Tent Hill Trail

Munson Road

80

Sleepy Hollow Trail

Amphitheater

Tent Hill Trail

Ski Slope Trail

Abandoned Ski Lifts

P

Ski Slope Trail

Swimming

504

Rattlesnake Road

504

Snowmobile Trail

North Run Road

Seneca Trail

Indian Trail

Seneca Trail

Hay Road Trail

West Side Road

Indian Trail

Julian Pike

North Run

Lake

Star Mill Trail

Bog Trail

Moss-hanne Trail

Black Moshannon

BLACK MOSHANNON STATE PARK

Walk along the shoreline to the Bog Trail, where you'll find an elevated boardwalk and wildlife-viewing platform. Be sure to take your binoculars and camera. Depending on the season and time of day, you're liable to see beavers, porcupines, pickerel frogs, and even a black bear. Waterfowl you're likely to see include migrating ospreys, wood ducks, tundra swans, and great blue herons. The best times for watching wildlife are mornings and evenings.

Feeding wildlife is prohibited, and there are a number of reasons for this. Some are just nuisance issues: Feeding waterfowl like Canada geese ensures that they return to the same spot year after year, leaving enormous amounts of droppings. Some concerns are more serious: Black bears, searching for food, damage park equipment and can even injure visitors. In any area where bears are present, keep food and food scraps in your car or camper. Never keep foodstuffs in a tent or in an open garbage can.

Miles and Directions

0.0 Start at the boat launch area No. 1 parking lot. Walk to PA 504 and turn left to cross the bridge over Black Moshannon Lake. Once across the bridge, turn right onto the paved road at the campground sign. Turn right again at the yellow Tent Hill Trail marker and walk toward the Environmental Learning Center building.

0.1 Arrive at the Environmental Learning Center building. Veer to the right—stay between the building and the shore of the lake. Walk through the picnic area to the Tent Hill Trail sign and yellow blazes.

0.2 Pass an unmarked trail on your left. Continue straight along the lake.

0.4 The Tent Hill Trail goes off to the left. Continue straight toward the dam and spillway.

0.5 Cross a shale access road and walk to the blue-blazed Shingle Mill Trail sign. Continue straight.

2.4 Turn right onto Huckleberry Road. Cross the bridge over Black Moshannon Creek and turn right onto Black Moshannon Road.

3.5 Pass the Short Trail and the Dry Hollow Trail trailhead on your left. Continue straight.

4.0 Pass the Ski Slope Trail on your left. Veer right and walk through the picnic area.

4.2 Pass the beach area on your right.

4.3 Turn right onto PA 504 and cross the bridge over Black Moshannon Lake. On the other side, turn left onto the paved walkway and walk through the picnic area.

4.4 Turn left onto the West Side Road.

5.5 Pass Hay Road Trail on your right. Continue straight.

5.6 Walk through boat launch area No. 3 to the Bog Trail. Follow the yellow blazes onto the boardwalk.

5.9 Arrive at the Bog Trail viewing platform. Retrace your steps to the boardwalk and turn left. Pass the Indian Trail and the Moss-Hanne Trail trailhead on your left. Turn right onto the West Side Road and retrace your steps to the boat launch area No. 1 parking area.

7.3 Arrive back at the parking lot.

Local Information

Centre County Convention and Visitors Bureau, 800 E. Park Ave., State College 16803; (814) 231-1400; www.visitpennstate.org

Local Events/Attractions

Boalsburg Military Museum, 51 Boal Ave., Boalsburg; (814) 466-6263; www.pamil museum.org

Campgrounds

Black Moshannon State Park, 4216 Beaver Rd., Philipsburg; (814) 342-5960; (888) 727-2757 (camping information and reservations); www.dcnr.state.pa.us/stateparks/findapark/blackmoshannon

Restaurants

Sarina's Italian Pizza & Restaurant, Ames Shopping Plaza #101, Philipsburg; (814) 342-6237; www.sarinaspizza.com

Honorable Mentions

North Central Pennsylvania

Here are two great hikes in the North Central region that didn't make the A-list this time around but deserve recognition. Check them out and let us know what you think. You may decide that one or more of these hikes deserves higher status in future editions, or you may have a hike of your own that merits attention.

I The Elk Trail

This 17-mile trail in Elk County, designed to show off the county's namesake, is in Elk State Forest, north of I-80, southwest of St. Marys, and south of Emporium. The trail is simply out in the middle of nowhere. And that's precisely why the herd of 650 to 700 elk was reestablished here. These cousins of the white-tailed deer were once native to the area, but by the mid-1800s they were wiped out by overhunting and loss of habitat. From 1913 to 1926 elk were captured in Yellowstone National Park and reintroduced here. Even today, a struggle continues between farmers, who suffer crop damage, and elk advocates, who want to see the herd preserved.

From Dubois, drive north on PA 255 about 18 miles to the village of Weedville. Turn right onto PA 555 and drive about 6 miles to Benezette. In Benezette turn north onto the paved road opposite the Benezette General Store; pass the Benezette Hotel, drive to where the pavement ends, and park. To see elk without walking, drive north 3.5 miles on Winslow Hill Road. For more information call Parker Dam State Park (814-765-0630) or Elk State Forest (814-486-3353). *DeLorme: Pennsylvania Atlas & Gazetteer*: Page 47 B5

J Parker Dam State Park

This park is in Clearfield County, north of I-80. The Keystone Trails Association calls Parker Dam "a hikers' park." It's an outdoor lover's paradise. First there's a network of trails that include the Beaver Trail—a boardwalk trail that takes you through a beaver propagation area. Then there are the trails that take you on an outdoor tour of the logging industry, where you can see the old tools and the ingenious way loggers transported logs to market, William Parker built a number of splash dams to accomplish that. The park also offers fishing, a swimming beach, canoe rentals, rental cabins, camping, and a top-notch nature and education center in the park office.

From Dubois, drive east on I-80 for 17 miles to exit 111. Take PA 153 north for 10 miles and turn right onto Mud Run Road at the Parker Dam sign. Continue on Mud Run Road for 2 miles to the park and the park office on your right. For more information call Parker Dam State Park at (814) 765-0630. *DeLorme: Pennsylvania Atlas & Gazetteer*: Page 46 C3

South Central Pennsylvania

Pennsylvania's South Central region has so much going for it, it's hard to imagine why anyone would want to go anywhere else. Let's review: There's Gettysburg National Military Park, an extremely user-friendly area, where all you have to do is park your car and start walking. Hikers can explore the battlefield and examine the relics of one of the bloodiest and most important battles of the Civil War.

The two highest peaks in the state, Mount Davis and Blue Knob, are also here, as is Raystown Lake, the largest body of water in the state. You'll also see some of the state's oldest quartzite rocks (300 million years old) at Pole Steeple.

How about history? There are a number of state parks in the South Central region where historical iron furnaces, blacksmith shops, houses, and in some cases entire villages have been restored to show new generations what life was like when coal was king and manufacturing was the number-one employer in the area. Hikers can explore iron furnaces and learn how just one furnace consumed more than an acre of timber a day. (See Hike 34: Greenwood Furnace State Park.)

At Alan Seeger Natural Area in Centre County, visitors can marvel at how the giant hemlocks there survived the ax while the entire area around them was clear-cut. Not far from Alan Seeger, there lies another mystery: the Indian Steps. No one knows who built them, but what we do know is that they lead to the top of Brush Mountain, through some of the rockiest mountain slopes in the state.

Many of the South Central region's natural wonders are the handiwork of the mountain system known as the Ridge and Valley Province—a range of parallel ridges separated by valleys and covering 25 percent of the state and all or part of twenty-seven counties. Looking like a giant washboard, this range begins at the Maryland border and arcs northeast to the New Jersey border at the Delaware Water Gap. Climb any South Central mountain and you'll see one ridge after another and another, until they're lost to the horizon. But be careful: Once you've seen this sight, you may get hooked.

27 Gettysburg

When you've finished this hike, you'll have a comprehensive idea of what took place July 1 through July 3, 1863, at the Battle of Gettysburg, when more than 150,000 troops clashed on the rolling hills surrounding this small Pennsylvania town. Considered by most historians to be the turning point of the American Civil War, it was also one of the bloodiest conflicts in modern warfare.

Just like the auto and bus tours, this hike visits the important battle sites and monuments; however, the hike leads away from the paved roads and monuments and onto the battlefields. Hikers get a firsthand experience of what it was like for Confederate soldiers to charge through an open field with bullets whizzing by. Let your imagination take over as you position yourself behind a boulder on Little Round Top or walk along a line of cannons.

Start: National Parking Lot South on PA 134
Distance: 9.1-mile loop
Hiking time: 5 to 6 hours
Difficulty: Moderate, due to length; easy, flat trail except for a few brief climbs
Schedule: Open year-round
Season: Spring, summer, fall
Trail surface: Paved roads, abandoned trolley grade, and forest footpaths, and open-meadow battle sites
Elevation gain: 597 feet
Land status: National military park

Nearest town: Gettysburg
Fees and permits: No fees or permits required
Other trail users: Tourists, students, history buffs, equestrians
Canine compatibility: Leashed dogs permitted; no pets permitted in Soldiers' National Cemetery
Maps: USGS Gettysburg, PA; Fairfield, PA
Trail contacts: Gettysburg National Military Park, 1195 Baltimore Pike, Gettysburg 17325; (717) 338-1243; www.gettysburgfoundation.org

Finding the trailhead: From Philadelphia, drive west on I-76 past Harrisburg to exit 236. Drive south on US 15 for about 30 miles and merge onto US 15 Business. Drive to the traffic circle in the center of the city of Gettysburg. Once on the circle, turn right onto US 15 Business and drive south for 1 mile; turn left onto PA 134 and park in the National Parking Lot South, across from the Soldiers' National Cemetery. *DeLorme: Pennsylvania Atlas & Gazetteer.* Page 91 B7. GPS: N39 49.006' / W77 14.002'

The Hike

More than 172,000 men and 634 cannons were positioned in an area encompassing 25 square miles. It was estimated that 569 tons of ammunition was expended. There were more than 5,000 dead horses left on the battlefield. In three days there were 51,000 casualties, the bloodiest battle in American history.

The extent of death and destruction stemming from the American Civil War is truly staggering. In the four years the war raged, more than $5 billion in property

A monument to General George Meade of Pennsylvania

was damaged and more than 600,000 lives were lost. One of the bloodiest battles of the war was fought from July 1 through July 3, 1863, on the rolling hills surrounding the city of Gettysburg in Pennsylvania's South Central region. A trip to Gettysburg National Military Park offers visitors the chance to look beyond the textbook accounts and numbers and understand the devastation on a visceral level.

Most scholars consider the Battle of Gettysburg the turning point in the Civil War. The actions that set the stage for this momentous battle began about a month earlier with the Confederate victory at Chancellorsville, Virginia. On the strength of that victory, Confederate general Robert E. Lee decided to divide his army into three corps and invade Pennsylvania.

On June 30, Confederate troops spotted Union troops on their way to Gettysburg, but there was no encounter that night. Forewarned and anticipating battle, troops from both sides set up their positions through the night. On July 1 the fighting began, and by day's end, more than 7,000 Confederates were dead, wounded, or taken prisoner. The North's casualties were even higher—more than 9,000 dead, wounded, or taken prisoner.

Full-scale fighting didn't begin until late the next day. By that evening, Union general Daniel Sickles ordered his troops to abandon their post near Little Round Top and attack the Confederates at a wheat field and peach orchard. Sickles's troops were massacred; the losses were so great that the wheat field turned scarlet from the bloodshed.

But by the third and last day, the North was secure in its positions and the South had lost its offensive drive. Confederate troops made one final attempt to breach the North's line. Gen. George E. Pickett and 15,000 troops led a charge across an open field toward the Northern stronghold of Cemetery Ridge. Pickett's men were slaughtered, the attack was repulsed, and the Battle of Gettysburg was over.

The next day, during heavy rains, Lee led his men in retreat to Virginia. During the three-day battle, the Union Army had 23,000 casualties; the Confederates, at least 25,000.

Millions of people have visited Gettysburg National Military Park since it was dedicated in 1895, but the vast majority of visitors seldom venture past the popular monuments. You will. At key sites this hike leads away from the paved roads and monuments and onto the actual battlefields. (This hike follows the *Gettysburg Heritage Trail Guide*, published by the National Park Service and the Boy Scouts of America, which is available at the visitor center bookstore.)

The trail starts at the High Water Mark. This is the spot where the Union forces repulsed Pickett's Charge, which came to be known as the "high-water mark," or high point, of the Confederates' advances. After passing a few monuments, the trail crosses a field and you walk alongside a split-rail fence. If you can forget the paved roads and the glistening monuments, you might sense what the countryside was like in the 1860s. Out here in the fields, you get a feel of what it was like for soldiers on both sides. The trail leads you right through the once-bloodstained wheat field and on to the Devil's Den, scene of some of the fiercest fighting of the battle. Devil's Den is an outcrop of boulders at the base of Little Round Top. It was from here that the Union troops defended their left flank. During the battle here, the carnage was so massive that Plum Run ran red with blood, earning it the odious nickname "Bloody Run."

ABRAHAM LINCOLN AND THE GETTYSBURG ADDRESS

When the Battle of Gettysburg was over, many of the dead were buried in hastily dug, inadequate graves; some were not buried at all. Pennsylvania's governor, Andrew Curtin, stepped in and commissioned a local attorney to purchase a suitable spot for the Union dead. Four months after the Battle of Gettysburg, reinterment began on 17 acres, which became the Gettysburg National Cemetery.

On November 19, 1863, President Abraham Lincoln (and revered speaker of the day Edward Everett) spoke at the dedication ceremonies. Lincoln's speech—just 272 words—took 2 minutes to deliver and has since come to be regarded as a masterpiece of the English language.

Today visitors to Gettysburg can visit the Gettysburg National Cemetery and the Lincoln Speech Memorial, both located within the cemetery grounds.

When you climb Little Round Top, it's easy to see how Union sharpshooters positioned themselves behind the boulders to pick off Confederate soldiers as they attempted the uphill advance. The climb up Little Round Top is short—only about 0.2 mile—but it's steep. And if you're on the path, you're frightfully exposed, just as the Confederate soldiers were.

When you pass the monument to Robert E. Lee and his horse, Traveller, you're walking the very same field where Pickett's Charge took place. There's a small monument where the attack was staged. From that point it's about 0.5 mile across an open field to where the Union troops were poised on Cemetery Ridge. It was from this ridge that Pickett and about 15,000 troops made the attack against an overwhelming barrage of Union artillery and musket fire. It was here that the battle was finally lost.

Miles and Directions

0.0 Start at the National Parking Lot South. Walk toward the battlefield and take the sidewalk that arcs to the left.

0.1 Arrive at the High Water Mark Trailhead. Turn right onto the paved walkway.

0.2 Bear right at the fork and walk toward Hancock Avenue.

0.3 Turn left onto Hancock Avenue.

0.5 Pass a path on your left. Walk toward the Vermont Monument.

0.7 Turn left at the fork onto Pleasanton Avenue to visit the Pennsylvania Monument. Turn right onto Humphries Avenue.

0.9 Arrive at the Minnesota Monument. Turn right at the monument and follow the footpath through the field to the split-rail fence.

1.0 Turn left at the split-rail fence.

1.3 Turn right onto United States Avenue.

1.5 Cross the traffic bridge over Plum Run.

1.6 Pass the Trostle House on your right.

1.8 Turn left onto Sickles Avenue.

2.0 Turn left onto Wheatfield Road.

2.4 Arrive at the "Wheatfield" plaque. Face the plaque and walk past it to a footpath through the field.

2.5 Turn right onto Sickles Avenue. Turn left onto De Trobriand Avenue.

2.7 Pass the Pennsylvania 110th Regiment Monument. Turn left into the forest at a second sign for De Trobriand Avenue on your right. You are on an abandoned trolley grade.

2.8 Cross a footbridge over a tributary to Plum Run.

2.9 Cross a second footbridge over a tributary.

3.0 Cross Brooke Avenue.

3.4 Cross a footbridge over a Plum Run tributary and turn right onto Sickles Avenue.

3.5 Turn right onto Warren Avenue and cross Plum Run on a traffic bridge.

3.6 Turn left onto a footpath to the top of Little Round Top.

3.8 Turn right at the parking lot.

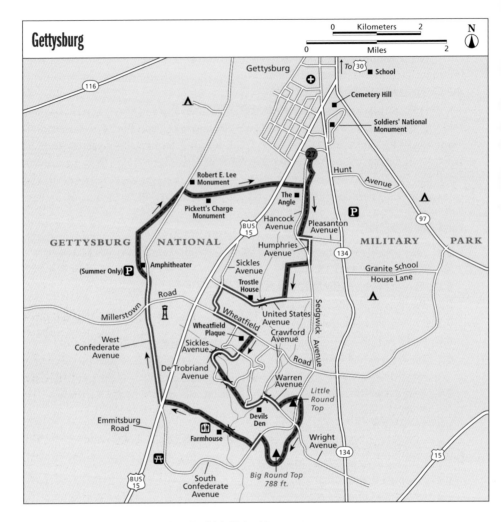

4.0 Turn left at the paved path to the 20th Maine Monument.

4.1 Turn left onto Wright Avenue and then right at the red-blazed horse trail into the forest.

4.3 Turn left onto the red-blazed Loop Trail.

4.7 Turn right on the Loop Trail.

4.9 Turn left at trail stanchion No. 14 and turn left onto South Confederate Avenue. Turn right onto a footpath beside a section of split-rail fence.

5.0 Arrive at the 1st Vermont Monument. Turn right; the trail goes downhill.

5.2 Cross a wooden footbridge over Plum Run and walk toward the white farmhouse. Turn right at the trail sign near the house.

5.3 Arrive at a rest area with a restroom and picnic table.

5.8 Cross Emmitsburg Road and turn right onto West Confederate Avenue.

5.9 Pass the horse trail on your left.

6.4 Pass the Lookout Tower on your right.

6.6 Cross Millerstown Road.

6.9 Turn left into the amphitheater parking lot. Walk to the left of the amphitheater and turn right onto the red-blazed horse trail.

7.1 Turn left at the sign for the hiking trail.

7.3 Turn right at the sign for hikers and horses.

7.6 Cross a small stream on a footbridge. Turn left at the fork.

7.9 Turn right onto a path that takes you back out to Confederate Avenue.

8.0 Arrive at the Robert E. Lee Monument. Walk to the right of the monument to get on the paved walkway.

8.1 The paved walkway ends at a small monument where Pickett's Charge began. Follow the footpath through the cornfields.

8.7 Cross Emmitsburg Road.

8.8 Arrive at the steps for "The Angle" Monument. Follow the path to the left.

9.0 Cross Hancock Avenue at Bryan House. Follow the sidewalk behind the Cyclorama.

9.1 Arrive back at the parking lot.

Local Information

Destination Gettysburg Visitor Center, 35 Carlisle St., Gettysburg 17325; (717) 334-6274; www.destinationgettysburg.com

Local Events/Attractions

Gettysburg Civil War Heritage Days, Gettysburg; (717) 334-6274; www.gettysburg reenactment.com

Accommodations

Dobbin House Tavern and B&B., 89 Steinwehr Ave., Gettysburg; (717) 334-2100; www.dobbinhouse.com

Campgrounds

Gettysburg Campground, 2030 Fairfield Rd., Gettysburg; (717) 334-3304; www .gettysburgcampground.com

Restaurants

Dobbin House Tavern, 89 Steinwehr Ave., Gettysburg; (717) 334-2100; www.dobbin house.com

POPULATION OF GETTYSBURG

In 1863: 2,400	In 1990: 7,025
In 1980: 7,194	In 2014: 7,620

28 Sunset Rocks

Walk a section of the Appalachian Trail to the ruins of a top-secret World War II POW camp. Climb Little Rocky Ridge for an exciting, hand-over-hand scramble through a narrow boulder outcrop for a mountaintop view.

Start: Parking lot for the furnace stack in Pine Grove Furnace State Park

Distance: 8.3-mile lollipop

Hiking time: About 5 hours

Difficulty: Moderate, due to short climbs; short section of two-handed climbing over boulders

Schedule: Open year-round

Season: Spring, summer, fall

Trail surface: Abandoned logging roads, paved roads, and forest footpaths

Elevation gain: 1,147 feet

Land status: State park and state forest

Nearest town: Shippensburg

Fees and permits: No fees or permits required

Other trail users: Thru-hikers, hunters (in season)

Canine compatibility: Leashed dogs permitted

Maps: USGS Dickinson, PA

Trail contacts: Pine Grove Furnace State Park, 1100 Pine Grove Rd., Gardners 17324; (717) 486-7174; www.dcnr.state.pa.us/stateparks/findapark/pinegrovefurnace

Michaux State Forest, 10099 Lincoln Way East, Fayetteville 17222; (717) 352-2211; www.dcnr.state.pa.us/forestry/stateforests/michaux

Special considerations: Although the boulder outcrop section is only 0.3 mile in length, hikers should be in good physical condition to attempt this. This section is not for inexperienced hikers or small children. For hikers who want to visit Sunset Rocks and don't feel comfortable with maneuvering through the outcrop, turn left onto the Sunset Trail at mile 1.4 and climb to the mountaintop, bypassing the outcrop.

Finding the trailhead: From Allentown, drive west on I-78 and connect with I-81 toward Harrisburg. Continue south on I-81 through Harrisburg to exit 37. Take exit 37 and drive south on PA 233 for 8.5 miles. Turn left into Pine Grove Furnace State Park and drive to the furnace stack. *DeLorme: Pennsylvania Atlas & Gazetteer:* Page 77 D6. GPS: N40 1.953' / W77 18.353'

The Hike

From the Revolutionary War period to the beginning of the twentieth century, the iron industry flourished in the mountains of Pennsylvania. The iron ore was extracted from the earth and the surrounding trees were harvested to produce charcoal to fire the furnaces, leaving behind denuded forests, abandoned quarry pits, the scarred earth of the charcoal flats, and a network of logging and mining roads. We'll hike these abandoned roads to explore the unusual history of this area.

In 1912 the South Mountain Mining & Iron Company sold 60 square miles of clear-cut forest and a 250-acre tenant farm to the state. The land was neglected and it steadily deteriorated until 1933, when President Franklin Roosevelt created the Civilian Conservation Corps (CCC). The CCC, which provided forestry work for

On your way to Sunset Rocks, stop at the newly opened Appalachian Trail Museum in Pine Grove Furnace State Park.

mostly unmarried young men, was one of the social programs established to allevi-ate the widespread unemployment during the Great Depression. Here in Pennsyl-vania, what came to be known as Camp Michaux was actually Camp S-51, the first CCC camp in the state. For the next nine years, the young men of Camp S-51 built themselves a home, improved old forest roads, and built new ones. In 1942, with the United States' involvement in World War II, young men were needed in Europe and the Pacific, so the camp was closed and Army Intelligence chose the site to set up the Michaux Prisoner of War Camp.

Just a 2-hour drive from the District of Columbia, the camp was also close to the Carlisle Army Post; because of the camp's remote location, the US Army felt it could keep the location a secret. Staffed by 150 soldiers, the camp, which first handled only German naval officers, was expanded to include officers from Rommel's African Corps as well as Japanese officers—for a total of 1,500 prisoners.

The POW camp was closed after the war. In 1948 a church coalition signed a 10-year lease to use the site as a church camp. When the lease expired, the land reverted to the state. In 1972 all the buildings were removed. Today all that remains

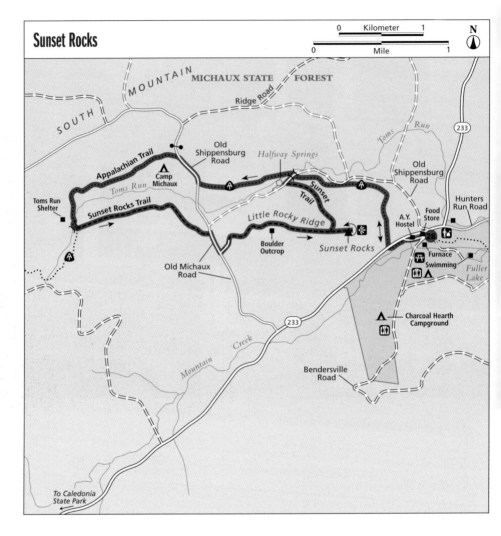

are the stone ruins of the barn foundation next to a giant spruce tree. Here and there along the trail, you may find posts from the barbwire fence that once surrounded the compound.

At a little more than 3.5 miles into the trail, you'll come to Toms Run Shelter. The shelter, part of the Appalachian Trail, is on the site where the tenant farmhouse was once located. There is a spring here and an outhouse and picnic tables. Local lore says that somewhere near the site are the unmarked graves of three children who died of smallpox.

After you've switchbacked your way to the summit of Little Rocky Ridge, you'll need both hands to navigate over a section of precariously perched boulders. The trail is well marked (blue blazes are painted right on the rocks); however, this section is not suitable for anyone who is not in good physical condition. Because the ridgetop

Sunset Rocks is one of the most popular vistas in the state.

is narrow, there is no way around the boulders—you either climb over them or turn around and go back the way you came.

Your hard work pays off soon enough, though. The view from Sunset Rocks is a spectacular south-facing view of the valley and the flat ridgetops spanning the 85,000-acre Michaux State Forest.

Miles and Directions

0.0 Start at the parking lot for the furnace stack. Walk across Quarry Road and turn left onto Bendersville Road. Walk past the American Youth Hostel to PA 233. Follow the white blazes.

0.1 Turn left at PA 233.

0.2 Turn right to cross PA 233 and arrive at the Appalachian Trail trailhead.

0.3 Turn right at the fork and arrive at a trail sign that reads "Appalachian Trail, Foot Traffic Only."

1.4 Bear left at the fork in the trail. Come to a trail intersection and continue straight on the white-blazed Appalachian Trail. (The blue-blazed Sunset Trail goes off to your left.) Cross Toms Run on a footbridge and turn left on the other side.

1.6 The trail merges onto a shale road.

2.1 Turn right at the double white blazes.

2.2 The trail merges onto the paved Old Shippensburg Road.

2.5 Turn left at a trail sign for the Appalachian Trail. Notice the log gate across the trail.

3.7 Arrive at Toms Run Shelter. Cross Toms Run.

3.8 Turn left at the double blue blazes onto the Sunset Rocks Trail.

4.4 Arrive at a clearing. Bear right at a fork in the trail.

4.9 Turn right onto the paved Old Michaux Road.

5.0 Turn left at a second gravel road. Look for the blue blazes.

5.4 Arrive at the Little Rocky Ridge trail sign.

5.5 Enter a boulder outcropping where the trail goes over the boulders.

5.7 At the intersection with the Sunset Trail, continue straight to Sunset Rocks. Retrace your steps back to the trail intersection.

6.2 Arrive back at the trail intersection and turn right.

6.7 Turn right at the intersection with the Appalachian Trail and retrace your steps back to PA 233.

8.0 Turn left at PA 233.

8.3 Arrive back at the parking lot.

Local Information

Hershey Harrisburg Regional Visitors Bureau, 3211 N. Front St., Ste. 301-A, Harrisburg 17101; (717) 231-7788; www.visithersheyharrisburg.org

Accommodations

American Youth Hostel/Ironmaster's Mansion, Pine Grove Furnace State Park, 1212 Pine Grove Rd., Gardners; (717) 486-4108; ironmastersmansion.com

Campgrounds

Pine Grove Furnace State Park, 1100 Pine Grove Rd., Gardners; (717) 486-7174; (888) 727-2757 (camping information and reservations); www.dcnr.state.pa.us/stateparks/findapark/pinegrovefurnace/

29 Pole Steeple

The rugged quartzite cliffs that cap off this hike are estimated to be at least 300 million years old. Pole Steeple Cliffs sit 526 feet above a pristine mountain lake and provide a spectacular view. If you're lucky enough to come at the right time, you'll see rock climbers all roped up and doing their thing.

For hikers there's a second highlight. This hike uses a section of the Appalachian Trail. Less than a mile from the start, hikers come to the halfway point of the roughly 2,190-mile-long trail. Check out the trail register to see what weary hikers have to say. The last 2.0 miles of this hike are flat and popular with cyclists, but the bicycle traffic is modest and shouldn't be a concern. Also, the rustic buildings, iron furnace, stables, and ironmaster's mansion have been designated a National Historic District. The overall length of the trail varies through the years. There can be washouts where the trail is re-routed, there can be property disputes, properties changing hands, et cetera.

Start: Fuller Lake day-use parking lot in Pine Grove Furnace State Park
Distance: 5.4-mile lollipop
Hiking time: About 3 hours
Difficulty: Moderate, due to the gradual climb and a short descent through an outcropping
Schedule: Open year-round
Season: Spring, summer, fall
Trail surface: Level railroad grade and an old logging road
Elevation gain: 779 feet
Land status: State park and state forest
Nearest town: Shippensburg

Fees and permits: No fees or permits required
Other trail users: Tourists, backpackers, hunters (in season)
Canine compatibility: Leashed dogs permitted
Maps: USGS Dickinson, PA
Trail contacts: Pine Grove Furnace State Park, 1100 Pine Grove Rd., Gardners 17324; (717) 486-7174; www.dcnr.state.pa.us/stateparks/findapark/pinegrovefurnace
Michaux State Forest, 10099 Lincoln Way East, Fayetteville 17222; (717) 352-2211; www.dcnr.state.pa.us/forestry/stateforests/michaux

Finding the trailhead: From Carlisle, drive south on I-81 for about 15 miles to exit 37. Take exit 37 and drive south on PA 233 for 8.5 miles to Pine Grove Furnace State Park. At the intersection of PA 233 North and PA 233 South, turn left onto Hunters Run Road. Drive for 0.2 mile and turn right at the Fuller Lake day-use parking lot sign. *DeLorme: Pennsylvania Atlas & Gazetteer:* Page 77 D6. GPS: N40 1.904' / W77 18.028'

The Hike

Because the Pennsylvania section of the Appalachian Trail (AT) is 232 miles long, it's not unusual to come across a day hike that uses a portion of the famed trail. This hike, however, not only uses a section of the AT but also leads you to one of its most famous spots—the halfway point. Less than 1.0 mile from the start, you'll reach the stanchion and sign that mark the midpoint of the roughly 2,180-mile trail. There's a

Climb to the top of these quartzite cliffs for a view that will take your breath away.

trail register where thru-hikers can leave messages, write wilderness-inspired poetry, or share their feelings about what it's like to have hiked 1,090 miles from either Springer Mountain, Georgia, or Mount Katahdin, Maine. Either way, reading the register can be enlightening.

For those who don't know, the Appalachian National Scenic Trail—the first national scenic trail in the United States—follows the Appalachian Mountain chain through fourteen eastern states. Trail construction began in 1921 and was completed more than fifteen years later. Today a total of more than 200 public agencies oversee the AT, while twelve volunteer hiking clubs totaling more than 4,000 volunteers maintain the trail under the leadership of the Appalachian Trail Conservancy.

Just south of the halfway marker, AT thru-hikers have a chance to slip back into civilization for a day or two. The Appalachian Trail leaves the forest and passes through Pine Grove Furnace State Park, where the first stop for hikers is the famous Pine Grove Store. Local folklore has it that once hikers hit the establishment, most immediately head for the freezer and begin gorging on family-size containers of ice cream.

The hikers' next stop is the American Youth Hostel. Right next door to the store, it's located in the refurbished ironmaster's mansion. The original Big House was a two-story wooden structure built in the 1790s. Unfortunately, it burned down sometime in the early 1800s. Based on comparisons with other area structures, scholars believe the current brick house—an example of the Federal style of architecture—was built between 1815 and 1820. The Big House was home to a string of ironmasters and was the scene of major social events and all sorts of business excitement. Prior to the Civil War, it was a stop on the Underground Railroad, where runaway slaves could find refuge in a hiding place that is still there today.

At the hostel, worn-out hikers can avail themselves of all the amenities of home, such as showers, laundry, cooking and living areas, and dining facilities. With their appetites finally sated, hikers can spend the night in dormitory-style rooms and then lounge around the next day on the expansive porch, which provides a sweeping view of the activity in the park.

Boy Scouts, most likely as a part of a badge-earning expedition, came to Pole Steeple awhile back to mount a flag on the cliffs. The flag is long gone, but the name has stuck and the cliffs remain popular with park visitors. Most who visit Pole Steeple walk or bike the 2.0 miles from the park to the base of the cliffs, make the steep climb up, and then return the same way. Our hike route is different—it allows you to get away from the crowd, enjoy the solitude of the forest, and arrive at the cliffs with plenty of energy for the descent.

The Pole Steeple cliffs are composed of erosion-resistant quartzite from the Cambrian period—that's nearly 300-million-year-old rock. This older quartzite is usually buried well within the rock strata, but here you'll find it right on the cliff face. A fault between Laurel Forge Pond and the cliffs moved the north side upward, depositing softer rock on top of the more-resistant quartzite. Millions of years of erosion have washed away the softer rock, leaving the Cambrian-era strata exposed.

On your way to the cliffs, the first stop is Fuller Lake. Everyone knows that the water in Pennsylvania's mountain lakes is . . . well, cold. The waters of Fuller are colder than most—a sign on the beach warns would-be swimmers. Even in the summer months the lake temperature can dip to the mid-60s. Before the lake was created, the area was the site of a 90-foot-deep iron ore quarry that supplied Pine Grove Furnace. The quarry was abandoned when it struck a spring and filled with water. Spring-fed and substantially deep, the lake remains chilly year-round.

The cliffs at Pole Steeple serve a dual role: They're pretty to look at, and they provide a top-notch view of the 25-acre Laurel Lake and Mountain Creek Valley. After visiting the cliffs, descend to Laurel Lake and walk the abandoned railroad bed beside Mountain Creek back to the park. This stretch alongside the dark, clear waters of Mountain Creek, with plenty of hemlocks growing along its banks, is one of the most picturesque hikes in the state.

Enjoy.

Miles and Directions

- **0.0** Start at the parking lot for Fuller Lake day use. Walk past the restroom and turn left onto the white-blazed gravel path.
- **0.1** The trail veers left at the fork in front of the food concession building. Cross Mountain Creek on a footbridge.
- **0.2** Cross the Fuller Lake outlet on a wooden bridge.

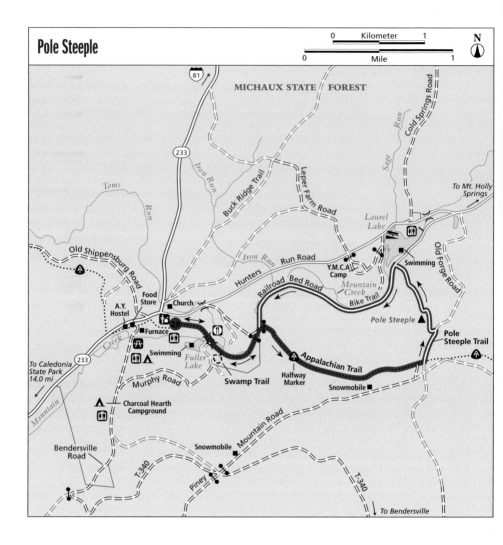

Pole Steeple

0   Kilometer   1

0   Mile   1

N

0.7   Arrive at an access gate; the trail turns right. Come to a second access gate.

0.9   Arrive at the Appalachian Trail halfway marker.

1.9   Turn left at the blue-blazed Pole Steeple Trail.

2.5   Arrive at the Pole Steeple outcropping. The trail goes down through the boulders.

2.7   Arrive at the base of the outcropping and begin your descent.

3.4   Turn left onto the paved Railroad Bed Road.

4.9   Pass the Appalachian Trail (where you started out) on your left. Retrace your steps back to the parking lot.

5.4   Arrive back at the parking lot.

Local Information

Hershey Harrisburg Regional Visitors Bureau, 3211 N. Front St., Ste. 301-A, Harrisburg 17101; (717) 231-7788; www.visithersheyharrisburg.org

Accommodations

American Youth Hostel/Ironmaster's Mansion, Pine Grove Furnace State Park, 1212 Pine Grove Rd., Gardners; (717) 486-4108; ironmastersmansion.com

Campgrounds

Pine Grove Furnace State Park, 1100 Pine Grove Rd., Gardners; (717) 486-7174; (888) 727-2757 (camping information and reservations); www.dcnr.state.pa.us/stateparks/findapark/pinegrovefurnace/

30 Flat Rock

A short, rocky climb leads to a springhouse for an icy drink then continues up Blue Mountain to Flat Rock for one of the top views in the state. From this overhanging ledge—one flat rock no bigger than your SUV—there is a 180-degree view of the majestic Cumberland Valley and (on a clear day) South Mountain. Tiny cars whiz along the roads, while tiny farm tractors stir up the dust in the fields. Along the trip you'll cross the famous 248-mile-long Tuscarora Trail.

Start: Colonel Denning State Park Nature Center parking lot off PA 233
Distance: 7.4-mile lollipop
Hiking time: About 4 hours
Difficulty: Moderate, due to uphill climbs, rocky footpaths and steep descents
Schedule: Open year-round
Season: Spring, summer, fall
Trail surface: Abandoned logging roads, improved shale roads, and some extremely rocky sections

Elevation gain: 825 feet
Land status: State park and state forest
Nearest town: Carlisle
Fees and permits: No fees or permits required
Other trail users: Tourists, backpackers
Canine compatibility: Leashed dogs permitted
Maps: USGS Andersonburg, PA
Trail contacts: Colonel Denning State Park, 1599 Doubling Gap Rd., Newville 17241; (717) 776-5272; www.dcnr.state.pa.us/stateparks/findapark/coloneldenning

Finding the trailhead: From Harrisburg, drive south on I-81 and take exit 37. Drive north on PA 233 for 6 miles. Turn right into Colonel Denning State Park and follow the signs to the nature center. *DeLorme: Pennsylvania Atlas & Gazetteer:* Page 77 B5. GPS: N40 16.911' / W77 24.965'

The Hike

The 273-acre Colonel Denning State Park is named for Revolutionary War veteran William Denning—which isn't very interesting except for the fact that Denning was never actually a colonel. Rather, Denning became famous as the manufacturer of an innovative, lightweight wrought-iron cannon.

The area around Colonel Denning State Park is known as Doubling Gap. Blue Mountain, one of a series of long parallel ridges that mark the beginning of Pennsylvania's Ridge and Valley Province, forms an "S," creating two gaps instead of just one. Our destination, the Flat Rock viewing area, lies in the center of the southern gap.

At the 1.0-mile mark, the trail intersects the famous 248-mile-long Tuscarora Trail, which was built in the 1960s as a bypass of the Appalachian Trail (AT) when it was thought that development in Virginia would reroute the AT. But as a result of the National Scenic Trails Act of 1968, the AT remained intact and the Tuscarora is now a side trail. Here you'll find a primitive shelter. If you've never slept in one of these before, you can get a feel for what it would be like to spend the night in your sleeping bag snuggled up on a real hardwood floor. There's no hot water or room service, but to the trail-weary thru-hiker, shelters like this seem palatial.

Flat Rock Overlook is one of the highest points in Pennsylvania's Ridge and Valley Province. Just yards before the view, there's a US Geological Survey benchmark embedded in a flat boulder. You just might step on it, but you probably can't read it—vandals have smashed it with a rock or a hammer, possibly in unsuccessful attempts to dislodge it.

From the edge of Flat Rock, there is a 180-degree view of the patchwork-quilt farmlands and roads of the Cumberland Valley. If it's a clear day, you can see South Mountain in the distance. Flat Rock is as good a place as any to eat your lunch, work on your tan, or watch the turkey buzzards swoop around, searching for their next meal. And those scraggly buzzards have a sizable area in which to search—Tuscarora State Forest is 91,165 acres of rugged, and sometimes remote, terrain. The name "Tuscarora" is taken from the Tuscarora Indians, a tribe adopted by the Iroquois Nation and allowed to migrate to this area in 1714. At that time the forests consisted of oak and chestnut, with hemlocks growing in the valleys. Like the rest of the forests in Pennsylvania, these forests were logged, one could say, almost to death. Logging began here in the early 1900s and ended in 1930.

Tuscarora State Forest is also home to a collection of undisturbed natural beauty; thousands of acres within the forest have been officially designated a part of either Wild or Natural Areas. Wild Area designation ensures that an area is allowed to retain its undeveloped character. The Tuscarora Wild Area, more than 5,000 acres located within the Tuscarora State Forest, was purchased by the state in 1964 and has been undisturbed since. Natural Areas are sites set aside for scientific study of natural systems and for their natural or unusual beauty. There are three Natural Areas in the Tuscarora State Forest. The most unusual of these by far is the Hoverter and Sholl Box Huckleberry Natural Area, an isolated 10-acre tract near New Bloomfield. Here you'll find a rare colony of box huckleberry—a single plant estimated to be 1,300 years old.

The box huckleberry is a member of the heath family, which includes mountain laurel, rhododendrons, azaleas, and species that produce berries, such as the blueberry and the cranberry. The box huckleberry grows about 6 inches a year by producing runners that fan out from the core. At the Natural Area, what looks like thousands of plants is actually just one plant that has been growing for 1,300 years.

Miles and Directions

0.0 Start at the nature center parking lot and walk to the Flat Rock Trail. Turn right and cross Doubling Gap Run on a footbridge. Climb the wooden steps and look for double red blazes.

0.2 Turn left onto a forest road and begin your ascent.

0.3 Come to a springhouse.

1.0 Arrive at a major trail intersection. Continue straight, following the "Flat Rock One Mile" sign. The Flat Rock Trail becomes part of the Tuscarora Trail. Follow the red and the blue blazes.

It's never easy getting to the top.

1.1 Pass a Tuscarora Trail thru-hiker shelter on your left.

1.3 Stay to the right at the fork. Cross a washout stream on a footbridge.

1.9 Walk over a USGS benchmark embedded in a boulder.

2.0 Arrive at Flat Rock. Retrace your steps to the trail intersection.

3.0 Arrive back at the major trail intersection; turn right onto the red-blazed Warner Trail.

3.5 Cross an open logging area. The trail becomes an improved road.

3.7 Turn right at the Warner Trail sign and begin your descent.

4.6 Turn left onto the Cider Path Trail.

5.2 Continue straight past the Cider Path Trail sign.

5.3 Arrive at the Cider Path Trail signpost and double red blazes. Turn left precisely beside the signpost.

6.2 Arrive at a Cider Path Trail and Shade Trail sign. Continue straight on the Cider Path Trail.

6.3 Turn left onto Doubling Gap Road.

6.7 Bear right at the fork in the road.

6.9 Bear right again at a second road fork.

7.1 Arrive at Doubling Gap Lake. Continue on the beach.

7.2 Pass through the beach parking lot and playground.

7.3 At the far end of the playground, turn left onto a wooden bridge across Doubling Gap Run. Turn right on the other side of the bridge and cross a tributary on a second footbridge.

7.4 Pass through the campgrounds. Turn right onto an auto bridge across Doubling Gap Run and arrive back at the nature center parking lot.

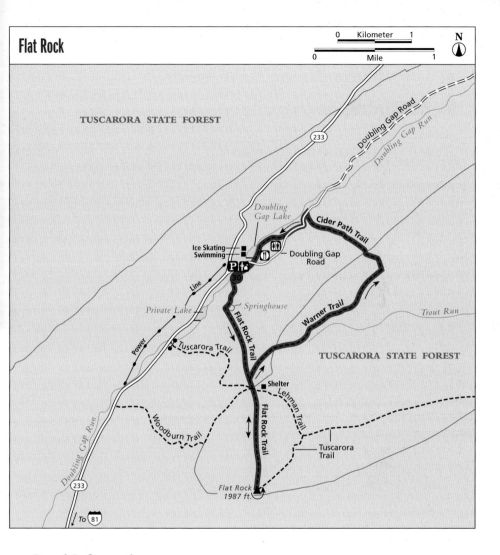

Flat Rock

0 Kilometer 1

0 Mile 1

N

TUSCARORA STATE FOREST

233

Doubling Gap Road

Doubling Gap Run

Doubling Gap Lake

Cider Path Trail

Ice Skating
Swimming

Doubling Gap
Road

30

P

Line

Springhouse

Private Lake

Flat Rock Trail

Warner Trail

Trout Run

Power

Tuscarora Trail

TUSCARORA STATE FOREST

Shelter

Lehman Trail

Woodburn Trail

Flat Rock Trail

Tuscarora
Trail

Doubling Gap Run

233

Flat Rock
1987 ft.

To 81

Local Information
Hershey Harrisburg Regional Visitors Bureau, 3211 N. Front St., Ste. 301-A, Harrisburg 17101; (717) 231-7788; www.visithersheyharrisburg.org

Campgrounds
Colonel Denning State Park, 1599 Doubling Gap Rd., Newville; (717) 776-5272; (888) 727-2757 (camping information and reservations); www.dcnr.state.pa.us/stateparks/findapark/coloneldenning

Local Outdoor Retailers
Dunham's Sports, 800 E. High St., Carlisle; (717) 249-7667; www.dunhamssports.com

31 Little Buffalo State Park

Bring your camera on this hike. It starts out on an 82-foot-long covered bridge—and not just any covered bridge. This is a Burr Truss, patented by Theodore Burr of Connecticut, architect and builder of the longest single-arch bridge in the world (also in Pennsylvania). How about a tour of a restored nineteenth-century gristmill, with one of the largest waterwheels east of the Mississippi?

Take a self-guided nature tour; then walk the path of a peculiar narrow-gauge railroad on your way to an inlet, where you might see a little green heron, an egret, or a blue-winged teal. End your hike at the Blue Ball Tavern, built in 1811, now the local historical society headquarters.

Start: Little Buffalo State Park parking lot off New Bloomfield Road
Distance: 6.2-mile loop
Hiking time: 3 to 4 hours
Difficulty: Moderate, due to the series of climbs up and down hollows
Schedule: Open year-round
Season: Spring, summer, fall
Trail surface: Abandoned railroad grades, pine needle nature trails, rocky footpaths, grassy paths, and blacktop
Elevation gain: 998 feet

Land status: State park
Nearest town: Newport
Fees and permits: No fees or permits required
Other trail users: Tourists, birders, hunters (in season)
Canine compatibility: Leashed dogs permitted
Maps: USGS Newport, PA
Trail contacts: Little Buffalo State Park, 1579 State Park Rd., Newport 17074; (717) 567-9255; www.dcnr.state.pa.us/stateparks/findapark/littlebuffalo/

Finding the trailhead: From Harrisburg, take US 22/322 North to the Newport/PA 34 exit. Turn left onto PA 34 and drive west for 3 miles to the intersection with Little Buffalo Creek Road. Turn right onto Little Buffalo Creek Road and drive 1.8 miles to the intersection with New Bloomfield Road. Turn left onto New Bloomfield Road and drive 0.4 mile to a parking lot near the breast of the dam on Holman Lake. *DeLorme: Pennsylvania Atlas & Gazetteer:* Page 77 A7. GPS: N40 27.320' / W77 10.286'

The Hike

No one really knows how Little Buffalo Creek or Buffalo Ridge got their names, but that doesn't seem to prevent folks from proposing theories. One theory—the one passed down and accepted by the local community—is that buffalo once inhabited the area.

The land on which the park is located was occupied by a succession of Native American tribes as they migrated westward, away from early colonists. In 1754 the provincial government of Pennsylvania, led by Ben Franklin and John Penn, purchased the land from the Iroquois League of Six Nations as part of the Albany Purchase.

Your hike starts with a visit to the 82-foot-long Clay's Covered Bridge.

Following the American Revolution, settlers moved onto the land and began farming. Not long after, John Koch opened the Blue Ball Tavern on the Carlisle Pike, the main road between Carlisle and Sunbury. The building, which has been restored and is open to visitors, now houses the Perry County Historical Society and an assortment of historical artifacts.

In 1808 the Juniata Iron Works commenced operations, smelting iron in charcoal-fired furnaces until 1848, when there was no more wood to burn. Evidence of charcoal making remains along the Buffalo Ridge Trail, where colliers stacked wood into piles, covered the piles with leaves, and then covered it all by packing soil on it. The piles were then burned for eight to ten days, turning the wood into charcoal. Look for the 20-foot-diameter flat areas along the trail—all that remains of the process.

Little Buffalo State Park opened in 1972, the result of an initiative that began in 1955, when the Department of Forests (now the Department of Conservation and Natural Resources) set a goal to provide a state park within 25 miles of every Pennsylvania resident. From 1955 to 1970 the state park system grew from forty-five to eighty-seven parks. Today more than 37 million people visit 117 Pennsylvania state parks annually.

Your first stop on this hike is Clay's Covered Bridge, an 82-foot-long covered bridge across Little Buffalo Creek. This bridge was designed and patented by Theodore Burr. Its innovative design involves one long arch extending from one side of the bridge to the other. The floor and the roof are attached to this arch by a series of king posts. Tied together, the structure provides superior strength. Because of his unique arch, Burr was able to build the longest single-arch wooden bridge in the world at nearby McCall's Ferry. Clay's Covered Bridge is one of fourteen covered bridges that can still be found in Perry County.

Shoaff's Mill has been grinding away since the early 1800s, churning out wheat and buckwheat flour, cornmeal, and livestock feed. Although the mill closed as a business in 1940, it has been completely restored, and today visitors can watch as its gigantic waterwheel grinds cornmeal and cracked corn—occasionally apples for apple cider—as part of the park's educational programs.

After crossing Clay's Covered Bridge and visiting Shoaff's Mill, the trail follows the grade of the defunct Newport & Sherman's Valley Railroad. The Newport was one of many narrow-gauge railroads built throughout the state in the nineteenth century to haul logs and freight for the logging industry. These narrow-gauge railroads were smaller than standard-size railroads—standard track width is 56.5 inches; a narrow gauge is 36 inches wide, with its engines and cars proportionally smaller as well. The Newport operated here from 1890 to 1937, when it went bankrupt, losing out to a standard-size railroad.

VOLKSMARCHING

The hike through Little Buffalo State Park has been chosen by the American Volkssport Association (AVA) as one of its 10-kilometer volksmarching hikes. The AVA, which has more than 500 walking clubs nationwide, is allied with the Europe-based International Volkssport Federation, which has thousands of clubs worldwide. AVA hikes are located throughout the United States.

The AVA selects a trail based on its safety, scenic interest, historic areas, natural beauty, and walkability. The chosen hikes are noncompetitive 10-kilometer walks designed for anybody and everybody, children and pets included. The hikes are mapped out, and there are Volksmarch signs and white arrows placed along their chosen trails. As you hike the Little Buffalo hike outlined in this book, you'll notice the club's brown hiker signs and white arrows along the trail. However, the hike in this book is slightly different from the volksmarch hike.

Some hikes, like the one at Little Buffalo, are year-round events. This means the hike is self-guided: Hikers sign in at the registration site, do the hike at their own pace, and then contact the group to get credit for the walk. Members can receive awards and special recognition for milestone events, such as ten events or 500 kilometers.

For more information contact the Keystone State Volkssport Association, 4230 B, Menno Village, Chambersburg; (717) 677-6511; www.ksva.net.

For the self-guided nature trail section of this hike, you need a pamphlet (available at the park office), which guides you past a series of numbered stanchions along the trail. This section is less than 1.0 mile long and passes through a magnificent hemlock forest. After the nature walk, the trail reconnects with the railroad bed to the west end of Holman Lake.

The 88-acre Holman Lake is an angler's delight—fish year-round for largemouth bass, catfish, panfish, and adult brook, brown, and rainbow trout. Holman has been designated a Big Bass Lake. Bass must be at least 15 inches to keep, and there is a daily limit of four. Electric and nonmotorized boats are permitted, and a boat rental operates from Memorial Day to Labor Day, 11 a.m. to 7 p.m.

The trail parallels the Holman Lake inlet and Little Buffalo Creek. This section of the trail is a flat walk on a grass path that leads you through the marsh-like area. Here is where you'll almost certainly see a little green heron, a great blue heron, or wood ducks. During migration, many waterfowl use the lake as a rest stop. There have been sightings of Canada geese, mallards, blue-winged teal, mergansers, buffleheads, common loons, and ring-necked ducks.

Once you cross Little Buffalo Creek Road, your real workout begins. Simply put: You go up one ravine then down the next, ad infinitum. In this section of the hike, you cross a total of seven wooden bridges, over seven washout streams, over five major ridges. There are also about a million short switchbacks. Yes, it's repetitive and grueling—even tortuous—but it's totally worth it because, hey, that's what hiking is, right?

If your legs can carry you back to the road, you'll find yourself, ironically, on the Exercise Trail. Eighteen permanent stations along this short stretch offer such delights as a balance beam, a pull-up bar, and bar vaults. If you've got anything left, give it a whirl. If, however, you need a little rest, you can slow down and check out the bluebird nesting boxes. Little Buffalo, along with fifty other state parks, is part of a bluebird rescue program that began in 1981. One of the problems for bluebirds, as well as other nesting birds, is that they need to nest in open cavities in trees. As civilization continues to encroach on the bluebird's habitat, nests are eliminated. Nesting boxes are provided to replace tree cavity nests. More than 25,000 bluebirds have fledged since the program began.

From the bluebird trail it's a short walk to the Blue Ball Tavern and back to the parking lot.

Miles and Directions

0.0 Start from the bulletin board in the parking lot near the restrooms. Turn left onto the sidewalk and walk past the restrooms toward the playground. Turn left again at the sign that reads "Mill & Covered Bridge."

0.1 Turn right at the sign for Shoaff's Mill. Cross Clay's Covered Bridge and turn left at the sign for Shoaff's Mill. After visiting the mill, return to the trail and turn left.

0.2 Pass the visitor center on your right.

Little Buffalo State Park

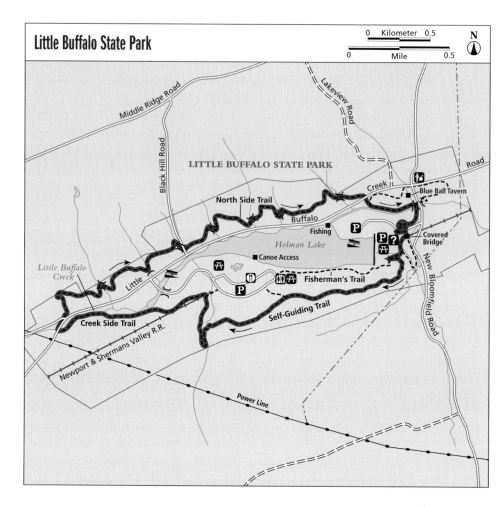

0.3 Pass the Mill Race Trail on your left.

0.4 Turn left at the brown hiker sign. Go up the wooden steps and turn left onto the Self-Guiding Trail.

1.2 Arrive at a trail intersection with the Buffalo Ridge Trail. Turn right at the "Shortcut to Main Area" sign.

1.3 Pass a water tank on your left.

1.4 Pass a forest road with a white arrow and continue straight toward the picnic area.

1.5 Come to an access gate and turn left onto the abandoned railroad bed.

1.8 Cross a park service road. Cross a tributary on a wooden footbridge and enter the forest.

1.9 Pass the Buffalo Ridge Trail on your left; continue straight onto the Little Buffalo Creek Trail.

2.0 Turn right onto the mowed path.

2.1 Arrive at the marsh of Holman Lake; turn left.

2.4 Cross a tributary to Little Buffalo Creek on a wooden footbridge.

2.6 A trail merges from your right. Continue to walk upstream alongside Little Buffalo Creek.

2.7 Pass under the power line. Turn right onto the wooden steps and arrive at Little Buffalo State Park Road. Turn right at the brown hiker sign and walk alongside the road.

2.8 Come to a brown hiker sign and turn left to cross the road. Then turn right at the Mineral Ridge Trail sign. Follow the red blazes and white arrows.

2.9 Continue straight where the trail forks.

3.1 The trail turns left on a dirt road.

3.7 Stay to the left at the fork in the trail.

3.9 Cross Black Hill Road.

5.6 Stay to the right at the fork.

5.7 Cross Little Buffalo State Park Road and turn right at the brown hiker sign. The trail becomes part of the Exercise Trail.

5.8 Cross a tributary stream on a wooden bridge and turn right onto the hikers' bridge over Little Buffalo Creek. The trail is now blacktop.

6.2 Cross the paved park road and arrive back at the parking lot.

Local Information

Hershey Harrisburg Regional Visitors Bureau, 3211 N. Front St., Ste. 301-A, Harrisburg 17101; (717) 231-7788; www.visithersheyharrisburg.org

Accommodations

Bridgeview B & B, 810 South Main Street, Marysville, PA 17053; (717) 957-2438; www.bridgeviewbnb.com

Campgrounds

Siler Valley Campsites 101 Silver Valley Circle, Saylorsburg; (570) 992-4824; www .silvervalleycamp.com

Riverfront Campground, 9 Newport Rd., Duncannon; (717) 834-5252; www .riverfrontcampground.com

32 Trough Creek State Park

Bring your camera on this hike and get a picture of the famous Balanced Rock—a rock hanging on the edge of the cliff and looking like it could topple into the valley at any moment. Along the way you'll cross a bridge at Rainbow Falls for another great photo opportunity. The trail then descends into the valley for an exploration of a cavelike hole in the ground known as the Ice Mine.

Start: Trough Creek State Park picnic area No. 5 on Trough Creek Drive
Distance: 4.3-mile lollipop
Hiking time: 2 to 3 hours
Difficulty: Moderate, due to a long, steep climb
Schedule: Open year-round. Park trails are closed during the winter months for safety reasons, generally mid-December through March, so call before planning this hike.
Season: Spring, summer, fall
Trail surface: Abandoned jeep roads, rocky footpaths, stone steps, and streamside paths

Elevation gain: 500 feet
Land status: State park and state forest
Nearest town: Huntingdon
Fees and permits: No fees or permits required
Other trail users: Tourists, hunters (in season)
Canine compatibility: Leashed dogs permitted
Maps: USGS Cassville, PA; Entriken, PA
Trail contacts: Trough Creek State Park, 16362 Little Valley Rd., James Creek 16657; (814) 658-3847; www.dcnr.state.pa.us/stateparks/findapark/troughcreek

Finding the trailhead: From Altoona, drive south on US 220/I-99 to the East Freedom exit. In East Freedom get on PA 164 and drive east about 15 miles through Martinsburg to PA 26. Turn left onto PA 26 and drive about 7 miles to Entriken and PA 994. Turn right onto PA 994 and cross Raystown Lake. Drive about 2 miles to Farm Hill Road. Turn left onto Farm Hill Road, drive about 2 miles, and turn left at the Trough Creek State Park sign. Drive all the way to the north end of the park to picnic area No. 5, on your left. *DeLorme: Pennsylvania Atlas & Gazetteer:* Page 75 B6. GPS: N40 19.865' / W78 7.504'

The Hike

Hiking the trails of Trough Creek State Park gives you firsthand knowledge of the ridge and valley system of Pennsylvania's mountains. One early Pennsylvania traveler wrote in his journal: "Pennsylvania's mountains are old and ornery, and equally inaccessible in all directions." When you begin the steep ascent up the Boulder Trail, you learn right off that what makes the mountains so ornery is that they're steep and, in many places, rocky.

Hikers won't see it much inside the state park borders, but the forests surrounding Trough Creek State Park have been hard hit by the gypsy moth infestation. The gypsy moth is native to China, but in 1863 a French scientist brought some to his laboratory in Massachusetts in an attempt to crossbreed them with silkworms. Some moths escaped and began infesting New England and eastern seaboard states, arriving

Sooner or later every hiker gets a turn on a swinging bridge.

in Pennsylvania in the 1960s. But it's the gypsy moth caterpillar, which eats tree leaves, that is the real culprit. The most affected trees are oaks, sugar maples, beech, and aspen. When 30 percent of a tree's foliage is destroyed, the tree is sufficiently weakened that it becomes susceptible to disease and attack from other insects and can eventually die.

At one point in the 1990s, more than 280,000 acres in Pennsylvania were defoliated by the gypsy moth caterpillar. Without a natural predator to control the population, alien species like the gypsy moth can cause virtually unlimited devastation. Fortunately, they do have a natural enemy—an infectious disease caused by a fungus that essentially eats the caterpillar. The fungus thrives on moisture, so when there's a dry season, the fungus is curtailed and more gypsy moths survive. Leaving little to chance, the Department of Conservation and Natural Resources sprays a biological insecticide from helicopters and small airplanes, flying 50 feet above the treetops. The insecticide is *Bacillus thuringiensis*, variety *kurstaki*, or Btk.

When you reach Balanced Rock, you can read all about it at the educational plaque near the viewing area. But to anyone in his right mind, it looks like a giant boulder that is about ready to topple into the gorge below. The truth is, however, that Balanced Rock (an erosion element) has been hanging on for thousands of years. It was once part of a much higher cliff composed of hard rock and softer rock, which has eroded away. In the process the precariously perched rock was eased into its current position.

Begin your descent into the gorge and pick up the appropriately named Copperas Rock Trail. This trail is named for the coppery-yellow stain on the cliff surface. The stain is actually ferrous sulfate, which is yellow precipitate that leaches out from a small pocket of coal in the cliff.

As you might guess, the Ice Mine Trail leads to the Ice Mine, a hole in the gorge bottom that functions as a natural refrigerator. An interpretive station explains this phenomenon. In short, winter air enters the mine opening and diffuses up the hillside. In spring and summer, cold air flows down the slope and into the hole; this keeps the mine cold. When melting snow water runoff gets inside the hole, the cold air inside freezes the water into ice.

Perhaps all state parks have at least one unique feature—Trough Creek certainly has a few, but it also has its own legend. The story goes that after visiting the park and seeing the ravens that nested on the cliffs of Raven Trail, renowned American author Edgar Allen Poe wrote his famous poem, "The Raven."

Before heading home, be sure to drive to one of the overlooks on PA 26. There are two overlooks near the Entriken Bridge (the PA 994 bridge). The Entriken Bridge Overlook is just south of the bridge, and the Coffee Run Overlook is just north of the bridge. From either of these you're rewarded with a spectacular view of Raystown Lake. The lake, which was created when the US Army Corps of Engineers built a dam across the Juniata River in the mid-1970s, is 30 miles long and covers 8,300 acres, making it the largest body of water in the state. With thirteen public-use areas, boat launches, a marina, a swimming beach, and plenty of fishing, Raystown is the top recreational spot in South Central Pennsylvania.

Miles and Directions

0.0 Start at the picnic area No. 5 parking lot. Walk to Trough Creek Drive; turn left and walk to the Ice Mine.

0.1 After exploring the Ice Mine, get on the red-blazed Boulder Trail and begin your ascent.

0.3 Reach the intersection with Laurel Run Trail. Keep right and stay on the Boulder Trail.

0.8 Cross Terrace Mountain Road and come to a trail sign for Laurel Run Trail, Ice Mine Trail, and Trough Creek Drive. Continue toward Trough Creek Drive, following the red blazes.

1.0 Arrive at Trough Creek Drive. Turn left and walk about 50 feet to the trail sign for Suspension Bridge, Rainbow Falls, and Balanced Rock. Cross the suspension bridge and turn right onto the white-blazed Abbot Run Trail.

1.3 Arrive at the bridge at Rainbow Falls.

1.4 Turn right at the steps and arrive at Balanced Rock. Return down the steps, turn right, and cross a second bridge. Immediately make a hairpin left turn onto the blue-blazed Ledges Trail and begin an uphill climb.

1.8 Turn left onto the red-blazed Copperas Rock Trail.

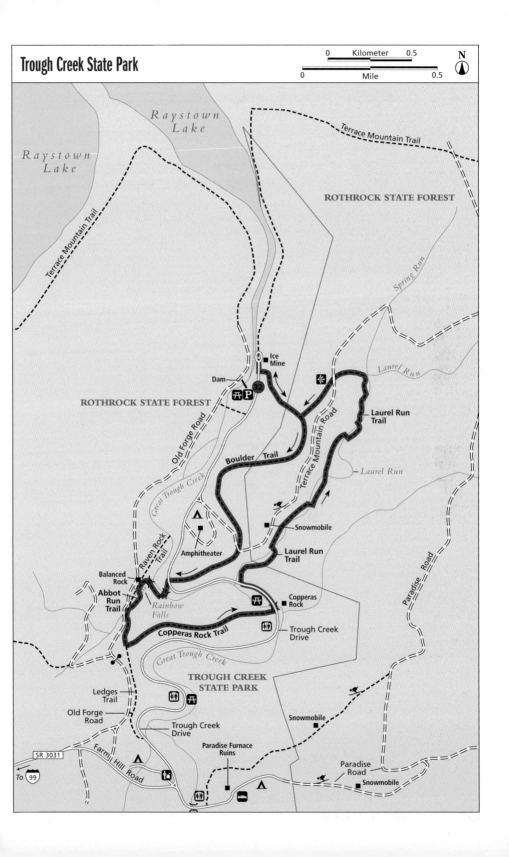

Trough Creek State Park

Kilometer
0   0.5

Mile
0   0.5

N

Raystown Lake

Raystown Lake

Terrace Mountain Trail

Terrace Mountain Trail

Spring Run

ROTHROCK STATE FOREST

Laurel Run

Ice Mine

Dam

32

ROTHROCK STATE FOREST

Old Forge Road

Great Trough Creek

Boulder   Trail

Terrace Mountain Road

Laurel Run Trail

Laurel Run

Raven Rock Trail

Amphitheater

Snowmobile

Laurel Run Trail

Balanced Rock

Abbot Run Trail

Rainbow Falls

Copperas Rock

Trough Creek Drive

Copperas Rock Trail

Great Trough Creek

TROUGH CREEK STATE PARK

Paradise Road

Snowmobile

Ledges Trail

Old Forge Road

Trough Creek Drive

Paradise Furnace Ruins

SR 3031

To 99

Farm Hill Road

Paradise Road

Snowmobile

2.2 Arrive at a major trail intersection and continue downhill to Trough Creek Drive. Turn left on Trough Creek Drive.

2.4 Turn right onto the Laurel Run Trail. You will cross Laurel Run on wooden bridges a number of times.

3.0 Pass a set of stone steps and a Laurel Run Trail sign on your right. Continue straight on the Laurel Run Trail. Look for green blazes.

3.1 Cross the final bridge and turn left, heading uphill and away from Laurel Run.

3.3 Arrive at a trail sign and turn left onto Terrace Mountain Road. Pick up the trail on your right.

3.7 Arrive at a trail sign. Take the Laurel Run Trail to your left. Arrive at the Ice Mine Trail sign and turn right, retracing your steps downhill to the Ice Mine.

4.2 Arrive back at the Ice Mine.

4.3 Arrive back at the parking lot.

Local Information

Huntingdon County Visitors Bureau, 6993 Seven Points Rd., Ste 2, Hesston 16647; (814) 658-0060; (888) 729-7869; www.visitpa.com/pa-local-resources/huntingdon -county-visitors-bureau

Campgrounds

Trough Creek State Park, 16362 Little Valley Rd., James Creek; (814) 658-3847; (888) 727-2757 (camping information and reservations); www.dcnr.state.pa.us/stateparks/ findapark/troughcreek

33 Canoe Creek State Park

This is an easy, pleasant hike where you can explore the limestone kilns used in the early 1900s to supply limestone for the bustling iron and steel industries. Visit an abandoned quarry operation, now a bat colony, then make your way up a knoll for views of the valley. Walk alongside Canoe Creek on its way to Canoe Lake. Both bodies of water are good for fishing.

Start: Visitor center parking lot
Distance: 4.6-mile loop
Hiking time: About 2 hours
Difficulty: Easy, due to mostly short climbs over knolls
Schedule: Open year-round
Season: Spring, summer, fall
Trail surface: Shale walkways, forest footpaths, abandoned dirt roads, and a boardwalk
Elevation gain: 969 feet

Land status: State park
Nearest town: Altoona
Fees and permits: No fees or permits required
Other trail users: Tourists, anglers, equestrians
Canine compatibility: Leashed dogs permitted
Maps: USGS Frankstown, PA
Trail contacts: Canoe Creek State Park, 205 Canoe Creek Rd., Hollidaysburg 16648; (814) 695-6807; www.dcnr.state.pa.us/stateparks/findapark/canoecreek

Finding the trailhead: From Altoona, drive south on PA 36 for approximately 4 miles to the intersection with US 22. Turn left onto US 22 and drive past the first sign for Canoe Creek State Park (0.9 mile from the intersection with PA 36). Drive 3.5 miles from the first park sign to the second park sign. Turn left at the second park sign onto Turkey Valley Road and into Canoe Creek State Park. Park in the lot near the Education Center. *DeLorme: Pennsylvania Atlas & Gazetteer:* Page 75 A5. GPS: N40 29.096' / W078 17.000'

The Hike

Canoe Creek State Park is a jewel in the crown of the state park system. At 958 acres it's small, but it's loaded with features. There are modern rental cabins, a food concession, and hot showers in the beach changing bathhouse.

Canoe Lake is a 155-acre lake that provides crystal-clear, icy cold water for swimming, canoeing, and fishing. It's stocked with walleye, muskellunge, bass, trout, chain pickerel, catfish, crappies, and other panfish. There is also ice fishing when there is an extended trout season. All Pennsylvania Fish & Boat Commission laws apply. Visitors wishing to fish need to get a Pennsylvania fishing license. The lake is open to non-powered and registered electric boats. Non-powered boats must display a State Park Launching Permit, a State Park Mooring Permit, or a current Pennsylvania registration. Boats registered in other states must display a Pennsylvania State Park Launch Permit as well as current registration.

This hike, which includes a visit to the historic Blair Limestone Company Kilns, is part of the "Path of Progress," a 500-mile automobile route that passes through nine

Limestone kilns still stand tall at Canoe Creek State Park.

southwestern Pennsylvania counties. It leads the traveler on a journey through the area's industrial past and, in doing so, teaches visitors how major industries, such as coal mining and steel production, helped create a cultural heritage.

As you begin this hike, you pass a number of educational kiosks, which explain limestone mining and the role of limestone in the production of steel. Leaving the kilns, a spur leads to a quarry. At the quarry, what appear to be small caves are actually entrances to limestone mines. These openings lead to a 1.5-mile-long network of tunnels. Miners went into the mine on a 45-degree tramway that led to four different levels, the deepest of which is 300 feet below the surface.

Nowadays, these abandoned mines are home to six species of bats, including the Indiana bat, which is on the Endangered Species List. The bats hibernate in the mines over the winter. In June the females roost in the attic of the abandoned church on Turkey Road, across from the park office. The young are born, and the cycle begins again.

If you want to learn more about bats, attend one of the park's bat walks, held at 8 p.m. during the summer months. Park employees or guest lecturers will tell you everything you've always wanted to know about bats. And they'll lead you to the church building across from the park office, where you'll see the largest colony of brown bats in the state—18,000 bats, just hanging around.

BAT KNOWLEDGE

If you want to get a head start on your bat knowledge, below are the questions and correct answers to Pennsylvania's Department of Conservation and Natural Resources true-or-false bat test.

1. **Bats really are blind.**
False. Though they don't see in color, they see better than we do at night! And many bats can "see" by sonar.

2. **The world's smallest bat weighs less than a penny.**
True. It's the bumblebee bat of Thailand, the world's smallest mammal.

3. **Some bats' hearing is so keen they can hear the footsteps of an insect walking on sand more than 6 feet away.**
True. Many bats find their way and locate prey using the sound of echoes.

4. **Bats are cruel by nature.**
False. Some bats are so kind they adopt orphans and will risk their lives to share food with less-fortunate bats.

5. **Vampire bats are the only mammals that feed on nothing but blood.**
True. By the way, vampire bats live only in Latin America, where most people will never even see one.

6. **Bats hang by their nose.**
False. They hang by their toes, counterbalanced by their upside-down weight.

7. **Bats get tangled in your hair.**
False. People may have thought this because bats fly over our heads hunting bugs. If a bat flies by you, it's probably chasing a mosquito.

8. **All bats live in attics and caves.**
False. Some choose trees or other sites; tropical bats make homes everywhere from banana leaves to spiderwebs.

9. **Bats are vicious.**
False. Bats pose little threat to people who leave them alone; they will bite in self-defense if mishandled.

Miles and Directions

0.0 Start from the parking lot near the visitor center. Walk to a small footbridge and sign for the visitor center. Walk through a small picnic area and turn right at the Limestone Trail trailhead sign.

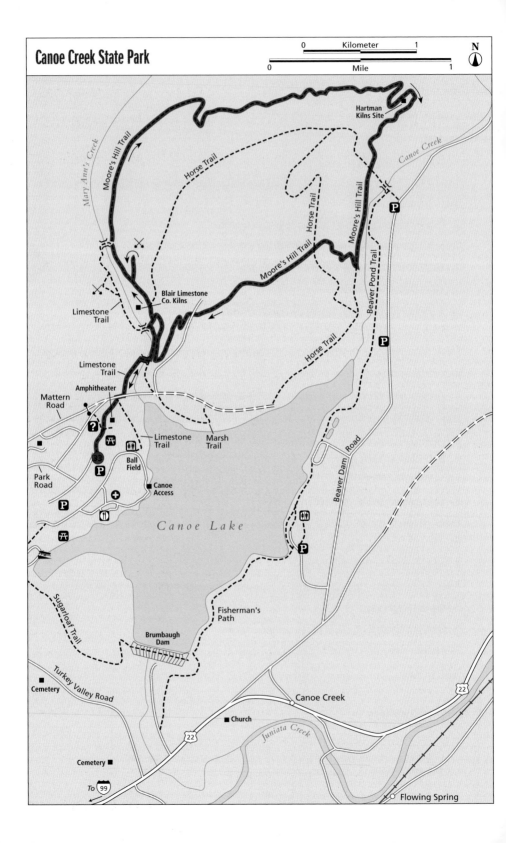

Canoe Creek State Park

Kilometer

0   1

0   Mile   1

N

Hartman Kilns Site

Mary Ann's Creek

Moore's Hill Trail

Horse Trail

Horse Trail

Moore's Hill Trail

Moore's Hill Trail

Canoe Creek

P

Beaver Pond Trail

Blair Limestone Co. Kilns

Limestone Trail

Limestone Trail

Horse Trail

P

Amphitheater

Mattern Road

?

Limestone Trail

Marsh Trail

Ball Field

Canoe Access

Canoe Lake

P

Park Road

P

Beaver Dam Road

P

Sugarloaf Trail

Fisherman's Path

Brumbaugh Dam

Turkey Valley Road

Cemetery

Canoe Creek

22

Church

Juniata Creek

22

Cemetery

To 99

Flowing Spring

0.1 Pass a water fountain and an amphitheater on your right. At the first trail fork, bear right. At the second trail fork, bear left.

0.2 Come to the Limestone Trail sign. Turn right onto the paved park road and take a quick left to the Limestone Trail kiosk.

0.3 Turn right onto the footbridge over Mary Ann's Creek; then turn left at the Limestone Kilns sign.

0.4 Arrive at the Limestone Kilns and kiosk. Turn right and walk uphill behind the kilns. Pass the Moore's Hill Trail on your right.

0.5 The horse trail goes off to your right; veer left onto the Limestone Trail.

0.6 Come to kiosk No. 3. Take the right fork to the stone quarry.

0.7 Arrive at an open area and the quarry.

0.8 Come to a lookout bench; retrace your steps downhill to the Limestone Trail.

0.9 Arrive back at kiosk No. 3. Turn right onto the Limestone Trail and look for the blue blazes.

1.1 Turn right onto Moore's Hill Trail.

1.2 Turn right at the fork in the trail and begin an uphill climb.

2.4 The trail turns left at a blue arrow.

2.8 Pass a kiln on your right.

3.0 Pass an intersection with the horse trail and then turn right. Follow the blue blazes. Canoe Creek is on your left.

3.2 Turn right onto the boardwalk.

3.4 Pass another intersection with the horse trail. Continue straight.

3.6 The trail turns right. Look for the blue blaze and a yellow arrow. Pass a jeep trail on your left and continue straight into forest.

3.8 Pass an intersection with an unnamed trail. Continue straight.

3.9 Cross the paved access road to the water tower.

4.2 Arrive back at the limestone kilns and kiosk. Turn left onto the Limestone Trail. Retrace your steps back to the visitor center parking lot.

4.6 Arrive back at the parking lot.

Local Information

Allegheny Mountain Convention & Visitors Bureau, 1216 11th Ave., Ste. 216, Altoona 16601; (814) 943-4183; www.explorealtoona.com

Local Events/Attractions

Horseshoe Curve National Historic Landmark, Kittaning Point, Altoona; (814) 941-7743; www.railroadcity.com/visit/world-famous-horseshoe-curve/

Campgrounds

Canoe Creek State Park, 205 Canoe Creek Rd., Hollidaysburg; (814) 695-6807; (888) 727-2757 (camping information and reservations); www.dcnr.state.pa.us/stateparks/findapark/canoecreek

Restaurants

The Dream Family Restaurant, 1500 Allegheny St., Hollidaysburg; (814) 696-3384

34 Greenwood Furnace State Park

This is simply a great hike. It starts in a restored nineteenth-century village that was once the company town for Greenwood Furnace Iron Works. The entire village has been designated a National Historic District. Old wagon roads and tramway trails lead hikers through the village and into the surrounding mountains, where the remains of charcoal pads can still be seen. There are visits to a historic cemetery and a pristine mountain lake, and, believe it or not, there's even a top-notch view. Bring your camera and your children on this one.

Start: Greenwood Furnace State Park office parking lot
Distance: 5.5-mile loop
Hiking time: About 3 hours
Difficulty: Moderate, due to a long gradual climb, followed by a rocky footpath, then a very steep descent
Schedule: Open year-round
Season: Spring, summer, fall
Trail surface: Abandoned wagon trails, forest footpaths, rocky outcroppings, and shale roads

Elevation gain: 1,007 feet
Land status: State park
Nearest town: State College
Fees and permits: No fees or permits required
Other trail users: Tourists, backpackers
Canine compatibility: Leashed dogs permitted
Maps: USGS McAlevys Fort, PA; Barrville, PA
Trail contacts: Greenwood Furnace State Park, 15795 Greenwood Rd., Huntingdon 16652; (814) 667-1800; www.dcnr.state.pa.us/stateparks/findapark/greenwoodfurnace

Finding the trailhead: From State College, drive south on PA 26 to the flashing yellow traffic light in Pine Grove Mills. From the traffic light, drive 9.6 miles south on PA 26 and turn left onto PA 305. Drive 4.5 miles to the Greenwood Furnace State Park office parking lot, on your left. *DeLorme: Pennsylvania Atlas & Gazetteer:* Page 62 C2. GPS: N40 39.022' / W077 45.270'

The Hike

This hike has a lot going for it. It's located in a National Historic District, the trails are well maintained, there's an excellent view, and the area is just plain beautiful. If you were interested in introducing someone to hiking, this hike would be an excellent choice. It's one of the few hikes in the state where just about anyone—experienced hiker or not—can get to a breathtaking vista without an exhaustive uphill climb.

Greenwood Furnace State Park offers a number of hikes with a historical flavor. Once upon a time, teams of mules pulled small railcars loaded with iron ore along a wooden-railed tramway from the Brush Ridge Ore Banks to the furnaces. Today hikers can walk this same tramway and its connected roadways. Another short hike guides visitors through the historic village, past the company meat house, furnace stacks, wagon and blacksmith shop, and the six-acre lake created to supply power for the company gristmill and water for the iron furnaces.

Relics of the past abound as you make your way to this hike.

Our hike begins on the old wagon road that linked Greenwood Furnace to Belleville. Pig iron ingots were hauled over this road to the steelworks (today Standard Steel) in Burnham. It's a little less than 3.0 miles from the trailhead to the Stone Valley Vista, where the first 1.5 miles is a gentle climb on a grassy wagon road. The trail gets a little rocky in the last mile, but the view from the vista, which stretches 10 to 20 miles on a clear day, is more than worth the effort.

Standing on the rocks of Stone Valley Vista and surveying the valley and mountains, it's hard to believe that a thick black smoke filled this valley during the seven decades the Greenwood Furnace Iron Works operated, from 1834 to 1904. Greenwood Furnace State Park was once the site of a booming nineteenth-century industrial village. Three hundred employees and their families lived and worked in this company town that produced iron for the burgeoning national railroad system.

The main fuel of the iron maker's furnace was charcoal. During its heyday, the Greenwood Furnace Company owned nearly 40,000 acres of forest, which it harvested for the charcoal furnaces. These furnaces consumed timber at the remarkable rate of an acre of forest per day. And though the area was clear-cut, not all trees were harvested for charcoal. The preferred trees were hickory and oak. The other timber was used in constructing the village.

HOW TO GROW A STATE FOREST

Dr. Joseph Trimble Rothrock may not have been one of Pennsylvania's most notable residents on a national or international level, but within the state—and especially within the state forest and conservation community—he was the major force. His efforts earned him the title the Father of Pennsylvania Forestry.

Rothrock was accomplished in a number of disciplines: medical doctor and surgeon, explorer, botanist, and university professor. Rothrock's father, the son of a German immigrant who had settled his family in Berks County, Pennsylvania, was also a physician. Rothrock was born in Mifflin County in 1839 and went on to graduate from Harvard in 1862 with a degree in botany. The next year he enlisted in the Union Army and saw action at Antietam and Fredericksburg, where he was wounded. By the end of the Civil War, he was a captain in the 20th Pennsylvania Cavalry.

In 1867 he received his medical degree from the University of Pennsylvania and became one of the founders of the Wilkes-Barre Hospital. From 1867 to 1869 he was professor of botany and human anatomy and physiology at the Agricultural College of Pennsylvania (now Penn State).

In 1880 Dr. Rothrock left Pennsylvania to study botany at the University of Strassburg in Germany, where he had a chance to study the managed forests of Europe. Obviously affected by what he had seen in Germany, Rothrock returned to Pennsylvania and began his campaign to save the state's forests. In 1895 he became the first commissioner of forestry, setting in motion the purchase of lands for state forestry reservations (now called state forests). He also initiated programs for the training of state foresters, the establishment of forest nurseries for reforestation, and the establishment of an agency to detect and extinguish forest fires.

During Rothrock's lifetime he witnessed the clear-cutting of Pennsylvania's forests. In a 1915 speech he stated, "Sixty years ago I walked from Clearfield to St. Marys; thence on to Smethport—60 miles; most of the way through glorious white pine and hemlock forests. Now these forests are gone. [Today] 6,400 square miles; more than 4 million acres of the state are desolated, cut and unprotected from fire."

Rothrock's namesake, the 94,287-acre Rothrock State Forest, located in Huntingdon, Mifflin, and Centre Counties, began its existence in 1903. At that time the forests in the area had been stripped bare to provide charcoal for the furnaces at the Greenwood Furnace Iron Works. When two furnaces were shut down, Rothrock was instrumental in helping the Bureau of Forestry purchase 35,000 acres. Other land purchases followed, and in 1953, after various forest districts were combined or eliminated, Rothrock State Forest was named.

What could be better than a lunch break under the pines?

Aside from its historical grandeur and picturesque setting, there's another reason Greenwood Furnace is popular with hikers and backpackers: It's an access point for two major backpacking trails. This particular trail is the northern terminus of the 72-mile Link Trail, which continues south to Cowans Gap State Park, where it links to the Tuscarora Trail. Going in the opposite direction, hikers use the Greenwood Spur to connect with the Mid State Trail, which runs from the Pennsylvania–Maryland border near the town of Artemas to the Pennsylvania–New York border near Wellsboro in Tioga County.

Miles and Directions

0.0 Start from the park office parking lot and walk east alongside PA 305.

0.1 Arrive at the historic Greenwood Furnace Church. Turn right to cross PA 305 and walk to the Link Trail trailhead. Follow the orange blazes.

0.2 Come to a gate across the trail.

0.8 The trail runs along the ridge.

1.5 The trail turns left and becomes a footpath.

2.1 The trail turns right. Begin an uphill climb.

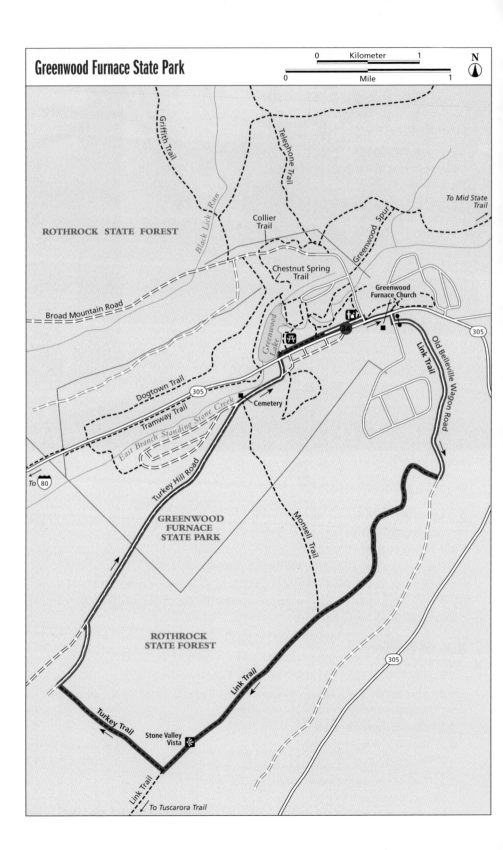

Greenwood Furnace State Park

0   Kilometer   1

0   Mile   1

N

Griffith Trail

Black Lick Run

Telephone Trail

ROTHROCK STATE FOREST

Collier Trail

Chestnut Spring Trail

Greenwood Spur

To Mid State Trail

Greenwood Furnace Church

Broad Mountain Road

Greenwood Lake

305

Link Trail

Old Belleville Wagon Road

305

Dogtown Trail

305

Tramway Trail

Cemetery

East Branch Standing Stone Creek

To 80

Turkey Hill Road

GREENWOOD FURNACE STATE PARK

Monsell Trail

ROTHROCK STATE FOREST

305

Link Trail

Turkey Trail

Stone Valley Vista

Link Trail

To Tuscarora Trail

2.9 Arrive at Stone Valley Vista.

3.1 Arrive at an intersection with the Turkey Trail. Turn right and follow the blue blazes, beginning your descent.

3.5 Pass the trail marker for the Link and Turkey Trails and arrive at the base of the mountain.

4.0 Turn right onto Turkey Hill Road.

4.4 Pass the Greenwood Furnace State Park boundary sign.

5.0 Pass the campground contact station.

5.1 Arrive at the historic Greenwood Furnace Cemetery.

5.2 Cross PA 305 and follow the walkway through the picnic area.

5.4 Come to the wooden steps to the park office parking lot.

5.5 Arrive back at the parking lot.

Local Information

Centre County Convention and Visitors Bureau, 800 E. Park Ave., State College 16803; (814) 231-1400; www.visitpennstate.org

Local Events/Attractions

Central PA Festival of Arts, first Wednesday of the first full week after the Fourth of July, State College; (814) 231-1400; www.visitpennstate.org/calendar/central-pa -arts-fest.php. More than 1,000 artists and vendors.

Campgrounds

Greenwood Furnace State Park, 15795 Greenwood Rd., Huntingdon; (814) 667-1800; (888) 727-2757 (camping information and reservations); www.dcnr.state.pa.us/ stateparks/findapark/greenwoodfurnace

Organizations

Penn State Outing Club, State College; sites.psu.edu/outingclub; e-mail: psouting club@gmail.com

35 Indian Steps

The major highlight of this hike is the mystery of a series of large stone steps erected on the side of a steep mountain. The hike begins with a gradual ascent to the summit, where the clearings above talus slopes provide sweeping panoramic vistas. Once on top of the mountain, the trail connects with a popular backpacking trail and skirts the ridge flank. Your descent includes the mysterious Indian Steps.

Start: Designated parking area on Harrys Valley Road
Distance: 4.1-mile loop
Hiking time: About 3 hours
Difficulty: Moderate, due to a rugged descent over a rocky trail
Schedule: Open year-round
Season: Spring, summer, fall
Trail surface: A series of improved shale and forest jeep roads, rocky trail, and stone steps
Elevation gain: 1,480 feet

Land status: State forest
Nearest town: State College
Fees and permits: No fees or permits required
Other trail users: Backpackers, hunters (in season)
Canine compatibility: Leashed dogs permitted
Maps: USGS Pine Grove Mills, PA
Trail contacts: Rothrock State Forest, 181 Rothrock Ln., Huntingdon 16652; (814) 643-2340; www.dcnr.state.pa.us/forestry/state forests/rothrock/index.htm

Finding the trailhead: From State College, drive south on PA 26 to the flashing yellow traffic light in Pine Grove Mills. From the traffic light, drive 3.1 miles south on PA 26 and turn right onto Harrys Valley Road. Drive exactly 2.0 miles and park on the jeep road on your left that is blocked with boulders. *DeLorme: Pennsylvania Atlas & Gazetteer.* Page 62 C1. GPS: N40 41.453' / W077 56.132'

The Hike

The highlight of this hike is undoubtedly the mystery of the Indian Steps. Someone, no one knows just who for sure, built these steps using enormous flat rocks found alongside the trail. One theory holds that Native Americans, probably the Kishacoquillas, built the steps. Dissenters argue that most Native American trails were chosen because they were the easiest routes, and these steps are not the easiest way to cross this mountain.

Regardless, there are clearly man-made steps crossing Tussey Mountain. Our hike will only cover half the steps. To see the steps on the other side, which are purportedly in better condition, leave PA 26 and drive in on Kepler Road to where the Indian Steps Trail crosses it. From there it's a short out-and-back—walk up the steps and then back down to your car.

This hike has been designed so that you can walk down, as opposed to walking up, the steps. The ravine on which the steps are located is extremely steep, and even though the steps are a little more than 0.1 mile long, going down them is a challenge. Be sure to wear good hiking boots with good tread. Small rocks and pebbles on the

No one knows who built these steps.

steps can create a kind of "walking on marbles" hazard. If you're carrying a camera or other gear, stow it in your pack before beginning this section. It's only a little more than 0.5 mile, but it's going to seem longer.

The trail runs through a steep washout ravine that is at times muddy and always rocky. As for the steps themselves, the rocks are thick and wide, too wide for one person to have maneuvered. Placing these steps was the work of two or three (or perhaps more) workers. And no matter how long ago the steps were built, in the places where they have held up, they do help hikers on their way.

There are a number of spectacular views all along this trail. The first one is at about the 1.0-mile mark, on the Pump House Road Trail—an abandoned dirt road that is now a grassy footpath. The ridgeline hike along the paved Pennsylvania Furnace Road is startlingly open. As with many forest roads, there are no guardrails; consequently, you can walk to the very edge of a number of steep talus slopes, with nothing in front of you but sky.

When you reach the top of the mountain and turn right onto the Mid State Trail, there's a large, flat boulder—a good place to stop and eat your lunch. Your next stop is a visit to the Tussey Mountain Fire Tower ruins and vista; from there it's on to the Schalls Gap Overlook. Both of these views are on your left.

It's easy to see why the Mid State Trail is a popular backpacking trail. It's well marked and well maintained. At this point on the Mid State Trail, you're nearer the southern terminus, which is near Artemas at the Maryland border. The northern terminus is at the New York border near Wellsboro.

On the 2.0-mile stretch of the Mid State Trail between Pennsylvania Furnace Road and the Indian Steps turnoff, the trail runs along a ridge flank on the mountaintop. At points the trail runs over large boulder outcroppings; the ridge is narrow, and there is no forest canopy overhead. Walking along these open areas, you get a feeling of freedom—like it's just you and the mountain and the sky.

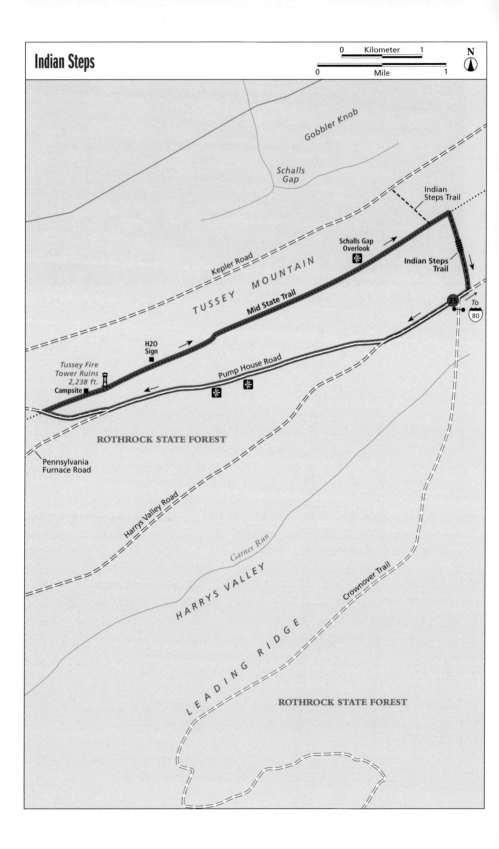

Indian Steps

0   Kilometer   1

0   Mile   1

N

Gobbler Knob

Schalls Gap

Indian Steps Trail

Kepler Road

TUSSEY MOUNTAIN

Schalls Gap Overlook

Indian Steps Trail

Mid State Trail

Indian Steps Trail

35

To 80

H2O Sign

Tussey Fire Tower Ruins 2,238 ft.

Campsite

Pump House Road

ROTHROCK STATE FOREST

Pennsylvania Furnace Road

Harrys Valley Road

Garner Run

HARRYS VALLEY

Crownover Trail

LEADING RIDGE

ROTHROCK STATE FOREST

Miles and Directions

0.0 Start at the blocked-off jeep road on Harrys Valley Road. To begin the hike, walk on Harrys Valley Road in the same direction you were driving.

0.2 Pass a blocked jeep road on your left.

0.4 Bear right onto the Pump House Road Trail. Look for two large boulders blocking vehicle traffic. Begin your ascent and note the pole gate stanchions.

1.0 Come to a rocky area on your right and your first view, on your left.

1.3 Connect with the Pennsylvania Furnace Road.

1.5 Arrive at the mountaintop. Turn right onto the orange-blazed Mid State Trail.

1.8 Arrive at the Tussey Fire Tower ruins.

1.9 The trail gets rocky. Pass an open area on flat boulders. Look for the orange blazes in the forest ahead.

2.9 Arrive at the Schalls Gap Overlook.

3.4 Come to the sign on the left that reads "Indian Steps Trail to Kepler Road." Do not take this trail; continue straight.

3.5 Come to the trail post that reads "Harrys Valley Road 1 Mile" on one side and "Indian Steps Trail" on the other side. Turn right and begin your descent.

3.6 Arrive at Indian Steps.

4.0 Turn right onto Harrys Valley Road.

4.1 Arrive back at your vehicle.

Local Information

Centre County Convention and Visitors Bureau, 800 E. Park Ave., State College 16803; (814) 231-1400; www.visitpennstate.org

Local Events/Attractions

Indian Caverns, 5386 Indian Trail, Spruce Creek; (814) 632-7578; www.indiancaverns .com

Penn's Cave & Wildlife Park, 222 Penn's Cave Rd., Centre Hall; (814) 364-1664; www.pennscave.com

Lincoln Caverns, 7703 William Penn Hwy. (US 22), Huntingdon; (814) 643-0268; www.lincolncaverns.com

Campgrounds

Greenwood Furnace State Park, 15795 Greenwood Rd., Huntingdon; (814) 667-1800; (888) 727-2757 (camping information and reservations); www.dcnr.state.pa.us/stateparks/findapark/greenwoodfurnace

Organizations

Penn State Outing Club, State College; sites.psu.edu/outingclub; e-mail: psoutingclub @gmail.com

36 Alan Seeger Natural Area to Greenwood Fire Tower

The hike begins as a gentle nature walk on a pine needle path that leads to some of the oldest trees in the state. You crisscross a delightful mountain stream as you wind your way through tunnels of rhododendrons, some as high as 20 feet with a 4-inch diameter. You make a major climb as you ascend to the mountaintop and a fire tower, which provides a panoramic view.

Start: Alan Seeger Natural Area picnic area parking lot
Distance: 5.1 miles out and back
Hiking time: About 4 hours
Difficulty: Moderate, due to a steep, strenuous climb
Schedule: Open year-round
Season: Spring, summer, fall
Trail surface: Pine needle nature trail; steep, rocky footpath; and a high plateau path
Elevation gain: 1,018 feet

Land status: State forest
Nearest town: State College
Fees and permits: No fees or permits required
Other trail users: Backpackers, picnickers
Canine compatibility: Leashed dogs permitted
Maps: USGS McAlevys Fort, PA; Barrville, PA
Trail contacts: Rothrock State Forest, 181 Rothrock Ln., Huntingdon 16652; (814) 643-2340; www.dcnr.state.pa.us/forestry/state forests/rothrock/index.htm

Finding the trailhead: From State College, drive south on PA 26 to the flashing yellow traffic light in Pine Grove Mills. Continue south 8.5 miles on PA 26 and turn left at the sign for Alan Seeger Road. Drive 5.9 miles to the Alan Seeger Natural Area picnic and parking area. *DeLorme: Pennsylvania Atlas & Gazetteer.* Page 62 C3. GPS: N40 41.743' / W77 45.9673'

The Hike

Like unsolved mysteries? On this hike there are two. The first concerns the area's namesake, Alan Seeger. Seeger was an American who moved to Paris to become a poet. When World War I broke out, he joined the French Foreign Legion and received a number of medals for his courage. His claim to fame came about as a result of his poem, "I Have a Rendezvous with Death," which eerily came true when he was killed in battle on July 4, 1916. Today, no one knows why his name was attached to this natural area. There are no available records to show if or when Seeger ever visited this part of the state.

The second mystery revolves around the very existence of the Alan Seeger Natural Area. From 1834 to 1903 the entire area surrounding Alan Seeger was clear-cut to produce charcoal for the furnaces at nearby Greenwood Furnace Iron Works. For some reason—no one knows why—118 acres of old-growth forest were spared the ax. This tract served as the foundation for the 368-acre park. As a result, you can see some of the oldest trees in Pennsylvania along the natural area's short interpretive trail. At one point you come face to face with a 500-year-old eastern hemlock that was

It's a long and winding road that takes you to the top of Broad Mountain.

struck by lightning in 1982 and lies across the trail. Also in this first section of your hike, you'll see some of the largest rhododendrons in the state. With trunks thicker than your arm, these shrubs have intertwined themselves and created tunnels that are in some places 20 feet high.

After the interpretive trail, begin a 1,000-foot climb up a ravine to the top of Broad Mountain. Along the way you pass through a second-growth forest of oak, hemlock, pine, black birch, and white birch. Striped maples can also be seen growing along boulder outcroppings. This species, with its distinctive vertical stripes, is right at home here. It thrives on shaded slopes and deep ravines.

Near the top of the mountain, you'll work your way through a series of short switchbacks. The reason for these closely spaced switchbacks is simple: The trail is very, very steep at this point, as opposed to lower down the ravine, where the trail is just very steep. But no matter how many times you do it, it's always exhilarating to reach the top of a climb. Broad Mountain is no exception. As soon as the trail levels off, you're cooled by a high-mountain breeze—welcome in the warmer months. (If you make this hike in the cooler months, be sure to layer clothing so you can add and remove them as necessary.) Walking through the dense huckleberry patches in the sunlight, you can almost forget that you just climbed up a rocky ravine that, in short order, you must hike back down.

Alan Seeger Natural Area to Greenwood Fire Tower

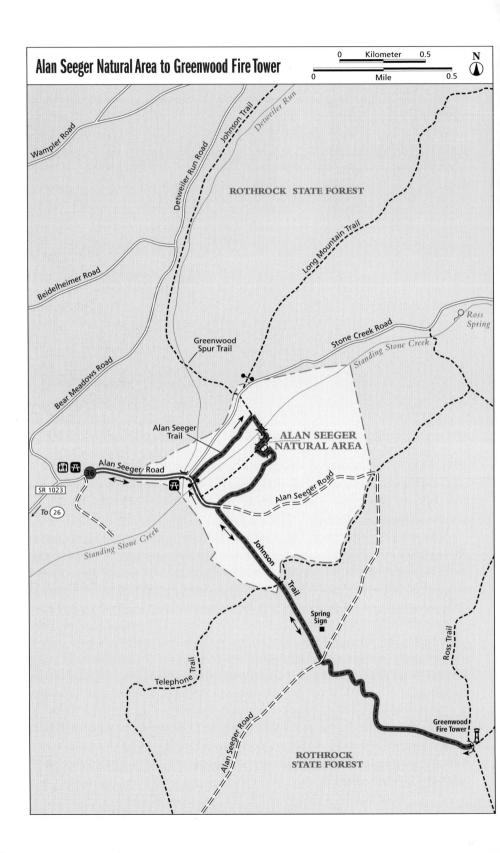

Enjoy yourself while you can. The flat area around the Greenwood Fire Tower is grassy, a natural spot for lunch and a little R&R. If you want to see why this section of Pennsylvania is known as the Ridge and Valley Province, climb the fire tower. On a clear day you can see a number of ridges separated by broad valleys. In this area, however, you may notice the pattern is irregular. Some ridges do not run parallel, and some of the valleys are deep and narrow as opposed to being wide, which is the norm.

Much of the area you are viewing from the tower lies within the 94,264-acre Rothrock State Forest, named for Dr. Joseph Rothrock, a professor at the University of Pennsylvania. As early as the late 1800s, Rothrock championed two ideas: He warned of the problems that would occur as a result of clear-cutting, and he believed in Pennsylvania's public ownership of forests. For his efforts, Rothrock was elected the first president of the Pennsylvania Forestry Association, forerunner of the Bureau of Forestry.

Miles and Directions

0.0 Start from the picnic area parking lot and turn left onto the paved road.

0.4 Cross the bridge over Detweiler Run and enter the original picnic area parking lot. Walk to the Alan Seeger Trail sign beside the trail bulletin board.

0.6 Arrive at the intersection with the Mid State Trail North. Turn left and veer right onto the Greenwood Spur South. Cross the first wooden bridge over Standing Stone Creek and enter an area of dense rhododendron.

0.7 Cross a second bridge over Standing Stone Creek and come to a sign for the giant eastern hemlock. Cross a third bridge over Standing Stone Creek.

0.8 Turn left onto a wooden truss bridge over Standing Stone Creek and enter a hemlock forest.

1.2 Cross Alan Seeger Road and arrive at the trailhead for the Mid State Trail and Greenwood Spur and the Johnson Trail. Turn left onto the Johnson Trail and follow the blue blazes.

1.7 Begin a serious uphill climb.

1.9 Cross Alan Seeger Road.

2.1 Come to a series of switchbacks.

2.9 Arrive at the Greenwood Fire Tower. Retrace your steps and cross Alan Seeger Road.

4.6 Reach Alan Seeger Road a second time. This time turn left onto the bridge over Standing Stone Creek.

4.7 Cross the bridge over Detweiler Run and retrace your steps to the parking lot.

5.1 Arrive back at the picnic area parking lot.

Local Information
Centre County Convention and Visitors Bureau, 800 E. Park Ave., State College 16803; (814) 231-1400; www.visitpennstate.org

Local Events/Attractions
Shaver's Creek Environmental Center, 3400 Discovery Rd., Petersburg; (814) 863-2000; http://shaverscreek.org

Pennsylvania Military Museum, 51 Boal Ave., Boalsburg; (814) 466-6263; http://pamilmuseum.org

Campgrounds

Greenwood Furnace State Park, 15795 Greenwood Rd., Huntingdon; (814) 667-1800; (888) 727-2757 (camping information and reservations); www.dcnr.state.pa.us/stateparks/findapark/greenwoodfurnace

Organizations

Penn State Outing Club, State College; sites.psu.edu/outingclub; e-mail: psouting club@gmail.com

Honorable Mentions

South Central Pennsylvania

Here are two great hikes in the South Central region that didn't make the A-list this time around but deserve recognition. Check them out and let us know what you think. You may decide that one or more of these hikes deserves higher status in future editions, or you may have a hike of your own that merits some attention.

K Caledonia State Park

Located in Adams and Franklin Counties, midway between Chambersburg and Gettysburg on US 30, Caledonia is the second-oldest park in the state system and one of the most popular. I'm sure Thaddeus Stevens didn't consider the beauty of his location when he built an iron furnace here in 1837, but as you'll discover even before you get into the park, the hemlock forests, historical buildings, and creeks with man-made spillways make the area picture-postcard perfect. There are more than 10 miles of trails in the park, plus a short section of the Appalachian Trail.

From Chambersburg, drive east on US 30 for 11 miles and turn left at the park sign on PA 233. For more information call Caledonia State Park at (717) 352-2161. *DeLorme: Pennsylvania Atlas & Gazetteer*: Page 91 5A

L Blue Knob State Park

Situated in the northwestern tip of Bedford County, west of I-99, this park boasts the second-highest peak in the state. Its namesake, a majestic quartzite peak called Blue Knob, is 3,146 feet above sea level, just 67 feet below the highest point in the state, Mount Davis. Blue Knob is situated on a spur of the Allegheny Front, providing spectacular views and abundant photo opportunities—plus some premiere downhill skiing in season.

From Altoona, drive south on I-99 and take the Roaring Springs exit. Follow Old Route 220 south to Route 164 west. Turn right onto PA 164 west and drive about 5 miles to the town of Blue Knob. In Blue Knob turn left onto Blue Knob Road and drive 5 miles to the park entrance. For more information call Blue Knob State Park at (814) 276-3576. *DeLorme: Pennsylvania Atlas & Gazetteer*: Page 74 B3

Southwest Pennsylvania

For sheer beauty, it would be hard to beat the Laurel Highlands of Southwest Pennsylvania. Here hikers can walk to the edge of the 1,000-foot-deep Conemaugh Gorge; or, if that's too tame, they can peer into the 1,700-foot-deep Youghiogheny River Gorge. For the backpacker in the family, there's the 70-mile-long Laurel Highlands Trail, which begins in the Youghiogheny Gorge, traverses the Laurel Ridge, and ends at the Conemaugh Gorge.

Do this or any part of the Laurel Ridge Trail when the mountain laurel is in bloom (usually from the middle of June to the end of the month) and you'll be awestruck by the spectacularly beautiful blooms. Mountain laurel didn't get to be the state flower for nothing. (See Hike 37: Conemaugh Gorge.)

If the gorges don't get your blood moving, you could join the 100,000 people who raft the Youghiogheny River every year. Or if you just want an easy hike, you can walk across the flat rocks leading over the river and get right up close to the famous Ohiopyle Falls. (See Hike 42: Ferncliff Peninsula Natural Area.)

Before leaving the subject of the Ohiopyle area, it should be said that Ohiopyle State Park may just be the nicest state park in the system. It should also be pointed out, however, that if you are towing a big camper, you'll need to call the park first to determine the best way to get to the campground. The drive out of the gorge bottom is so steep and so long, there may be some vehicles that just can't make it up.

There are two hikes in the Southwest region where you'll be able to leave the crowds behind. Mount Davis, the highest point in the state, confirms the old saw that it's lonely at the top. It's not the easiest drive, and the weather can change rapidly, but what hiker in his or her right mind would pass up a chance to reach the state's pinnacle?

Ryerson Station State Park sits all alone on the western fringes of the state, proving once again that it's location, location, location. It was precisely the remote location that prompted the government to build a fort here to protect early settlers. Now you can get away from the crowds and commune with bluebirds and the great blue heron or climb one of the steepest slopes around to an old family cemetery.

Finally, there is nowhere else in the country where you can hike one day and visit what scholars have declared "the only real piece of art created in America." If you live anywhere near the Laurel Highlands (or anywhere in Pennsylvania, for that matter) and you've never been to Fallingwater, take a hike up to Frank Lloyd Wright's masterpiece. (See Hike 40: Bear Run Nature Reserve.) Actually, there are two of his works here; Kentuck Knob is out of the gorge, not 5 minutes from the Ohiopyle Campgrounds.

37 Conemaugh Gorge

The highlights of this hike are a visit to Big Spring Reservoir and the views of Conemaugh River Gorge. Pass through a dense understory of rhododendron and mountain laurel to get to the gorge's edge, where outcroppings provide excellent places to relax and take in the deep gorge panorama.

Start: Seward Trailhead parking area off PA 56
Distance: 7.2 miles out and back
Hiking time: About 4 hours
Difficulty: Moderate, due to the steady uphill climb to the edge of the gorge
Schedule: Open year-round
Season: Best mid-June to see mountain laurel in bloom
Trail surface: Rocky footpath and dirt road
Elevation gain: 1,281 feet
Land status: State park
Nearest town: Johnstown

Fees and permits: There is a fee to use the overnight camping areas. Call Laurel Ridge State Park for more information: (724) 455-3744.
Other trail users: Backpackers
Canine compatibility: Leashed dogs permitted
Maps: USGS New Florence, PA; Vintondale, PA
Trail contacts: Laurel Ridge State Park, 1117 Jim Mountain Rd., Rockwood 15557; (724) 455-3744; www.dcnr.state.pa.us/stateparks/findapark/laurelridge/

Finding the trailhead: From Altoona, drive west on US 22. Take the PA 56 exit and drive south to Seward. Drive 1 mile past the intersection with PA 711 to an access road, on the right. Turn right onto the access road and drive 0.4 mile to the trailhead parking area where the road ends. *DeLorme: Pennsylvania Atlas & Gazetteer:* Page 73 A6. GPS: N40 24.503' / W79 00.328'

The Hike

Looking into this great gorge, it's difficult not to be awestruck by the forces that have steadily worked for millennia to create this giant gash in the earth. For all its serenity, it's equally difficult to imagine that you're looking down on the site of one of the most disastrous events in US history—the Johnstown Flood.

For residents of southwestern Pennsylvania, the summer of 1889 will forever be memorable for its unprecedented flooding and natural disasters. While the flooding was devastating on both sides of the Alleghenies, it was staggering in the Conemaugh Valley. On May 31, 1889, more than 2,200 people lost their lives when the South Fork Dam on the Conemaugh River burst, sending a 35-foot-high wall of water 14 miles downstream to the city of Johnstown. By the time it reached the unsuspecting city, it struck with enough force to carry a 48-ton locomotive more than a mile. Tens of thousands of people lost their homes, and 3 square miles of the city were destroyed.

Newspaper reports and eyewitness accounts describe a level of destruction so complete that the town seemed never to have existed. Buildings, bridges, utility infrastructure, streetcar lines, and stone sidewalks were destroyed and so thoroughly buried

Big Spring Reservoir

that residents could no longer even trace the lines of the once-busy and crowded downtown streets.

Remarkably, the city began rebuilding. With supplies sent in from all over the country, the mills that were left standing were opened, and those men who could went back to work. Clara Barton, who had founded the American Red Cross just seven years earlier, set up hospitals throughout the city. There is a flood museum in Johnstown, as well as a national monument at the sight of the dam. Surprisingly, the dam, with the exception of the center part that gave way, is still standing; visitors can walk out on it.

This hike begins at the northern terminus of the 70-mile-long Laurel Highlands Trail. (You can find the southern trailhead in the Youghiogheny River Gorge in Ohiopyle.) The trail is well maintained and popular with backpackers. It has mile markers and eight overnight camping areas (each with potable water, restrooms, tent pads, and shelters). Whether you do the entire 70 miles of the trail, or just the 7.2 miles of this hike, you soon learn that the Laurel Highlands section of the Allegheny Mountains is just what the name implies: a high plateau covered with wall-to-wall mountain laurel.

But there's more to this hike than just views from the ridge. Your first treat is the pristine Big Spring Reservoir and its emerald water. If you take this hike in mid-June, you'll be rewarded with a wonderland of mountain laurel in full bloom. Sassafras, tulip poplar, beech, oak, and maple trees provide plenty of shade, while the tenacious

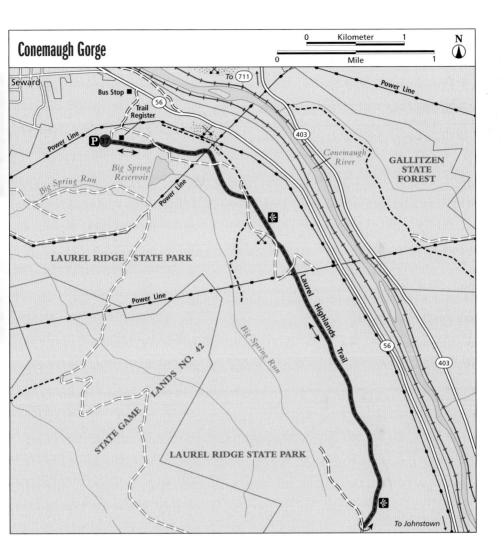

hemlocks cling to the ravines. Exposed limestone and sandstone boulders provide plenty of natural viewing areas, so sit back and enjoy.

Miles and Directions

0.0 Start at the trailhead in the parking area. Look for the yellow blazes.

0.1 Come to a concrete 70-mile marker, a trailhead bulletin board, and a sign-in register.

0.2 Pass the Big Spring Reservoir on your right.

0.6 Cross a power line swath.

0.7 Cross a dirt road. Come to milepost 69. Begin a climb.

0.9 Cross the dirt road a second time.

1.1 Reach a rock outcropping for a view of the gorge.

1.5 Cross dirt road the third time.

1.7 Come to milepost 68.

2.7 Reach milepost 67.

3.0 Come to a view of Johnstown.

3.6 Arrive at a dirt road. Turn around and retrace your steps back to the trailhead.

7.2 Arrive back at the trailhead.

Local Information

Greater Johnstown/Cambria County Convention & Business Bureau, 111 Roosevelt Blvd., Ste. A, Johnstown 15906; (814) 536-7993 or (800) 237-8590; www.visitjohns townpa.com

Local Events/Attractions

Johnstown National Flood Memorial, 733 Lake Rd., South Fork; (814) 495-4643; www.nps.gov/jofl

Johnstown Flood Museum, 304 Washington St., Johnstown; (814) 539-1889; www .jaha.org/contact.html

Campgrounds

Laurel Hill State Park, 1454 Laurel Hill Park Rd., Somerset; (814) 445-7725; (888) 727-2757 (camping and cottages information and reservations); www.dcnr.state.pa .us/stateparks/findapark/laurelhill

Restaurants

Pine Grill Restaurant, 800 North Center Ave., Somerset; (814) 445-2102; www.pine grill.com

38 Linn Run State Park

There are some strenuous climbs as the trail makes its way alongside a stream, past a waterfall, and out of the first valley. Above the falls, smaller feeder streams wash over mossy rock outcroppings, creating grotto-like falls.

Start: Grove Run Picnic Area parking lot
Distance: 4.2-mile loop
Hiking time: About 3 hours
Difficulty: Moderate, due to a strenuous climb out of the stream valley
Schedule: Open year-round
Season: Spring, summer, fall
Trail surface: Rocky footpath and washouts
Elevation gain: 919 feet
Land status: State park
Nearest town: Ligonier

Fees and permits: No fees or permits required
Other trail users: Hunters (in season)
Canine compatibility: Leashed dogs permitted
Maps: USGS Ligonier, PA
Trail contacts: Linn Run State Park, PO Box 50, Rector 15677; (724) 238-6623; www.dcnr .state.pa.us/stateparks/findapark/linnrun/ Forbes State Forest, 1291 Route 30 (PO Box 519), Laughlintown 15655; (724) 238-1200; www.dcnr.state.pa.us/forestry/state forests/forbes/

Finding the trailhead: From Pittsburgh, drive east on US 30 to Ligonier. Continue 2 miles past Ligonier and turn right on PA 381. Continue 4 miles to the village of Rector and turn left onto Linn Run Road. Drive 4 miles and enter Linn Run State Park. Turn right into the Grove Run Picnic Area. *DeLorme: Pennsylvania Atlas & Gazetteer:* Page 73 C5. GPS: N40 09.113' / W079 13.591'

The Hike

If you've never been to this area of the Laurel Highlands, you're in for a treat. Driving the last few miles on PA 381 to the tiny village of Rector makes the whole trip worthwhile—and you don't even have to get out of your car. In this remote area it's hard to know where the countryside ends and the state parks begin.

As Linn Run makes its way down the gorge from the Laurel Highlands to the Ligonier Valley, it widens substantially and takes on a more serene feel. Eastern hemlocks line both banks, creating a deep green shade. Mature maples and oaks create a canopy across the road as you drive by hundreds of acres of rustic-fenced horse property. It feels as though you're driving on a movie set that was designed to give the impression of wealth. What you're passing is Rolling Rock Farms, the private enclave of the Mellon family, owners of (among other things) the Pittsburgh-based Mellon National Bank and Rolling Rock Beer.

The founder of this dynasty was Andrew William Mellon, financier, industrialist, and statesman. Like most other magnates of the early twentieth century, Mellon made his money in the coal, oil, and iron industries. Eventually he crossed over into politics and served as secretary of the treasury under three consecutive presidents:

Linn Run is one of the most picturesque streams in Pennsylvania.

Warren Harding, Calvin Coolidge, and Herbert Hoover. In 1932 and 1933 he was the American ambassador to Britain.

Mellon is also remembered as a philanthropist. He was instrumental in the establishment of the Mellon Institute in Pittsburgh, which merged with the Carnegie Institute in 1967 to become Carnegie Mellon University. But perhaps his most important philanthropic act came about in 1937, when he decided to donate his vast art collection to the people of the United States. The result: the establishment of the National Gallery of Art in Washington, DC.

Alas, we leave all this behind when we exit the world of the rich and famous and reenter the real world of Linn Run State Park. Not far from the park entrance you'll find the Grove Run Picnic Area on your right. The highlight of this picnic area is a large stone fountain of free-flowing water from Grove Run Spring. It's ice cold and sparkling clear, and by the look of the traffic to the fountain, it may be the most popular attraction in the park. There is a steady stream of water gatherers with dozens of containers.

Fill up your water bottle and start your climb up the ravine. On your way up the gorge, there are a number of cool places to rest. You'll find cavelike pockets in the outcropping along the trail, where a steady stream of water trickles from one mossy ledge to the next. You'll find that you can hear the waterfall at Grove Run long before you can see it. Like the smaller washout falls along the trail, it's set in a deep pocket of outcropping. This causes the sound of the falls to echo off the walls, making it sound much larger than it is.

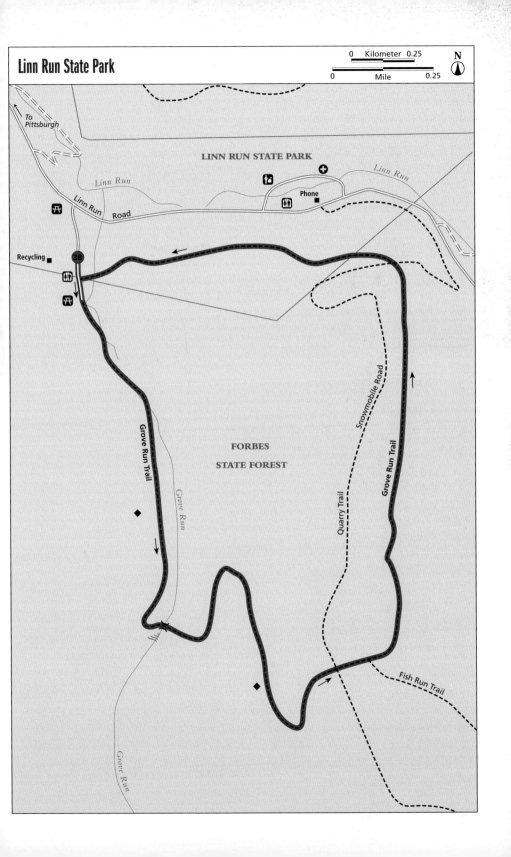

Linn Run State Park

0   Kilometer 0.25

0   Mile   0.25

N

To Pittsburgh

LINN RUN STATE PARK

Linn Run

Linn Run

Phone

Linn Run   Road

Recycling

38

FORBES

STATE FOREST

Grove Run Trail

Grove Run

Snowmobile Road

Quarry Trail

Grove Run Trail

Fish Run Trail

Grove Run

This hike is sure to provide a good workout. There is a steep, unrelenting, 2.0-mile climb out of the valley before you reach the grassy plateau where the trail levels off. From there, cut across another ridge overlooking Linn Run Valley. In sections along this ridge, wild grapevines are the predominate vegetation. There is also an abundance of catbrier, a prickly vine that you wouldn't think would be much good for anything except snagging your clothes; however, its bluish to black seeds, greenish leaves, and flowers provide food for grouse, deer, and smaller animals.

The trail skirts along a slope high above Linn Run and Linn Run Road before you dip back into the valley, ford Grove Run on the exposed rocks, and come out at the picnic area, where you can refill your water bottle.

Miles and Directions

0.0 Start at the Grove Run Picnic Area parking lot. Walk to the Grove Run Trail sign at the west end of the lot and pick up the blue blazes.

0.1 Cross two small runs that drain into Grove Run.

0.3 Grove Run is on your right.

0.4 Bear right and begin an uphill climb.

0.9 Come to a wooden bridge across Grove Run and a waterfall. Cross the stream and turn left.

1.1 Ford two tributaries of Grove Run.

1.8 Cross Quarry Trail snowmobile road. Come to a sign that reads "Fish Run Trail." Stay on the Grove Run Trail, continuing straight ahead.

3.1 Cross the Quarry Trail a second time. Come to a sign for the Grove Run Trail.

3.2 Come to a sign that says "Grove Run Picnic Area" to the left and "Linn Run Road" to the right. Go left to the picnic area.

4.0 Ford Grove Run on the exposed rocks.

4.2 Arrive at the picnic area and parking lot.

Local Information
Laurel Highlands Visitors Bureau, 120 E. Main St., Ligonier 15658; (800) 333-5661; www.laurelhighlands.org

Local Events/Attractions
Laurel Highlands Bluegrass Festival, June, Ligonier; (724) 238-4200; www.laurelhighlandsbluegrass.com

Autumnfest, October, Seven Springs Mountain Resort, 777 Waterwheel Dr., Seven Springs; (800) 452-2223; www.7springs.com

Campgrounds
Linn Run State Park, Linn Run Rd., Rector; (724) 238-6623; www.dcnr.state.pa.us/stateparks/findapark/linnrun/; rustic cabins available year-round

Laurel Hill State Park, 1454 Laurel Hill Park Rd., Somerset; (814) 445-7725; (888) 727-2757 (camping and cottages information and reservations); www.dcnr.state.pa.us/stateparks/findapark/laurelhill

39 Wolf Rocks Trail

This hike is in the heart of the Laurel Highlands region of the Allegheny Mountains. There are two highlights: the blooming mountain laurel and Wolf Rocks, an outcropping of boulders along the edge of Laurel Summit that provides an impressive view of Linn Run Valley and Chestnut Ridge. If you choose, there is also a short side trip—after the hike—to Spruce Flats Bog.

Start: Laurel Summit State Park picnic area parking lot
Distance: 4.3-mile circuit
Hiking time: About 2.5 hours
Difficulty: Moderate, due to an extremely rocky section
Schedule: Open year-round
Season: Spring, summer, fall
Trail surface: Rock- and root-covered footpath and cross-country ski trails
Elevation gain: 311 feet
Land status: State park
Nearest town: Ligonier

Fees and permits: No fees or permits required
Other trail users: Cross-country skiers, hunters (in season)
Canine compatibility: Leashed dogs permitted
Maps: USGS Bakersville, PA; Ligonier, PA
Trail contacts: Laurel Summit State Park; c/o Linn Run State Park, PO Box 50, Rector 15677; (724) 238-6623; www.dcnr.state.pa .us/stateparks/findapark/laurelsummit/ Forbes State Forest, 1291 Route 30 (PO Box 519) Laughlintown 15655; (724) 238-1200; www.dcnr.state.pa.us/forestry/state forests/forbes

Finding the trailhead: From Pittsburgh, drive east on US 30 to Ligonier. Continue 2 miles past Ligonier and turn right on PA 381. Continue 4 miles to Rector and turn left onto Linn Run Road. After 4 miles, enter Linn Run State Park. Continue on Linn Run Road for 5 miles to Laurel Summit State Park and turn left into the park and picnic area. *DeLorme: Pennsylvania Atlas & Gazetteer:* Page 73 C5. GPS: N40 07.105' / W79 10.595'

The Hike

Laurel Summit State Park lies within the 58,000-acre Forbes State Forest. Comprising a mere 15 acres, Laurel Summit State Park basically constitutes the area surrounding Wolf Rocks Trail. Nearby are three other Laurel state parks: Laurel Mountain, Laurel Hill, and Laurel Ridge. The other Laurel parks are considerably larger, and it's easy to get these parks confused. Your best bet is to get a Pennsylvania State Parks and Forests Map and highlight or circle the parks in different colors.

"Gnarly" comes to mind when describing Wolf Rocks. Plenty of trails have roots and rocks underfoot, but this trail, for the most part, has you stepping from root to rock without pause for dirt. But before long, you'll get into the rhythm of stepping from one rock to the next. In fact, once you pass through the delicate white and pink mountain laurel blossoms, it's possible to forget the trail completely.

It's a rocky trail leading to the Wolfs Rock Overlook. DEBRA YOUNG

The showstopping highlight on this hike is the Wolf Rocks overlook. These sandstone and limestone boulders were heaved to the mountaintop during one of the more recent tectonic events. Along most mountain ridges, boulders like those at Wolf Rocks remain underground; however, in rare instances they may erupt to the surface. Evidence of this eruption lies all about. The smaller rocks, which are farther inland from the edge, have ragged edges and are scattered every which way. The larger rocks that sit right on the edge are flat rocks split apart by horizontal cracks. In some places the larger rocks look as though they were crudely stacked, one on top of the other. The rocks are a great place for lunch. If you come at the right time of day, they're an absolutely fabulous spot to stretch out, listen to the wind whistle up out of the valley, and get a tan.

On your return to the picnic area, you'll pass the mysterious 28-acre Spruce Flats Bog, part of the 305-acre Spruce Flats Wildlife Management Area. When loggers arrived in the area, they found a stand of hemlock in the swampy woodland—which, incidentally, they mistook for spruce, forever mislabeling the bog. And once they had harvested the trees, the swampy woodland reverted to a bog, which scientists believe it was originally. It has remained a bog ever since. The existence of a bog is by no means mysterious; the existence of one this far south, however, is curious. Here's the problem: Nearly all bogs are formed as the result of glaciation, which occurs when a glacier melts or retreats and, in doing so, alters the underlying topography and environment. When scientists mapped the southern reach of the glaciers during the last ice age, none extended this far south—hence the confusion. Some experts suggest,

THE WHISKEY REBELLION

As you hike along the trails of the Laurel Highlands, the last thing you'd think of is a riot—you know, the kind of thing where people are angry and shots are fired and federal troops are sent out. Believe it or not, that's exactly what took place in southwestern Pennsylvania in the 1790s.

The farmers who settled this corner of the state, many of whom were of Irish and Scottish descent, were famous for their rye whiskey. Rye is a cereal grass that, once ground into flour, is used to make bread and other baked items. It's also used as livestock feed. But despite its many uses, it was not a terrific cash crop—that is, unless it was sold as alcohol. And so the majority of these grain farmers received the bulk of their incomes from the sale of whiskey.

In 1791 Federalist leader and Secretary of the Treasury Alexander Hamilton imposed an excise tax on whiskey sales. The farmers felt this tax was unwarranted and organized a resistance, which included the tarring and feathering of federal revenue officials.

It all came to a head in the spring of 1794, when arrest warrants were issued for the farmers who refused to pay the tax. In the riot that ensued, one federal official was killed, and the home of the regional excise tax inspector was burned. In August of that year, President George Washington stepped in, first by sending negotiators to the area and then, when that failed, by mobilizing the militia.

His troops marched to the area and set up camp on the hilltop where Laurel Hill State Park is today. There was no bloodshed, and the rebellion ended with Washington making a deal with the farmers. If they would grow only corn, he said, they would be given free land in Virginia (what is now Kentucky). The farmers agreed . . . and soon began making corn whiskey—better known as Kentucky bourbon.

with rather obvious logic, that the bog is simply the result of an earlier ice age; but until this is proven, the bog's presence here remains a mystery.

Regardless of its convoluted history, there are a number of interesting plants growing in Spruce Flats Bog's acidic and nutrient-poor ecosystem today. Representing the heath family of evergreen bushes is the cranberry, cousin to the ubiquitous mountain laurel and rhododendron. But don't pick the red berries and expect them to taste like the stuff you eat at Thanksgiving: Cranberries are bitter and need to be processed before humans can eat them. Wildlife, on the other hand, love the wild berries.

Two of the region's most common insect-eating plants can be found in the bog as well: the sundew and the pitcher plant. The sundew usually has an 8-inch stalk

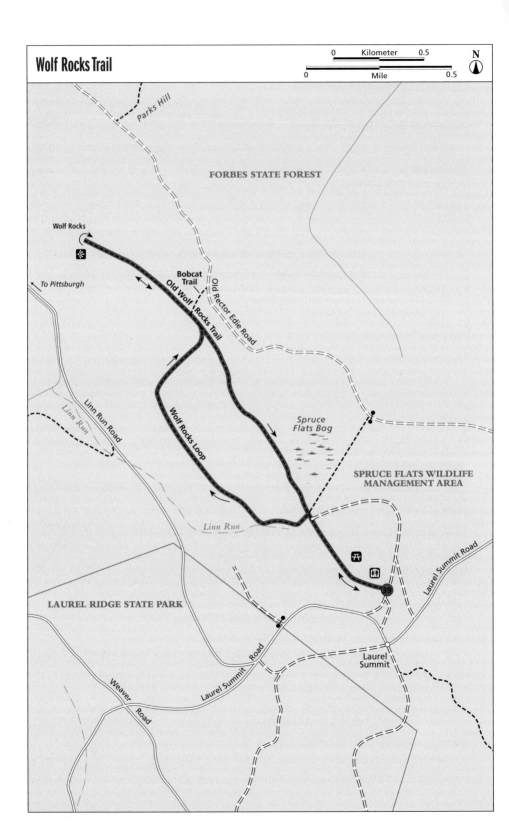

Wolf Rocks Trail

0   Kilometer   0.5

0   Mile   0.5

N

FORBES STATE FOREST

Parks Hill

Wolf Rocks

To Pittsburgh

Bobcat Trail

Old Wolf Rocks Trail

Old Rector Edie Road

Linn Run

Linn Run Road

Wolf Rocks Loop

Spruce Flats Bog

SPRUCE FLATS WILDLIFE MANAGEMENT AREA

Linn Run

39

Laurel Summit Road

LAUREL RIDGE STATE PARK

Laurel Summit Road

Laurel Summit

Weaver Road

that supports a pink rosette covered with sticky hairs. These hairs trap insects, and the plant devours them. The pitcher plant is appreciably larger. It has a 20-inch stalk with red vaselike leaves filled with water and sticky hairs. Insects, attracted to the plant's bright color, venture inside the leaves and are trapped by the plant's hairs and subsequently drowned and consumed.

The best way to visit Spruce Flats Bog is to return to the picnic area parking lot and get on the short trail that leads to it. If you visit the bog, keep your eyes open for wildlife and birds. This special management area has been set up specifically to improve wildlife habitat, and all the trails within the area are used as viewing trails. Look for small clearings where the trees have been removed. These areas were created to provide the appropriate environment for grouse and songbirds.

Foresters from the Forbes State Forest monitor the wildlife activity here and conduct mammal track counts after January and February snowstorms to see if their efforts are paying off. In addition, the Audubon Society of Western Pennsylvania conducts annual bird surveys here in late spring.

Miles and Directions

0.0 Start at the parking area of the Laurel Summit State Park picnic area. Look for the red blazes.

0.2 Cross over a pipeline swath.

0.4 Come to a culvert over a small run.

0.6 Turn left at the sign for Wolf Rock Loop.

1.2 Pass through a fern-covered open area.

1.5 Turn right at the double red blazes.

2.1 Turn left onto the Old Wolf Rocks Trail.

2.4 Arrive at the Wolf Rocks overlook. Retrace your steps.

2.7 Come to a fork, where a grassy path goes off to the left. Stay to the right on the red-blazed footpath. Come to a trail intersection and a sign that reads "Wolfs Rocks Loop Trail Turn Right." Do not turn right; continue on the Old Wolf Rocks Trail.

3.9 Arrive back at the Wolf Rocks Loop Trail intersection. Continue straight.

4.0 Cross the pipeline swath.

4.3 Arrive back at the parking area.

Local Information
Laurel Highlands Visitors Bureau, 120 E. Main St., Ligonier 15658; (800) 333-5661; www.laurelhighlands.org

Local Events/Attractions
Fort Ligonier, 200 S. Market St., Ligonier; (724) 238-9701; http://fortligonier.org

Campgrounds
Laurel Hill State Park, 1454 Laurel Hill Park Rd., Somerset; (814) 445-7725; (888) 727-2757 (camping and cottages information and reservations); www.dcnr.state.pa.us/stateparks/findapark/laurelhill

40 Bear Run Nature Reserve

There are a number of highlights on this hike. The trail begins in a pristine stand of pines, continues on gently rolling grassy roads, and finally leads to a heart-stopping view into the 1,700-foot-deep Youghiogheny River Gorge. Returning from the gorge, you pass Fallingwater, Frank Lloyd Wright's architectural masterpiece.

Start: Bear Run Nature Reserve parking lot off PA 381
Distance: 8.0-mile loop
Hiking time: About 5 hours
Difficulty: Moderate, due to a section of strenuous climbing
Schedule: Open year-round
Season: Spring, summer, fall
Trail surface: Grassy jeep roads, forest footpath, and rocky ridge path
Elevation gain: 1,038 feet

Land status: Western Pennsylvania Conservancy property
Nearest town: Ohiopyle
Fees and permits: No fees or permits required
Other trail users: Cross-country skiers, hunters (in season)
Canine compatibility: Dogs not permitted
Maps: USGS Mill Run, PA
Trail contacts: The Western Pennsylvania Conservancy, 800 Waterfront Dr., Pittsburgh 15222; (412) 288-2777; www.paconserve.org

Finding the trailhead: From Pittsburgh, drive east on I-70/76 and take exit 91 at Donegal. Drive east on PA 31 to Jones Mills. Turn right onto PA 381 and drive south to Normalville. Continue south on PA 381 to Mill Run. Drive 3.5 miles past the village of Mill Run and turn left into the Bear Run Nature Reserve. The parking lot is behind the buildings. *DeLorme: Pennsylvania Atlas & Gazetteer:* Page 86 B3. GPS: N39 54.401' / W79 27.574'

The Hike

The Bear Run Nature Reserve is a 5,000-acre natural area owned and maintained by The Western Pennsylvania Conservancy. On the east side of the reserve, you'll find gently rolling grassy terrain, the visitor center, and a bulletin board of information about the trails. Across PA 381, on the western side of the reserve, it's rugged, rocky terrain that ends at the Youghiogheny River Gorge. Here you'll also find an unusual treat for a woodland hike: The conservancy also owns and operates Frank Lloyd Wright's famous structure Fallingwater, built of local sandstone and cantilevered over a waterfall on Bear Run.

The conservancy buildings are rustic. Near the trailhead there's an old-fashioned hand pump where you can fill your water bottle and rest in the shade of the gently swaying pines. The informative bulletin board, which holds maps and brochures, can be found at the southeast corner of the parking lot.

Though the trails are well marked, it's a good idea to get one of the conservancy's trail maps. Some of the trails are blazed with the same color and shape; others have the same color blaze with either a rectangular or circular-shaped blaze to set them apart.

The Barn is the centerpiece of the Bear Run Nature Reserve.

The hikes on the east side of PA 381 are quite hiker-friendly. These are short, easy nature trails that showcase their namesakes, such as the Tulip Tree Trail, the Aspen Trail, etc. You might see a warbler on the Warbler Trail, or be moved to write a verse or two on the Poetry Trail. Dotted along the trails are group camping sites where naturalists from the conservancy have set up youth programs to study the surrounding wildlife, flora, ecosystems, and geology.

Once you cross PA 381, it's a whole different matter. You won't have time to write poetry over here. After following Laurel Run into the valley bottom, taking in the beauty of the rhododendron and hemlocks, you begin a strenuous, rocky climb to the top of Laurel Ridge and a view of the 1,700-foot-deep Youghiogheny River Gorge.

As you near the summit, the trail passes beneath the telephone lines that run along one side of the ridge and down the other. Along the ridge the trail gets close to the edge, where natural overlooks provide the best views of the gorge. Paradise Overlook is a great spot to rest and eat your lunch.

The Peninsula Trail takes you on a loop around one of the many peninsulas on the Youghiogheny River. These peninsulas were created as the river ran through the valley bottom, cutting its snakelike design into the soft sandstone that lined the river's edge. Leaving the forest, you pass through a meadow and connect with a farm road, which takes you back to PA 381 and the parking lot.

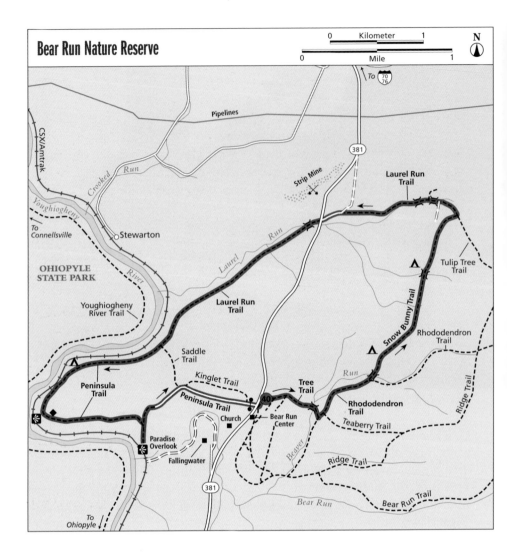

Bear Run Nature Reserve

OHIOPYLE STATE PARK

Miles and Directions

0.0 Start at the parking area behind the buildings. Walk to the north end of the parking lot to signs reading "Tree Trail" and "Skiing Area." Follow the arrows to a stand of pines. Look for yellow circle-blazes. Pass by an unmarked trail on your left. Veer right and begin an uphill climb.

0.1 Pass Pine Trail intersection on your right. Continue through the pine trees.

0.2 Come to an intersection with the Aspen Trail on your right. Look for yellow-rectangle blazes. Continue straight.

0.4 The Tree Trail ends at an intersection with the Rhododendron Trail. Turn left onto the Rhododendron Trail. Look for white-circle blazes.

0.7 Arrive at an intersection where the Rhododendron Trail turns right. Continue straight onto the Snow Bunny Trail and follow the orange-rectangle blazes.

2.1 Snow Bunny Trail ends at the intersection with the Tulip Tree and Laurel Run Trails. Turn left onto Laurel Run Trail; look for white-rectangle blazes.

2.7 Turn right at the double white blazes onto a jeep road.

2.8 Turn left at the marker for the Laurel Run Trail.

3.1 Cross PA 381 and look for the Laurel Run Trail signpost.

4.2 Trail veers left. Begin ascent through rocks. Come to a signpost; Laurel Run is to the right.

4.4 Pass a signpost for Laurel Glen on your right. Continue straight.

4.8 Arrive at an intersection with Saddle Trail. Continue straight onto the Peninsula Trail. Look for white-rectangle blazes.

5.4 Reach the ridgetop. This is the first view of the river gorge.

5.5 The trail turns left into the forest.

5.8 Arrive at the telephone line swath and turn left onto the swath. Look for a white blaze on a telephone pole.

6.1 Come to the first overlook.

6.8 Arrive at Paradise Overlook. Turn right to the overlook and then retrace your steps back to the trail.

7.1 Trail brings you to the edge of a meadow. Turn right and follow the trail to the corner of the field, keeping the meadow on your left.

7.9 Arrive at and cross PA 381.

8.0 Arrive back at the parking area.

Local Information

Laurel Highlands Visitors Bureau, 120 E. Main St., Ligonier 15658; (724) 238-5661 or (800) 333-5661; www.laurelhighlands.org

Local Events/Attractions

Frank Lloyd Wright's Fallingwater, 1491 Mill Run Rd., Mill Run; (724) 329-8501; www.fallingwater.org

Frank Lloyd Wright's Kentuck Knob, 723 Kentuck Rd., Chalk Hill; (724) 329-1901; www.kentuckknob.com

Accommodations

Ohiopyle State Park, PA 381, Ohiopyle; (724) 329-8591; (888) 727-2757 (camping information and reservations); www.dcnr.state.pa.us/stateparks/findapark/ohiopyle

Restaurants

Fallingwater Cafe (at Fallingwater), 1491 Mill Run Rd., Mill Run; (724) 329-8501, ext. 1400; www.fallingwater.org/12/fallingwater-cafe

41 Mount Davis Natural Area

Here's your chance to rise above it all, to the highest point in all of Pennsylvania, Mount Davis (3,213 feet). Because of its altitude, the area surrounding this hike is different than the typical mountain trails at lower elevations. You'll see trees charred from lightning fires, peculiar rock circles, and stunted trees. The immediate area around the "highest point" monument and tower is tourist-friendly: flat and paved. But the majority of this hike is ideal for those who want to rough it a bit and explore the unusual high-mountain ecosystem.

Start: Mount Davis Picnic Area
Distance: 3.4-mile loop
Hiking time: About 2.5 hours
Difficulty: Easy, due to a level terrain
Schedule: Open year-round
Season: Spring, summer, fall
Trail surface: Grassy road; rocky, rugged footpaths; and improved shale road
Elevation gain: 384 feet
Land status: State forest

Nearest town: Somerset
Fees and permits: No fees or permits required
Other trail users: Tourists, hunters (in season)
Canine compatibility: Leashed dogs permitted
Maps: USGS Markleton, PA
Trail contacts: Forbes State Forest, 1291 Rte. 30 (PO Box 519), Laughlintown 15655; (724) 238-1200; www.dcnr.state.pa.us/forestry/stateforests/forbes/

Finding the trailhead: From Pittsburgh, drive east on I-70/76 and take exit 110 at Somerset. Get on US 219 and drive south 22 miles to Meyersdale. In Meyersdale turn right on Broadway Street and follow the signs for Mount Davis. It is 8.5 miles from the right turn on Broadway to the Mount Davis Monument sign. Drive 0.5 mile past the sign (you will be hiking back to the monument) and turn right into the Mount Davis Picnic Area. *DeLorme: Pennsylvania Atlas & Gazetteer.* Page 87 B5. GPS: N39 47.612' / W79 10.093'

The Hike

At 3,213 feet above sea level, Mount Davis is the highest point in Pennsylvania. There are plenty of geological features unique to this lonely spot to lure the undecided hiker, but it's probably enough to say that you're going to the top of it all.

Mount Davis Natural Area lies within the 30-mile-long Negro Mountain Range of the Allegheny Plateau. The 581-acre natural area surrounds a 7-acre tract where you'll find the observation tower, monument, and tourist parking lot.

The climate on Mount Davis can be summed up in one word: awful. Annual temperatures range from –30°F to 95°F. There are plenty of high winds, more than 3 feet of both rain and snow a year, and a frost in every month. The best time to visit is in late spring or early summer. At other times of the year, the weather can be miserable with cold, rainy winds—and of course snowstorms in the winter.

A GEOLOGIC FEATURE

MT. DAVIS

MT. DAVIS 3213 FEET ABOVE SEA LEVEL IS THE HIGHEST POINT IN PENNSYLVANIA. THE EROSION-RESISTANT SANDSTONE AT THE SURFACE BELONGS TO THE POTTSVILLE GROUP FORMED ABOUT 230 MILLION YEARS AGO. THESE LAYERS OF SEDIMENTARY ROCK WERE PUSHED UP AS AN UPFOLD 200 MILLION YEARS AGO DURING THE UPHEAVAL CALLED THE APPALACHIAN REVOLUTION.

At 3,213 feet above sea level, Mt. Davis is the highest point in Pennsylvania.

This miserable climate, however, has created a number of geological and natural features worth noting. The natural area is home to the pitch pine, a stubby-looking tree with limbs that reach out like gnarled fingers. Early settlers to the region extracted the pitch from the pine, also known as pine tar, by burning pine knots and catching the residual tar. At the Tar Kiln Site, visitors can see how a tar kiln was built on top of a huge boulder and a trough was hollowed out to guide the tar to containers. The pitch was used as a lubricant for wagon axles, to mark sheep, and as a cure for distemper in horses.

On the geologic end, the continual freezing and thawing during the Pleistocene (some 70,000 years ago) caused the Pottsville sandstone of the mountaintop to break up into stone circles. There are educational plaques embedded on the rocks around the tower to explain this phenomenon, but the best way to see the extent of these circles is to view them from the 40-foot tower. And it's from atop this tower that you'll have a chance to experience another local phenomenon. From the observation tower, a number of the surrounding peaks appear to be higher than Mount Davis. Plaques on the tower platform assure that, while there are nearby peaks more than 3,000 feet high, none of the surrounding mountains are taller than Mount Davis. It's merely an optical illusion.

The area is also rich in history and folklore. Mount Davis is named for former landowner John Davis, one of the last surviving veterans of the Civil War. Davis was a land surveyor and a naturalist adept at identifying all the plants and animals in the area. It was he who surveyed the area and determined that this one particular rock was the highest point in the state.

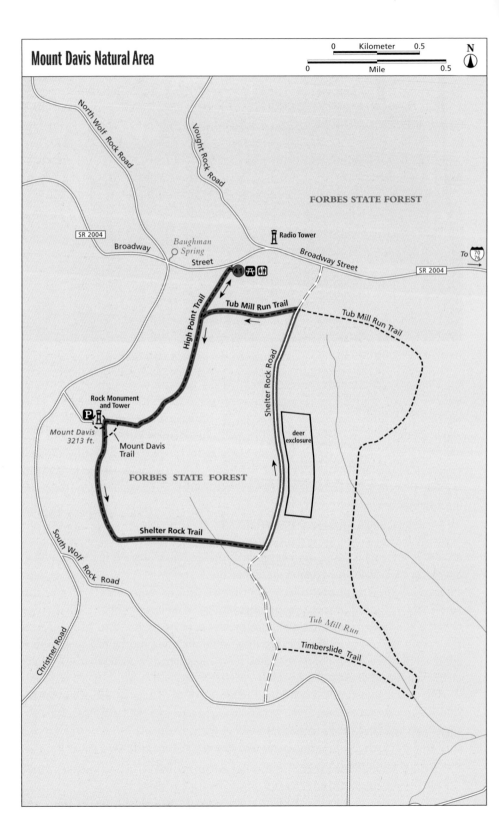

Mount Davis Natural Area

0   Kilometer   0.5

0   Mile   0.5

N

North Wolf Rock Road

Vought Rock Road

FORBES STATE FOREST

SR 2004

Broadway

Baughman Spring Street

Radio Tower

Broadway Street

To 70 76

SR 2004

41

High Point Trail

Tub Mill Run Trail

Tub Mill Run Trail

Shelter Rock Road

Rock Monument and Tower

P

Mount Davis 3213 ft.

Mount Davis Trail

deer exclosure

FORBES STATE FOREST

Shelter Rock Trail

South Wolf Rock Road

Christner Road

Tub Mill Run

Timberslide Trail

And according to folklore, even George Washington slept here. In 1753, during the French and Indian War, the twenty-one-year-old lieutenant passed through here and along Negro Mountain as part of a supply train aiding troops in Pittsburgh. (Incidentally, Negro Mountain, though at risk of being politically incorrect, was named for an African-American soldier who distinguished himself before dying in battle. He was buried on the mountain.)

Just as the name implies, the natural area has been left to nature—for the most part. As you walk the Shelter Rock Road on the return loop, you'll notice a white-tailed deer exclusion area. Just as you'd fence out rabbits from your garden, the USDA Forest Service has erected this fenced barrier to keep the pesky whitetail from devouring the newly planted trees.

Miles and Directions

0.0 Start by walking uphill in the parking lot to the northwest corner of the picnic area. Look for the trail sign. Turn left onto the High Point Trail and follow the blue blazes.

0.1 Pass the Tub Mill Run Trail on your left. Continue straight.

0.7 Pass the Mount Davis Trail on your left. Continue straight.

0.8 Arrive at the rock monument and the tower. Retrace your steps to the circular paved road. Turn right onto the paved road then turn left on the Shelter Rock Trail at the trail sign.

1.0 Pass the Mount Davis Trail on your left. Continue straight.

1.3 Begin a descent down a small ridge.

2.0 Cross Tub Mill Run.

2.1 Turn left onto Shelter Rock Road.

2.2 Pass a fenced-in deer exclusion area on your right.

2.4 The exclusion area ends. There are small boulders placed on the road at culverts; count four culverts.

2.9 Arrive at the Tub Mill Run Trail sign just before the fifth culvert on your left. (The sign is vertical and nailed to a tree set back from the road.) Turn left onto the Tub Mill Run Trail.

3.3 Come to an intersection with the High Point Trail. Turn right onto the High Point Trail.

3.4 Arrive back at the trailhead and retrace your steps to the parking lot.

Local Information
Laurel Highlands Visitors Bureau, 120 E. Main St., Ligonier 15658; (724) 238-5661 or (800) 847-4872; www.visitpa.com/regions/laurel-highlands

Local Events/Attractions
Windber Coal Heritage Center, 501 15th St., Windber; (814) 467-6680; http://echf .windberpa.org/index.php?option=com_content&view=article&id=142&Ite mid=353

Campgrounds
Laurel Hill State Park, 1454 Laurel Hill Park Rd., Somerset; (814) 445-7725; (888) 727-2757 (camping and cottages information and reservations); www.dcnr.state.pa .us/stateparks/findapark/laurelhill

42 Ferncliff Peninsula Natural Area

This easy hike loops the 100-acre Ferncliff Peninsula, giving hikers the best views of the Youghiogheny River rapids and Ohiopyle Falls. The trail leads you right to the river's edge onto flat sandstone boulders, where you can examine tree fossils embedded in the rock. At points, a canopy of rhododendron shades the trail. At marked sites along the way, learn about the peninsula's unique environment, which includes Southern wildflowers and umbrella magnolia trees.

Start: Parking area off PA 381 near the railroad tracks
Distance: 2.4-mile loop
Hiking time: About 2 hours
Difficulty: Easy, due to the level terrain
Schedule: Open year-round
Season: Spring, summer, fall
Trail surface: Typical rocky footpath and flat boulders at the river's edge
Elevation gain: 172 feet
Land status: State park

Nearest town: Ohiopyle
Fees and permits: No fees or permits required
Other trail users: Naturalists, tourists, swimmers, anglers
Canine compatibility: Leashed dogs permitted
Maps: USGS Ohiopyle, PA; Fort Necessity, PA
Trail contacts: Ohiopyle State Park, PO Box 105, Ohiopyle 15470; (724) 329-8591; www.dcnr.state.pa.us/stateparks/findapark/ohiopyle

Finding the trailhead: From Pittsburgh, drive east on I-70/76 and take exit 91 at Donegal. Drive east on PA 31 to Jones Mills. Turn right onto PA 381 and drive 21 miles south to the village of Ohiopyle. As soon as you cross the two railroad tracks of the Baltimore & Ohio Railroad, turn right into the parking lot. Drive to where boulders block a shale road. Start hiking between the boulders on the shale road. *DeLorme: Pennsylvania Atlas & Gazetteer:* Page 86 A3. GPS: N39 52.311' / W79 29.646'

The Hike

Simply stated, this hike gives you an unparalleled view of Ohiopyle Falls. You're led right to the edge of the Youghiogheny (pronounced YAWK-a-gay-nee) River and onto a series of flat boulders, which at points jut into the river. You're as close to the falls as anyone is going to get. That is reason enough to lace up your boots.

Ohiopyle Falls is truly a showstopper—it even stopped a young George Washington. The year was 1754. While scouting for a route to get his British troops and supplies to Pittsburgh to capture Fort Duquesne from the French, he traced the Youghiogheny River as a supply route. Everything was fine until he came to Ohiopyle Falls, where he had to abandon his plans and go the rest of the way over land. Unfortunately, his bad luck continued, and his troops lost the Battle of Fort Duquesne—one of the early battles of the French and Indian War. Ultimately the British would defeat the French,

A view of Ohiopyle Falls on the Youghiogheny River

in 1763, to maintain control of the American colonies. And the hard-luck officer would go on to lead those colonies to independence.

In the 1800s renowned Scottish geologist Charles Lyell visited the area. Lyell, a major force in modern geology, was the founder of stratigraphy—the study of the earth's layers. But more important to the area, Lyell was also an inspiring artist. As a result of one of his sketches of the falls, Ohiopyle became a popular summer resort area, catering to more than 10,000 visitors each summer. The Baltimore & Ohio Railroad even ran Sunday excursion trips from Pittsburgh. Wealthy visitors preferred to stay at the one luxury hotel on Ferncliff Peninsula, which had all the amenities of its day, including a tennis court, a bowling alley, and a dance hall.

Today nothing remains of that time and place on the peninsula. In fact, because of Ferncliff's unusual ecosystem, the area has been designated a National Natural Landmark by the US Department of the Interior, as well as a Natural Area by the Pennsylvania Bureau of State Parks. These natural area designations ban new construction, and the entire peninsula has been allowed to return to its natural state.

The peninsula's ecosystem is unusual because of a horseshoe bend in the river. While this may not seem overly significant, it causes the flow of the river to slow as it makes the turn. This allows the seeds that have been suspended in the water to be deposited along the shore. And because the gorge provides a natural shelter from the weather, the climate is warmer on the peninsula. For those reasons, some species of Southern wildflowers have flourished here. If you slow your pace, and know what you're looking for, you can find the Carolina tassel-rue, also called false bugbane, and the large-flowered marshallia, also known as Barbara's buttons. The Carolina tassel-rue blooms in midsummer with a white composite flower on a separate flower stem. Barbara's buttons bloom in late June or early July with a pink flower the size and shape of a dandelion, three-ribbed leaves, and a 1- to 3-foot stem.

And of course, as its name suggests, you'll find a number of fern species growing on the peninsula. Christmas, marginal wood, and spinulose grow in the forest, while royal and cinnamon ferns grow along the river. There's also an abundance of rhodo-dendron here, as well as old-growth hemlock, white pine, oak, hickory, tulip trees, and maples; there is even a traditionally Southern tree, the southern magnolia. Along the trail there are a number of interpretive plaques that not only educate but also force you to slow down and smell the forest.

Miles and Directions

0.0 Start at the parking area off PA 381, beside the railroad tracks. This parking area is also for the Great Gorge Trail and the American Youth Hostel.

0.1 Pass under the old railroad bridge, now part of the Rails-to-Trails bicycle trail. Come to the Ferncliff Trail sign. Pick up the black blazes and veer left along the river out of the forest canopy and onto the boulders.

0.2 Arrive at the fossil education plaque on a flat boulder. The trail is on the boulders.

0.4 Turn left onto the steps at the Falls Overlook sign. After viewing the falls, retrace your steps to the trail, which begins a climb up the cliff edge.

0.6 Arrive at an intersection with the Butternut Trail. You'll see the Natural Overlook sign and an information plaque. Continue straight.

0.8 Arrive at an intersection with the Oakwood Trail. Continue straight.

0.9 Come to an unmarked river trail. Turn left for a view of the rapids.

1.0 Arrive at the rapids viewing area. Retrace your steps back to the trail and turn left.

1.3 Come to an intersection with Fern Wood Trail. Veer left on the Ferncliff Trail.

1.5 The trail veers left down the gorge toward the river.

1.8 Turn left onto an unmarked side trail for a view of the river. Retrace your steps.

1.9 Arrive back at the trail. Turn left.

2.0 The trail turns away from the river. Look for black blazes.

2.2 Arrive at the Ferncliff Peninsula Natural Area National Landmark plaque and trail intersection. Continue straight. The trail veers to the left.

2.3 Come to the intersection with the Fern Wood Trail and the Oakwood Trail to the right. Continue straight through the intersection. The trail veers to the left. Turn left onto the Ferncliff Trail and retrace your steps back to the parking area.

2.4 Arrive back at the parking area.

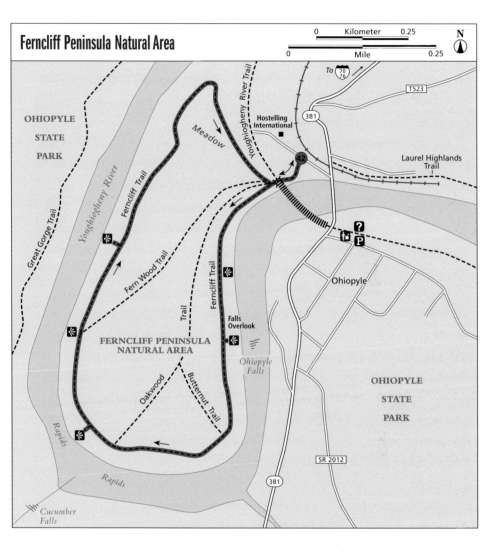

Local Information

Laurel Highlands Visitors Bureau, 120 E. Main St., Ligonier 15658; (724) 238-5661 or (800) 847-4872; www.laurelhighlands.org/outdoors/ohiopyle

Local Events/Attractions

Laurel Highlands River Tours, 4 Sherman St., Ohiopyle; (724) 329-8531 or (800) 472-3846; www.laurelhighlands.com. Whitewater rafting, rock climbing.

Accommodations

Ohiopyle Lodge, 138 Grant St., Ohiopyle; (800) 419-7599; www.ohiopylelodge.com

Campgrounds

Ohiopyle State Park, 124 Main St., Ohiopyle; (724) 329-8591; (888) 727-2757 (camping information and reservations); www.dcnr.state.pa.us/stateparks/findapark/ohiopyle

RAILS-TO-TRAILS

The mission of the Rails-to-Trails Conservancy is to "enhance America's communities and countryside by converting thousands of miles of abandoned rail corridors and connecting open spaces into a nationwide network of public trails."

By the early twentieth century, every large city and small town in the United States was connected by steel and railroad ties. In 1916 the United States had laid nearly 300,000 miles of track across the country, giving it the distinction of having the world's largest rail system. Since then, other forms of transportation, such as cars, trucks, and airplanes, have diminished the importance of the railroad, and that impressive network of rail lines has shrunk to less than 150,000 miles. Railroad companies abandon more than 2,000 miles of track each year, leaving unused rail corridors overgrown and idle.

The idea to refurbish these abandoned rail corridors into usable footpaths and trails was introduced in the mid-1960s. And in 1963 work began in Chicago and its suburbs on a 55-mile stretch of abandoned right-of-way to create the Illinois Prairie Path.

It took nearly two decades for the idea of converting old railways into footpaths to catch on. Then, in 1986, the Rails-to-Trails Conservancy was founded, its mission specifically to help communities see their dreams of having a usable rail corridor for recreation and nonmotorized travel become reality. At the time the conservancy began operations, only 100 open rail trails existed. Today there are 1,600 preserved pathways, totaling more than 20,000 miles, as well as 9,000 miles of potential rail trails.

Ultimately the conservancy's goal is to see a completely interconnected system of trails throughout the entire United States. If you're interested in learning more about rails-to-trails and wish to support the conservancy, contact them at:

Rails-to-Trails Conservancy
The Duke Ellington Building
2121 Ward Court, NW 5th Floor
Washington, DC 20037
(202) 331-9696
www.railtrails.org

43 Youghiogheny River Trail to Jonathan Run Falls

For an easy, Sunday-stroll-type hike, this one can't be beat. It starts at the refurbished train depot and traces an abandoned railroad grade. The path is, quite literally, flat the whole way. There are excellent river views en route, and at the end there's a deep forest waterfall.

Start: Visitor information center in Ohiopyle
Distance: 6.4 miles out and back
Hiking time: About 2 hours
Difficulty: Easy, due to the level trail
Schedule: Open year-round
Season: Spring, summer, fall
Trail surface: Rails-to-trails bridges, forest footpath, and a crushed limestone bicycle trail along an abandoned railroad grade
Elevation gain: 855 feet
Land status: State park

Nearest town: Ohiopyle
Fees and permits: No fees or permits required
Other trail users: Cyclists, tourists, swimmers, kayakers
Canine compatibility: Leashed dogs permitted
Maps: USGS Ohiopyle, PA; Fort Necessity, PA
Trail contacts: Ohiopyle State Park, PO Box 105, Ohiopyle 15470; (724) 329-8591; www.dcnr.state.pa.us/stateparks/findapark/ohiopyle

Finding the trailhead: From Pittsburgh, drive east on I-70/76 and take exit 91 at Donegal. Drive east on PA 31 to Jones Mills. Turn right onto PA 381 and drive 21 miles south to the city of Ohiopyle. Pass under the railroad bridge and turn right into the public parking lot. *DeLorme: Pennsylvania Atlas & Gazetteer.* Page 86 A3. GPS: N39 52.154' / W79 29.660'

The Hike

After you've spent a day or two watching bicyclists weave their way across the 600-foot-long rails-to-trails bridge, you'll want to get up there yourself. And it'll be worth it when you do. Two old railroad bridges span the river, each more than 100 feet above the water. From the first bridge you can watch swimmers wading in the wide, shallow waters to the east. But look the other way and the river narrows dramatically into the famous Ohiopyle Falls. It's here, to the west, that the river snakes around the Ferncliff Peninsula, so that when you are on the second bridge, you're just above the rafter put-in area on the peninsula. This provides a ringside seat to listen to the adrenaline screams and watch the kayakers and rafters as they are sent careening down the river.

More than 100,000 people ride the Youghiogheny River rapids every year. Half of these people opt to take a professionally guided tour; the other 50,000 brave it alone or with friends. This is not an insignificant fact: According to a random sampling conducted by American Whitewater, of the 30 years from 1976 to 2006, there were 2,000,000 river runners on the Youghiogheny River and there have been 17 deaths. These figures work out to be .85 fatalities per 100,000, which is considered a pretty good record by American Whitewater.

Rafters on the Youghiogheny River

Further research compiled in a five-year study by American Whitewater shows the risk of dying in a river is fifteen times lower than dying behind the wheel of a car. Easterners can rest easy; findings show that the Arkansas River in Colorado—with seventeen deaths in five years—is the country's most dangerous river for riding rapids.

This hike covers a short section of the Great Allegheny Passage Rails-to-Trails route that runs from McKeesport (near Pittsburgh) to Cumberland, Maryland. When the trail is completed, it will connect with the C&O Canal Towpath in Cumberland and continue to Washington, DC, for a total of 335 miles. Expect a well-groomed trail (a level, crunchy surface) with all the amenities—a restroom and drinking fountain at the start and a restroom along the route—and plenty of shade and views of the river. And you get to wander into the forest for a short distance to see the gently cascading Jonathan Run Falls.

On the return trip you don't even have to think. Just follow the bicyclists, joggers, and other walkers back to Ohiopyle. Once in this tiny and colorful village, you can reward yourself with some ice cream, available less than a block from the refurbished railroad station, which is now the visitor center.

Miles and Directions

0.0 Start at the public parking lot in downtown Ohiopyle. Cross PA 381 and walk to the visitor information center; the hike begins at the center. Walk across the first bridge.

0.1 Reach the other side of the bridge.

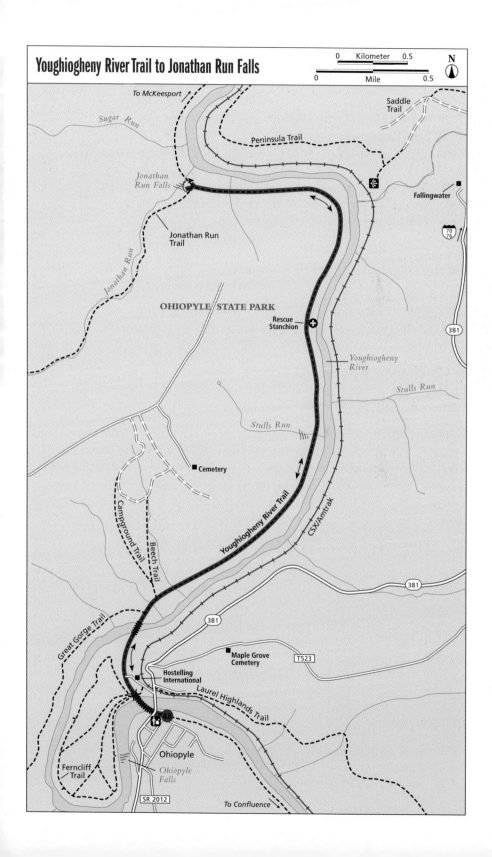

Youghiogheny River Trail to Jonathan Run Falls

0   Kilometer   0.5

0   Mile   0.5

N

To McKeesport

Saddle Trail

Sugar Run

Peninsula Trail

Jonathan Run Falls

Fallingwater

Jonathan Run Trail

Jonathan Run

70 76

OHIOPYLE STATE PARK

Rescue Stanchion

381

Youghiogheny River

Stulls Run

Stulls Run

Cemetery

Campground Trail

Beech Trail

Youghiogheny River Trail

CSX/Amtrak

381

Great Gorge Trail

381

Maple Grove Cemetery

T523

Hostelling International

Laurel Highlands Trail

Ohiopyle

Ferncliff Trail

Ohiopyle Falls

SR 2012

To Confluence

0.4 Arrive at the second bridge.

0.5 Reach the other side of the bridge. Pass the Great Gorge Trail on your left. Continue straight.

0.6 Pass a sign for the Campground Trail and the Beech Trail on your left.

2.0 Pass a rescue stanchion and bench.

3.1 Turn left onto the Jonathan Run Trail, entering the forest. (There's a sign for the Kentuck Trail.)

3.2 Turn right onto a short access path to Jonathan Run Falls. Turn around and retrace your steps to the visitor information center.

6.4 Arrive back at the visitor information center.

Local Information

Laurel Highlands Visitors Bureau, 120 E. Main St., Ligonier 15658; (724) 238-5661 or (800) 847-4872; www.laurelhighlands.org/outdoors/ohiopyle

Local Events/Attractions

Laurel Caverns Geological Park, 200 Caverns Park Rd., Farmington; (800) 515-4150; www.laurelcaverns.com

Accommodations

Cottages at Fayette Springs, 368/378 Fayette Springs Rd., Chalk Hill; (724) 437-2051; www.fayettesprings.com

Campgrounds

Ohiopyle State Park, 124 Main St., Ohiopyle; (724) 329-8591; (888) 727-2757 (camping information and reservations); www.dcnr.state.pa.us/stateparks/findapark/ohiopyle

Restaurants

The Stone House Restaurant and Country Inn, 3023 National Pike, Farmington, PA 15437; (724) 329-8876; www.stonehouseinn.com

44 Ryerson Station State Park

Ryerson is a pleasant hike in a small park. If you're looking to get away from the crowds and want to spend a day exploring nature and soaking up local history, this is the hike for you. The hike consists of a series of short climbs up extremely steep hollows. A 300-year-old wolf tree greets you on your first ascent to an overlook 400 feet above the park. Follow a mowed pathway alongside a lake inlet and into a meadow, where the vegetation is more than 6 feet high. Scan the inlet for the great blue heron, explore a bluebird box trail, and visit an old family cemetery.

Start: Third parking lot at the end of Fordway Road, near Pavilion No. 2
Distance: 5.4-mile circuit
Hiking time: About 3 hours
Difficulty: Moderate, due to climbs in and out of steep hollows
Schedule: Open year-round
Season: Spring, summer, fall
Trail surface: Smooth, well-groomed cross-country ski trails, snowmobile roads, and mowed walking paths
Elevation gain: 1,421 feet

Land status: State park
Nearest town: Waynesburg
Fees and permits: No fees or permits required
Other trail users: Cross-country skiers, snow-mobilers, anglers, birders, hunters (in season)
Canine compatibility: Leashed dogs permitted
Maps: USGS Wind Ridge, PA
Trail contacts: Ryerson Station State Park, 361 Bristoria Rd., Wind Ridge 15380; (724) 428-4254; www.dcnr.state.pa.us/stateparks/findapark/ryersonstation

Finding the trailhead: From Pittsburgh, drive south on I-79 and take exit 14 at Morrisville. Drive west on PA 21 for 22 miles to Bristoria Road and the park entrance. Turn left onto Bristoria Road and drive 0.8 mile to Fordway Road. Turn right on Fordway Road, just before the dam, and drive 0.7 mile to the large picnic area parking lot, on your left. Drive to the last row, near Pavilion No. 2. *DeLorme: Pennsylvania Atlas & Gazetteer:* Page 84 A2. GPS coordinates: N39 53.009' / W80 26.973'

The Hike

Ryerson Station State Park opened to the public in 1967, taking its name from nearby Fort Ryerson, a small refuge built in 1792 to defend then-frontier settlers against Native American raids. In this 1,100-acre park, you'll find a 10-mile network of trails available to hikers from spring through fall—cross-country skiers and snowmobilers take over the trails in winter.

One of the main attractions along this hike is the 300-year-old oak tree often referred to as the Wolf Tree. This is an expression used by foresters to describe a tree that has flourished for hundreds of years by wolfing down all the available sunlight in an area, essentially eliminating the possibility of any other tree growing near it.

The famous Wolf Tree of Ryerson Station State Park

At the top of the first ravine, you're treated to a view of the valley and 62-acre R. J. Duke Lake. (**Note:** Duke Lake was drained in 2005 but it is being reconstructed and is scheduled to be refilled and open to the public in the summer of 2017.) The North Fork of Dunkard Fork was dammed in 1960 to create the lake, and though it may be somewhat unnatural, the lake inlets are home to an immensely diverse wildlife population. Watch for ospreys during their spring migration. You're treated year-round to great blue herons, which have a rookery in a nearby grove of sycamore trees. In the open areas look for Carolina chickadees, Acadian flycatchers, and willow flycatchers. The wetlands are home to beaver, muskrat, deer, rabbit, squirrel, and skunk, as well as box and snapping turtles and the eastern spiny soft-shell turtle.

The trail takes you through thick meadow vegetation—look for Queen Anne's lace, nettles, fleabane, and spy lily. Cross the old iron bridge, which you'll cross again on your return. After a short jog to the right, you'll walk the paved road to the Pine Box Trail, which leads you up a steep ravine to Chess Cemetery. The pine box in the trail name, you now understand, refers to the coffins that, for some reason, the families felt compelled to trudge up this unmercifully steep grade to their final resting place.

It's all downhill from the cemetery as you make your way into the steep Applegate Hollow, across the hollow bottom, and on to Bristoria Road. Then it's across the iron bridge and back to the land of the living.

Miles and Directions

0.0 Start at the third and largest parking lot at the end of Fordway Road. Walk past Pavilion No. 3 to the Lazear and Fox Feather Trails.

0.1 Turn right onto the Lazear Trail.

0.3 Come to the 300-year-old oak Wolf Tree and a deer exclosure.

0.5 Arrive at the intersection with the Orchard Trail. Turn right onto the Lazear Trail.

0.8 Come to the overlook sign and walk to the overlook.

0.9 Begin your descent.

1.4 Come to an intersection with the Tiffany Ridge Trail. Continue straight on the Lazear Trail and descend into Munnell Hollow.

1.8 Pass the Tiffany Ridge Trail on your left and continue straight. Pass the Fox Feather Trail on your left and continue straight.

1.9 Turn right onto the Iron Bridge Trail. There is a trail sign that reads "To Campground."

2.3 Turn left on the Iron Bridge then turn right onto Bristoria Road and continue to the Pine Box Trail.

3.1 Turn left onto the Pine Box Trail. A sign reads "Chess Cemetery." Begin a serious uphill climb.

3.2 Come to the trail sign for Pine Box Trail and the cemetery to your right.

3.3 Come to a switchback and trail signs for the Pine Box Trail and cemetery; turn left.

3.4 Come to a signpost that reads cemetery straight ahead. Continue straight.

3.5 Arrive at the cemetery. Retrace your steps back to the Pine Box Trail.

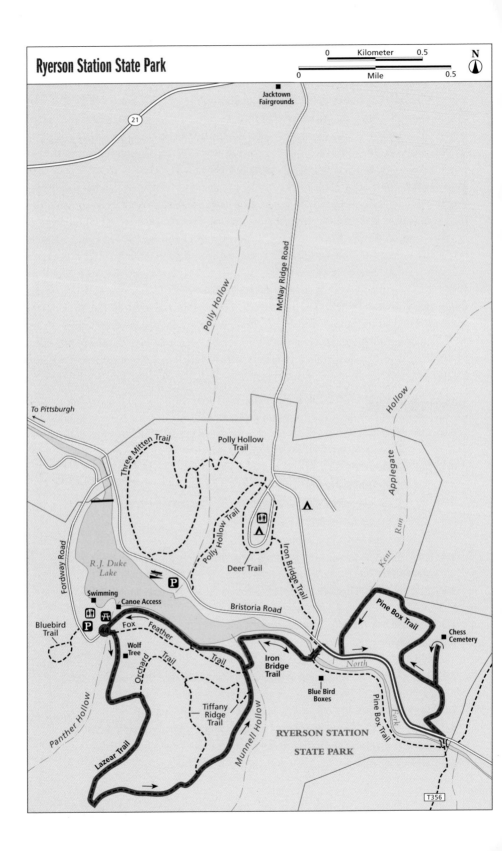

Ryerson Station State Park

0 Kilometer 0.5
0 Mile 0.5

N

Jacktown
Fairgrounds

21

McNay Ridge Road

Polly Hollow

Hollow

To Pittsburgh

Three Mitten Trail

Polly Hollow
Trail

Applegate

Polly Hollow Trail

Kent Run

Fordway Road

R.J. Duke
Lake

Deer Trail

Iron Bridge Trail

P

Pine Box Trail

Swimming

Canoe Access

Bristoria Road

Chess
Cemetery

Bluebird
Trail

P

Fox

Feather

Trail

Trail

Wolf
Tree

North

Iron
Bridge
Trail

Orchard

Trail

Blue Bird
Boxes

Tiffany
Ridge
Trail

Munnell Hollow

Pine Box Trail

Fork

Panther Hollow

RYERSON STATION

Lazear Trail

STATE PARK

T356

3.6 Turn right onto the Pine Box Trail and walk along a very steep ridge.

3.8 Begin your descent into Applegate Hollow.

4.2 Turn left at the yellow arrow sign at the hollow bottom.

4.5 Turn right at Bristoria Road.

4.6 Turn left to cross the Iron Bridge and then turn right onto the Iron Bridge Trail. Retrace your steps through the meadow and along the inlet.

5.0 Come to the intersection of the Fox Feather and Lazear Trails. Turn right onto the Lazear Trail, heading toward the lake.

5.2 Come to a trail intersection with signs for the Fox Feather Trail, the Long Loop, the Short Loop, and the Lazear Trail. Turn right toward the lake.

5.3 Pass behind the boat rental building and take the path through the picnic area.

5.4 Arrive back at the parking lot.

Local Information

Greene County Tourism Promotion Agency, Fort Jackson Building, 19 S. Washington St., Waynesburg 15370; (724) 627-8687; www.greenecountytourism.org

Local Events/Attractions

Greene County Fair, August, Waynesburg; (724) 852-5323; www.greenecountyfair .org

Greene County Historical Society Harvest Festival, October, Waynesburg; (724) 627-3204; www.greenecountyhistory.com

Campgrounds

Ryerson Station State Park, 361 Bristoria Rd., Wind Ridge; (724) 428-4254; (888) 727-2757 (camping information and reservations); www.dcnr.state.pa.us/stateparks/findapark/ryersonstation

Honorable Mentions

Southwest Pennsylvania

Here are two great hikes in the Southwest region that didn't make the A-list this time around but deserve recognition. Check them out and let us know what you think. You may decide that one or more of these hikes deserves higher status in future editions, or you may have a hike of your own that merits some attention.

M   Todd Sanctuary

Located in the southeast corner of Butler County, Todd Sanctuary has 5 miles of trails running over its 162 acres. The Audubon Society of Western Pennsylvania owns the sanctuary and welcomes public use. Started in 1942 by the late E. W. Clyde Todd, curator for the Carnegie Museum of Natural History, the sanctuary is one of the first natural areas to be preserved in the Pittsburgh area. This is an easy walk suitable for both children and seniors.

From Pittsburgh, drive north on PA 28 about 25 miles to exit 17. Drive west on PA 356 for 0.8 mile to Monroe Road. Turn right onto Monroe Road and drive 1.3 miles to Kepple Road. Turn right on Kepple Road and drive 1.9 miles to the sanctuary, on the right. For more information call the Audubon Society of Western Pennsylvania at (412) 963-6100. *DeLorme: Pennsylvania Atlas & Gazetteer.* Page 58 C1

N   The Beechwood Farms Nature Reserve

This reserve is located in Fox Chapel, 8 miles northeast of downtown Pittsburgh. There are 5 miles of interlocking trails on this 134-acre reserve. The Audubon Society of Western Pennsylvania leases the land from The Western Pennsylvania Conservancy. There are no dogs, bikes, or picnicking allowed. It's a great spot for hiking, birding, and, in season, viewing migratory birds.

From Butler, drive south on PA 8 to 3.1 miles past I-76; turn left on Harts Run Road and continue 3.5 miles to Dorseyville Road. Turn right on Dorseyville Road and drive 0.2 mile to the reserve, on your right. For more information call Beechwood Farms at (412) 963-6100. *DeLorme: Pennsylvania Atlas & Gazetteer.* Page 57 D7

Northwest Pennsylvania

Northwest Pennsylvania dips below I-80 to include Moraine and McConnells Mill State Parks. Aside from Presque Isle State Park, which is (pardon the pun) an island unto itself, the far northwestern corner of Pennsylvania is dominated by the Allegheny National Forest.

The 513,257-acre Allegheny National Forest is situated at the western end of the Allegheny Plateau. The ravines and peaks are not as deep and dramatic as those in the central and eastern parts of the state because the western end of the state was farther removed from the tectonic event that shaped the mountains we have today. The event took place along what is now the eastern seaboard; consequently, the eastern half of the state got the Bigger Bang.

Here's something to ponder: The Allegheny National Forest is, relatively speaking, lightly used, yet it's within a day's drive of one-third of the nation's population and half of Canada's. Despite the proximity, you'll find spots in the forest remarkably remote and unused. There are 201 miles of hiking trails, and if you get too tired to take another step, there are more than 500 miles of forest roads on which you can drive. There are also a number of paved state roads that traverse the park. Believe it or not, some park visitors just drive around in their cars from one area of interest to the next.

If you're too tired to hike and don't want to drive, consider renting a canoe and getting a friend to paddle you along the Allegheny River. While you've got the canoe, you could even try canoe camping along the shores of the 12,000-acre Allegheny Reservoir.

Speaking of water: More than 4 million people visit Erie's Presque Isle every year. The reason for that is very simple: It's the only place in the state where you can visit a great beach without having to fight the dreaded beach traffic. When you look at the ocean-like waves off Presque Isle, you'd swear you were at "the shore" somewhere on the Atlantic Ocean.

The hiking trails on the isle are flat, except for an occasional shifting sand dune. The level terrain makes the one multiuse trail a popular place for in-line skaters, cyclists, and joggers. In season and on weekends, this trail gets crowded; but if you're smart, you'll hike it on a weekday and do your weekend hiking on the network of trails that are more toward the isle's interior.

The land around McConnells Mill and Moraine State Parks has a little more relief than the rest of the northwestern corner—most folks are surprised when they visit McConnells Mill and see the deep gash. During the last ice age, a moraine was formed when a glacier retreated; this moraine not only stopped the natural flow of water but also actually reversed the flow—creating the unusual topography of Moraine State Park and Slippery Rock Gorge.

45 Presque Isle State Park

Walk the same rough-poured sidewalk that the old lighthouse keeper walked when he went from his home in the Presque Isle Lighthouse to his boat at the US Lighthouse Service boathouse on Misery Bay. Along the way, you'll pass a marsh with thriving vegetation and vernal ponds.

Start: Perry Monument parking lot
Distance: 5.0-mile loop
Hiking time: About 2 hours
Difficulty: Easy, due to the flat terrain
Schedule: Open daily dusk to dawn
Seasons: Best Apr to Nov
Trail surface: Rough sidewalk, beach, and sandy forest footpath
Elevation gain: 41 feet
Land status: State park

Nearest town: Erie
Fees and permits: No fees or permits required
Other trail users: Tourists
Canine compatibility: Leashed dogs permitted
Maps: USGS Erie North, PA
Trail contacts: Presque Isle State Park, 301 Peninsula Dr., Ste. 1, Erie 16505; (814) 833-7424; www.dcnr.state.pa.us/stateparks/findapark/presqueisle/index.htm

Finding the trailhead: From downtown Erie, drive west on PA 5 (which is also 12th Street) and turn right onto Peninsula Drive (also PA 832). Pass the main gate and drive 5.4 miles to the Perry Monument parking area on East Fisher Drive. *DeLorme: Pennsylvania Atlas & Gazetteer:* Page 27 C5. GPS: N42 09.321' / W80 05.474'

The Hike

There's a reason more than 4 million people visit Presque Isle every year. The phrase "something for everybody" has been bandied around, and though it's worn thin from overuse, nothing could be truer. There really is something for everyone, whether you're an outdoor lover, a history buff, a natural history student, a birder, or, of course, a hiker.

Thirteen miles of roads transport visitors from one end of this 3,200-acre park to the other. A 13.5-mile multipurpose trail runs along the bay, loops the far peninsula, and returns on the lakeside to its beginning point. You can hike the trail, but it is predominantly a bicyclist and in-line skater path.

Our hike, which combines the Sidewalk and Dead Pond Trails, gives you the opportunity to visit both the Presque Isle Lighthouse and the Perry Monument—the two centerpieces of the park. The 57-foot redbrick Presque Isle Lighthouse, situated on the shores of Lake Erie, was built in 1872 and is today a private residence—visitors, however, can use a nearby beachside path to access a photo site. Visit the educational gazebo at the lighthouse parking area for more information on this and other area lighthouses.

The Perry Monument, built in 1926, commemorates Commodore Matthew C. Perry and his men for their bravery during the War of 1812. Perry commanded the US fleet that defeated British forces in the Battle of Lake Erie in 1813. His report

The Presque Isle Lighthouse, first lit in July 1873

of the battle to General Harrison has become famous: "We have met the enemy and they are ours." Locals have another connection to Perry: Six of his eleven vessels were built in Erie with timber from Presque Isle.

After visiting the monument and the lighthouse, make your way onto the Dead Pond Trail for a decidedly different hiking experience. Though the Dead Pond Trail is only a little more than 2.0 miles long, it manages to span a number of distinct ecological zones. The terrain will go from sandy to grassy to a typical forest path, and then it's sandy again. In the forested areas are red and silver maples, pin oaks, and pine plantations, as well as stands of poplar and sassafras. Everywhere else you'll find chokecherry and serviceberry lining the path. There's also an assortment of honey-suckle along the trail, plus elderberry, hobblebush, viburnum, and arrowwood. But by far the most abundant (and least desirable) vegetation is the phragmite known as the common reed. It's still not known how this peevish plant, native to Europe and the Orient, made it into the United States, but as with most invasive species, the reed has thrived and taken over much of the landscape—or would if allowed to do so. On Presque Isle it's a full-time project trying to eradicate the plant. Park workers are routinely dispatched to cut the invader, which can reach heights of more than 12 feet, back away from the roadways and paths.

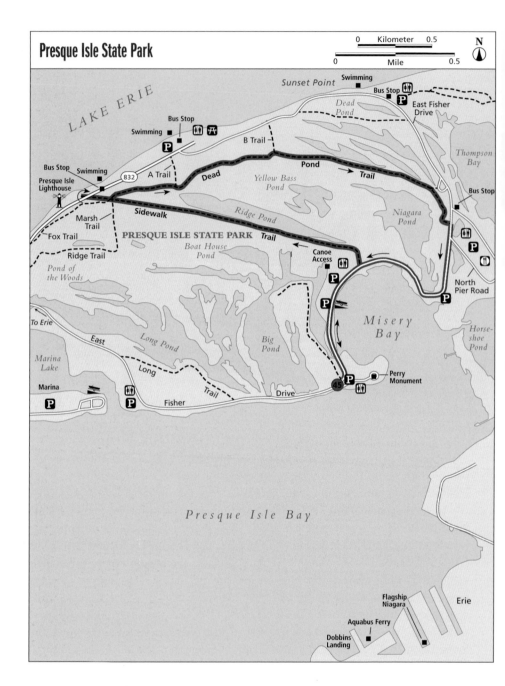

Presque Isle State Park

Before summarily dismissing this plant as an out-and-out pest, it should be said that the reed enjoys a better reputation in the Orient, where it has traditionally been used for thatch to build roofs. Today it's often used as a packing material. Try to keep this in mind when you're surrounded by this plague. The best place along this hike to see how this reed has taken over is while you're walking beside East Fisher Drive, from the Dead Pond Trail trailhead to the Perry Monument parking lot.

Presque Isle State Park is a hiker's utopia. You can experience all that the Erie area has to offer: excellent restaurants, a planetarium, and museums. And yet, in a matter of minutes, you can leave all this behind and enter another world of sand dunes, exotic flora, American history, and, best of all, solitude.

Miles and Directions

0.0 Start from the Perry Monument parking area. Walk out the main entrance, cross East Fisher Drive, and turn right. Cross the auto bridge over Misery Bay.

0.5 Turn left onto the Sidewalk Trail.

1.6 Arrive at an intersection with the Marsh, Fox, and Dead Pond Trails. Continue straight.

1.7 Cross Peninsula Drive and walk to the educational gazebo. Walk to the sign that reads "Beach View" and a photo opportunity; turn right toward the beach.

1.8 Turn left at a white stanchion with green arrow. View the lighthouse. Retrace your steps back to the educational gazebo.

2.0 Cross Peninsula Drive to the Sidewalk Trail bulletin board. Continue straight on the Sidewalk Trail and retrace your steps.

2.1 Turn left onto the Dead Pond Trail.

2.4 Pass intersection with the A Trail on your left.

2.9 Pass intersection with the B Trail on your left.

3.5 Veer right at the trail fork.

3.7 Arrive at East Fisher Drive. Turn right and walk on the right shoulder.

4.5 Pass Sidewalk Trailhead on your right.

5.0 Turn left into the Perry Monument parking lot.

Local Information
Visit Erie, 208 E. Bayfront Pkwy., Ste. 103, Erie 16507; (800) 524-3743; www.visit eriepa.com

Local Events/Attractions
Tom Ridge Environmental Center at Presque Isle, 301 Peninsula Dr., Ste. 1, Erie 16505; (814) 833-7424; http://trecpi.org
Flagship Niagara, Erie Maritime Museum, 150 E. Front St., Erie; (814) 452-2744; www.flagshipniagara.org

Campgrounds
Sara's Campground (Presque Isle), 50 Peninsula Dr., Erie; (814) 833-4560

Restaurants
Pufferbelly Restaurant, 414 French St., Erie; (814) 454-1557; http://thepufferbelly.com

Organizations
Erie Outing Club, PO Box 1163, Erie 16512; (814) 456-9775; www.erieoutingclub.org

46 Hemlock Run

There are two highlights to this hike that make it a must-do: the view of the sparkling green waters of Chappel Bay and the crystal-clear water of Chappel Fork feeding into that bay. This hike is mostly downhill, but it's not easy. The multiple stream crossings and the effort it takes to pick your way across the rocks make this a challenging—but rewarding—hike.

Start: North Country Trail parking area off PA 59
Distance: 6.8-mile shuttle
Hiking time: About 4 hours
Difficulty: Moderate, with short, difficult climbs
Season: Year-round
Trail surface: Abandoned logging roads, railroad grade, and forest trails
Elevation gain: 331 feet
Land status: National forest
Nearest town: Warren
Fees and permits: No fees or permits required

Other trail users: North Country Trail thru-hikers, backpackers, campers
Canine compatibility: Leashed dogs permitted
Maps: USGS Cornplanter Bridge, PA; Westline, PA
Trail contacts: Bradford Ranger District, 29 Forest Service Dr. (PO Box 88), Bradford 16701; (814) 363-6000
Allegheny National Forest, 4 Farm Colony Dr., Warren 16365; (814) 728-6100; www.fs .fed.us/r9/forests/allegheny

Finding the trailhead: To shuttle point: From Dubois, drive north on US 219 through Ridgway. Continue north to the intersection with PA 59. Turn left onto PA 59 and drive 8.1 miles to the intersection with PA 321. Turn left onto PA 321 and drive 4.5 miles south to the North Country Trail sign and the parking area, on your right. GPS: N41 48.687' / W078 52.297'
To start: Leave one vehicle at the parking area on PA 321. Drive north on PA 321 to the intersection of PA 59. Turn left and drive 2.3 miles to the North Country Trail sign and FS 265 on your left. Turn left on FS 265 and drive 300 feet to the parking area and trailhead. *DeLorme: Pennsylvania Atlas & Gazetteer:* Page 31 B7. GPS: N41 51.431' / W078 51.594'

The Hike

The North Country National Scenic Trail is one of the more ambitious trail-construction projects currently under way in our park system. When completed, the trail will stretch 4,400 miles through seven northern states—from the Adirondack Mountains in New York all the way to the vast plains of west-central North Dakota. Hemlock Run Trail is your opportunity to hike a part of this extensive trail system—and an immensely popular one among folks who should know. Parts of the 96-mile section of the North Country Trail in the Allegheny National Forest were built by the Allegheny Outdoor Club, headquartered 20 miles to the west in Warren. One member of this hiking club likes this trail so much that if he can't find a partner to do a car shuttle with him, he drops his bicycle off at the first parking area, does the hike, and then bikes the 6.8 miles back to his vehicle.

Starting out on Hemlock Run

One thing you learn when you hike this part of the state is that early settlers came here to harvest the timber. This region boasted giant white pines and hemlocks. The white pines were used to build houses and ships. The hemlocks were also valuable, but not for their wood, which, incredibly, was left discarded in the forest. Instead, the hemlock bark was harvested and made into tannin, the substance used to tan leather.

Though the giant white pines and hemlocks are no longer pervasive, hikers can still find one of the most valuable stands of hardwood in the world in the Allegheny National Forest. The most prized of these trees is the black cherry, which is used throughout the world to produce fine furniture and veneer. You'll also find yellow poplar, white ash, red maple, and sugar maple mixed in. Today, white ash is used to produce Louisville Slugger baseball bats.

Logging companies built networks of roads to get around in the forest and narrow-gauge railroads to haul the logs out to nearby sawmills or to a river, where the logs were floated downstream to cities like Pittsburgh. When the logging companies pulled out, their roads and railroads remained. In 1859, when the first commercial oil well in the world was drilled in nearby Titusville and the forests of northwestern Pennsylvania became a virtual oil field, oil companies used these same roads. Today, both the oil and logging industries continue to operate in the forest on a limited scale, but what most hikers encounter are the rusted remains of these once-flourishing industries. Just 0.5 mile into this trail, you can see for yourself the ruins of an oil field power station.

The hike in this section is little more than a leisurely stroll through a forest of tall hemlock trees. At intervals, you may emerge from the deep shade of the hemlocks and enter grassy meadows with odd-looking humps of earth. These are old oil well sites. The humps are piles of dirt that resulted as the area was cleared of trees and flora. Also in the meadows, look for the scarlet berries of the teaberry bush, a low-growing evergreen plant also known as wintergreen. Oil from these berries is used to make the popular wintergreen flavoring.

On your way down into the valley floor, look for beaver dams in Hemlock Run and its tributaries. Also on your way down, you pass through an area of hundreds of sandstone and conglomerate boulders, ranging in size from a Volkswagen to that of a small house. Look for "House Rock," a midsize boulder that because of its sloped top and straight sides is said to resemble a house.

At about the 4.0-mile mark, you pick up an abandoned railroad bed that was used to haul logs down this ravine to the Kinzua Mill. The mill, as well as the towns of Kinzua and Corydon, is long gone—submerged forever under the waters of the 27-mile-long, 12,000-acre Allegheny Reservoir, which was created when the US Army Corps of Engineers built the Kinzua Dam across the Allegheny River in 1968.

A little farther on, the trail parallels a pipeline path. Before you leave the pipeline, look for a bright blue patch of low-growing bluets. These low-lying plants, also known as Quaker-ladies, have four pale blue or violet flower petals with a yellow eye in the center. Shortly after this, you'll cross a power line swath and make your way to the edge of a giant open area that reflects the works of beavers on Chappel Fork. Head over to the wooden footbridge and take a seat. If you are quiet and very patient on this bridge, you may get to photograph a beaver at work. Good luck.

Miles and Directions

0.0 Start from the North Country Trail sign. Two flat boulders flank the trail. Look for blue blazes.

0.2 Turn right at the blue blaze with directional arrow.

0.4 Turn right onto the original trail. Look for the blue blazes.

0.6 Continue straight as another road cuts off to the left.

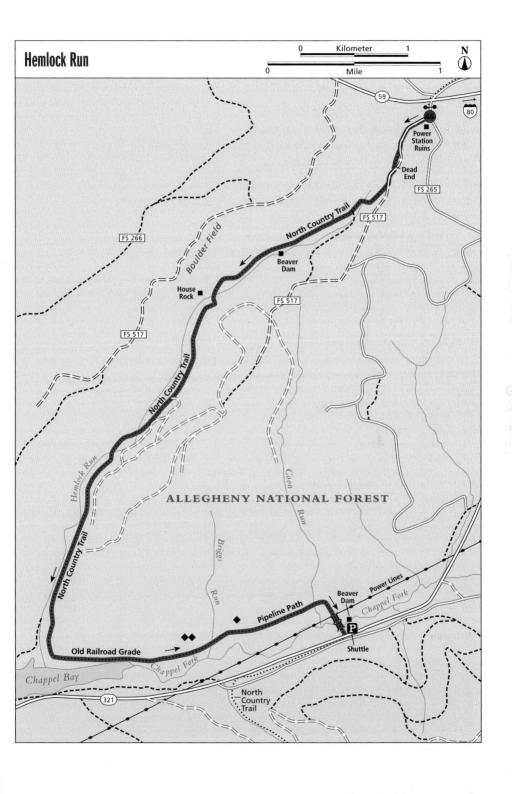

Hemlock Run

Power Station Ruins

Dead End

FS 265

North Country Trail

FS 517

FS 266

Boulder Field

Beaver Dam

House Rock

FS 517

FS 517

North Country Trail

Hemlock Run

Coon Run

ALLEGHENY NATIONAL FOREST

Briggs Run

North Country Trail

Power Lines

Beaver Dam

Chappel Fork

P

Pipeline Path

Shuttle

Old Railroad Grade

Chappel Fork

Chappel Bay

321

North Country Trail

0   Kilometer   1

0   Mile   1

N

1.3   Turn left onto FR 517. Walk on the road 100 feet and turn right at Hemlock Run (stream) and the trail sign.

2.1   Veer left into the ravine and cross the stream. (This is the first of many crossings; look for blue blazes on the other side of the stream.)

3.5   Pick up an abandoned railroad grade.

4.6   Turn left. You can see the waters of Chappel Bay.

4.8   The road veers off to the left. Continue straight; look for blue blazes.

5.2   Pick up the railroad grade through the bog.

5.7   Cross Briggs Run. Turn left and begin an uphill climb.

5.8   Turn right onto a pipeline swath. Continue through a stand of saplings onto an old road.

6.7   Come to a power line swath, beaver dams, and a footbridge over Coon Run then another footbridge over Chappel Fork.

6.8   Arrive at the parking area and your shuttle vehicle.

Local Information

Warren County Visitor Bureau, 22045 Route 6, Warren 16365; (800) 624-7802; www.wcvb.net

Local Events/Attractions

Kinzua Dam & Allegheny Reservoir, 1205 Kinzua Rd., Warren; (814) 726-0661; www .lrp.usace.army.mil/Missions/Recreation/Lakes/KinzuaDamAlleghenyReservoir .aspx

Kinzua Bridge State Park, Keating; (814) 966-2646; www.dcnr.state.pa.us/stateparks/ findapark/kinzuabridge/index.htm

Campgrounds

Kiasutha Camping Area, Allegheny National Forest, Warren; (814) 723-5150; www.fs .fed.us/r9/forests/allegheny

Organizations

Allegheny Outdoor Club, Warren; www.alleghenyoutdoorclub.org

47 Tom's Run

This easy hike leads you through a 120-acre parcel of old-growth forest—giant hemlocks and white pines—to an old railroad logging grade that parallels the white-capped waters of Tom's Run. The west branch of Tionesta Creek snakes its way down the slope and joins Tom's Run at the point where you begin your final ascent. Along the way you'll see sandstone boulders the size of small houses perched above. Let the rushing waters of the streams and the hemlock-scented breeze carry you away from the cares of the outside world.

Start: Picnic area at Hearts Content Recreation Area
Distance: 4.0-mile loop
Hiking time: 1.5 to 2 hours
Difficulty: Easy, with a short moderate climb over the ridge and an easy ascent in the last 1.5 miles
Schedule: Open year-round
Season: Spring, summer, fall
Trail surface: Footpath and an abandoned railroad grade groomed for cross-country skiing in winter

Elevation gain: 465 feet
Land status: National forest
Nearest town: Warren
Fees and permits: No fees or permits required
Other trail users: Anglers, cross-country skiers
Canine compatibility: Leashed dogs permitted
Maps: USGS Cherry Grove, PA; Cobham, PA
Trail contacts: Allegheny National Forest, 4 Farm Colony Dr., Warren 16365; (814) 728-6100; www.fs.fed.us/r9/forests/allegheny

Finding the trailhead: From Pittsburgh, drive north on I-79 to I-80. Drive east on I-80 and take exit 29 at Barkeyville. Drive north on PA 8 to Franklin. Take US 62 north to Tidioute. Turn right on Old PA 337 and drive 10.1 miles. Make a hard right onto Hearts Content–Sheffield Road and drive 3.7 miles to the trailhead. *DeLorme: Pennsylvania Atlas & Gazetteer:* Page 31 C4. GPS: N41 41.519' / W79 15.522'

The Hike

Hearts Content Recreation Area is a hiker's mecca. Aside from having great hikes like Tom's Run, the area is less than 0.5 mile from the trailhead for the popular Hickory Creek Wilderness Trail and affords connections with the more epic Tanbark and North Country Trails. The recreation area also offers a 1.0-mile interpretive trail as well.

You'll share parking with hikers using other trails, but don't worry; there's ample room. The Hickory Creek Trail leads hikers on an 11-mile loop through the 8,663 acres of old-growth forest in the Hickory Creek Wilderness Area. The estimated time for this hike is seven hours, but many hikers prefer to strap on a backpack and turn their hike into a one- or two-day overnight excursion.

Because of the popularity of the wilderness area, the picnic area at Hearts Content is one of the most comfortable trailheads in the state. There is a seasonal water fountain

Where the trails meet at Tom's Run

and a modern year-round restroom facility. The large bulletin board displays a detailed map, brochures, and all the necessary information about the trails and the adjacent area. There is also a Braille pad for the sight-impaired. The picnic area also has a pavilion and, of course, plenty of picnic tables. Check out the pavilion for an informative display on logging in the forest. It explains how early loggers in the area squared off white pine timbers by hand into giant sections that were hauled out on the logging railroad.

Hearts Content Campground is located less than 0.5 mile away. There are twenty-two campsites with picnic tables, electricity, and fire rings. There are also toilets and water. Some of the sites have camping pads and others have lean-to shelters. The campground operates on an honor system, so make sure you don't forget to pay the daily fee.

The Tom's Run hike departs from the picnic area and begins on a gently sloping trail. At about 0.25 mile, you cross the first of many small footbridges. At 0.5 mile you connect with the Tanbark Trail and begin a moderate climb across a ridge. Notice the abundance of ferns. They grow unmolested while deer feast on the young saplings, for the simple reason that deer don't like fern. To protect new seedlings from the deer, the forest service has fenced in hundreds of seedlings and shrubbery.

The trail leads you past hemlock, white pine, and beech trees that are 300 to 400 years old. Take a good look at the beech trees, though. Many of them have a disease called beech bark scale, which produces tiny white spots on their bark. It is predicted that within twenty years there will be no more living beech trees in this area.

Not long after reconnecting with the Tom's Run Trail, you'll come to your first meadow. Here the remains of the logging railroad begin. The corrugated-looking trail is where the railroad tracks used to be. When the tracks were pulled up, the railroad ties (no more than roughly hewn logs) were left in place. As the logs decomposed, they left behind a corrugated landscape. Keep an eye out; most have rotted away, but remnants of some logs remain.

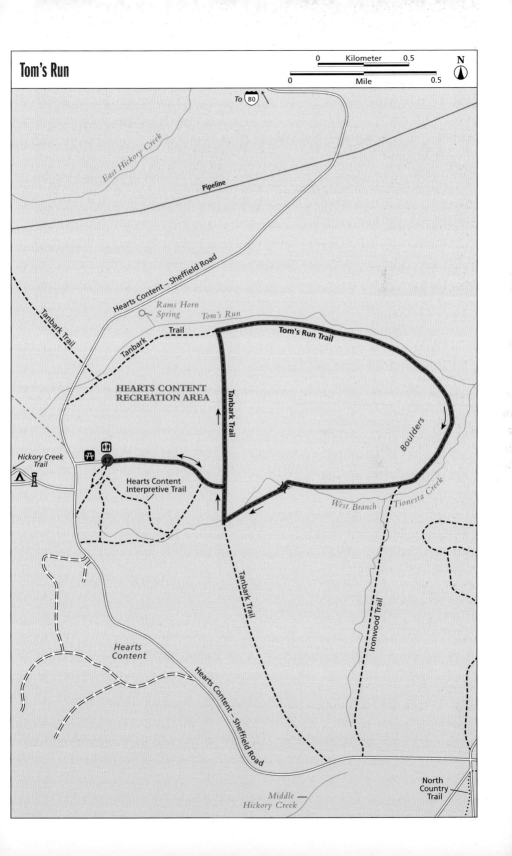

Tom's Run

0   Kilometer   0.5

0   Mile   0.5

N

To 80

East Hickory Creek

Pipeline

Hearts Content – Sheffield Road

Tanbark Trail

Rams Horn Spring

Tom's Run

Tanbark Trail

Tom's Run Trail

HEARTS CONTENT RECREATION AREA

Tanbark Trail

Boulders

Hickory Creek Trail

47

Hearts Content Interpretive Trail

West Branch Tionesta Creek

Tanbark Trail

Ironwood Trail

Hearts Content

Hearts Content – Sheffield Road

North Country Trail

Middle Hickory Creek

As you approach the stream, you'll hear the sound of the rushing waters of Tom's Run as it surges against, around, and under moss-covered boulders. These boulders look as if they might have slid down the ridge slope to rest precariously along the stream. On your right, up the slope, huge sandstone boulders are scattered about as if some giant of the forest had laid out his own rock garden. Here, overhanging hemlock branches form dark tunnels over the trail. At one point you'll pass through a patch of mountain laurel and cross perhaps a dozen small footbridges spanning the washes that empty into Tom's Run.

You come to a fork in the trail as Tom's Run Trail heads up the slope and the Ironwood Trail starts. You leave Tom's Run behind as the trail aligns itself with the west branch of Tionesta Creek. Shortly you come to the only handrail bridge, and shortly after that you retrace your steps back to the trailhead.

Miles and Directions

0.0 Start by walking to the sign that reads "Hearts Content Cross Country Ski Trails" at the east side of the parking lot. Walk 50 feet beyond that sign to the sign that reads "Tom's Run Skiing Trail." Look for blue blazes.

0.5 Turn left onto the white-blazed Tanbark Trail.

1.1 Turn right onto Tom's Run Trail.

2.2 Pass the Ironwood Trail on your left.

3.1 Cross the handrail footbridge.

3.4 Turn right at the sign that reads "Tom's Run Trail."

3.5 Come to the original point where Tom's Run Trail meets Tanbark Trail. Turn left.

4.0 Arrive back at the trailhead.

Local Information
Warren County Vacation Bureau, 22045 Route 6, Warren 16365; (800) 624-7802; www.wcvb.net

Local Events/Attractions
Warren County Fair, August, 371 Barton Run, Pittsfield; (814) 563-9386; www .warrencountyfair.net

Campgrounds
Hearts Content Campground, c/o Allegheny National Forest, Warren; (814) 723-5150; www.fs.fed.us/r9/forests/allegheny

Restaurants
Ribs & Bones, 6452 Jackson Run Rd., Warren; (814) 723-8205

Organizations
Allegheny Outdoor Club, Warren; www.alleghenyoutdoorclub.org

48 Minister Creek

Minister Creek Trail is one of the most popular trails in the Allegheny National Forest. After a 0.5-mile climb from the parking lot to the trailhead, you begin the rock-and-root-covered trail by heading into the valley for your first encounter with the crystal-clear waters of Minister Creek. As you ascend from the valley, you are in the midst of mammoth sandstone boulders, some 100 feet wide and 50 feet high. At one point the trail passes right through a fissure in one of these giants.

Start: Trailhead 0.5 mile from the Minister Creek Campground parking lot on PA 666

Distance: 8.0-mile loop

Hiking time: Experienced hikers, about 3 hours; beginners, about 4 hours

Difficulty: Moderate to strenuous, rugged uphill climbing

Schedule: Open year-round

Season: Spring, summer, fall

Trail surface: Well-maintained footpaths; opportunity to climb among huge boulders

Elevation gain: 1,362 feet

Land status: National forest

Nearest town: Sheffield

Fees and permits: No fees or permits required

Other trail users: Campers, anglers, thru-hikers, backpackers

Canine compatibility: Leashed dogs permitted

Maps: USGS Mayburg, PA; Cherry Grove, PA NW Hike # 50 Forest County

Trail contacts: Allegheny National Forest, 4 Farm Colony Dr., Warren 16365; (814) 728-6100; www.fs.fed.us/r9/forests/allegheny

Finding the trailhead: From I-80, take the Dubois exit 97 and drive north on US 219 to Ridgway. Take PA 948 north out of Ridgway and drive to the intersection of PA 948 and PA 666. Turn left on PA 666 and drive 14.7 miles to the Minister Creek Campground parking area, on your left. *DeLorme: Pennsylvania Atlas & Gazetteer:* Page 31 C5. GPS: N41 37.230' / W79 09.212'

The Hike

The centerpiece of this hike is, of course, Minister Creek—a crystal-clear, three-forked trout stream that converges here and meanders along the valley floor. Along the stream are gently swaying wheatgrass and fern and sturdy hemlocks that provide both shade and a deep sense of serenity.

Of course for every hiker who says the stream is the best part of this hike, there's another who'll tell you it's the Minister Valley Overlook. The overlook—the flat top of a giant boulder 0.8 mile from the trailhead—is considered the reward hikers get for climbing out of the deep valley. If you sit awhile on the overlook, and if you're lucky, you may see bald eagles floating on the thermal uplifts that rise out of the valley.

But the beauty of this hike really begins as soon as you get on PA 666, a gently winding road that runs alongside Tionesta Creek. While this stream is often too shallow to canoe, it's a favorite among anglers. The annual Pennsylvania State Championship Fishing Tournament is held on this stream in nearby Tidioute, the last full

Springtime on Minister Creek

weekend in September. This catch-and-release tournament has categories for all ages, from the Junior Derby (for ages 3 to 10) to a $100 prize for the oldest angler to catch a fish. There are also prizes for the largest muskellunge, northern pike, walleye, smallmouth bass, and trout.

Testimony to the abundant fishing and hunting in this area, both sides of PA 666 are dotted with rustic fishing and hunting cabins. There are villages and year-round houses here and there, but the traveler gets the distinct sense of leaving the modern world behind and entering a true forest sanctuary. Even the tiny Minister Creek Campground feels rustic; there are no fancy motor homes here. With just one road in and only six family campsites, this place is for serious campers who like to get away from it all, even if they have to rough it. In the campground, just past the second campsite, there is a hand-pumped water supply. Campers use pit toilets. There are no toilet facilities for hikers.

If the established campground isn't your thing, there are flat footpaths that lead to a series of excellent camping sites along Minister Creek. These are ideal during the summer months. Maple, black cherry, beech, basswood, and hemlock trees provide shade so that, aside from the slight dappling sunlight that sprinkles your path, you're

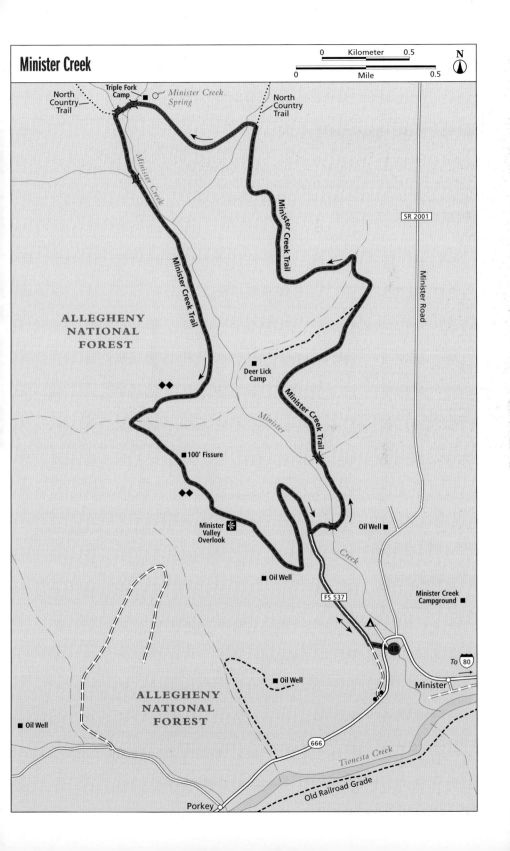

Minister Creek

0   Kilometer   0.5

0   Mile   0.5

N

North Country Trail

Triple Fork Camp

Minister Creek Spring

North Country Trail

SR 2001

Minister Creek

Minister Creek Trail

Minister Creek Trail

ALLEGHENY NATIONAL FOREST

Minister Road

Deer Lick Camp

Minister

100' Fissure

Minister Creek Trail

Minister Valley Overlook

Oil Well

Creek

Oil Well

FS 537

Minister Creek Campground

To 80

666

Oil Well

Minister

ALLEGHENY NATIONAL FOREST

Oil Well

Tionesta Creek

Old Railroad Grade

Porkey

protected from the sun from one end of the trail to the other. Also, there is an almost constant breeze to cool you off, which is nice on those hot summer days when the dense growth takes on a junglelike mugginess.

Out on the trail, one of the first things you're bound to notice is the way in which the trees, ferns, and moss grow on the sandstone boulders. Look around; despite the variety of species, almost all the trees on the boulders are the same height. A closer examination of the system reveals why. Lichen and moss form on the boulder first, creating a pocket in which to catch rain and other detritus essential for tree growth. But there are limited nutrients and resources here on the sandstone surface. With only so much food to go around, young trees cannot reach their full potential. The trees grow only to a certain height, and there they stop. Don't be fooled; despite their size, these trees can be quite old. This phenomenon, called suppression, is the reason the broad top of a boulder seems to support a garden of trees all the same height.

The species of trees that survive on these boulders are the more adaptable species, such as beech, hemlock, and maples. More particular species, like black walnut, ash, and some oaks, would not survive on the boulders because they could not compete with their less-fussy neighbors.

As you make your final ascent past the silent monolithic boulders, you may get the feeling you've stumbled back in time to another era. Or you may feel you have stumbled forward, into the middle of the next Indiana Jones movie. Either way, enjoy the solitude.

Believe it or not, the best is yet to come. Even after your hike is finished, there is one more treat to look forward to. Jump in your car and continue on PA 666 about 17 miles to US 62. Turn left at the intersection and go less than 1 mile to George's Little Store, which has everything from fishing tackle to cold cuts to ice cream served in their giant, homemade waffle cones (sometimes still warm from the oven). From this point, with your waffle cone in hand, you can either retrace the route you came in on or, as many sightseers do, opt for a leisurely drive on US 62, enjoying the many vistas along the Allegheny River.

Miles and Directions

0.0 Start from the parking area and walk across PA 666 to the trail sign.

0.1 Bear right at FS 537 and take the Middle Loop Trail. White-diamond blazes mark the trail.

0.5 Arrive at the trailhead. Turn right on North Loop Trail and descend to the valley floor.

0.9 Cross Minister Creek on a small footbridge.

1.6 Pass the sign for Deer Lick Camp.

2.6 Meet North Country Trail for the first time and turn left. The trails combine for 0.4 mile.

2.9 Reach Minister Creek Spring.

3.0 Come to Triple Fork Camp and cross two forks of Minister Creek. The North Country Trail (blue blazes) takes off to the right. Continue to follow the Minister Creek Trail (look for the white blazes).

3.3 Cross a third bridge over Minister Creek. Follow the white blazes.

4.8 Begin your ascent through giant boulders.

5.0 Reach the top of the ridge.

5.4 Follow the trail to Minister Valley Overlook.

6.7 Reach Minister Valley Overlook.

7.5 Reach the trailhead. Retrace the way you came in.

8.0 Arrive back at the parking lot.

Local Information

Warren County Vacation Bureau, 22045 Route 6, Warren 16365; (800) 624-7802; www.wcvb.net

Local Events/Attractions

Pennsylvania State Championship Fishing Tournament, last full weekend in September, Tidioute; (814) 484-3585; e-mail: pascft1959@verizon.net

Campgrounds

Minister Creek Campground, c/o Allegheny National Forest, Warren; (814) 723-5150; www.fs.fed.us/r9/forests/allegheny

Restaurants

George's Little Store, US 62, East Hickory; (814) 463-7660

Organizations

Allegheny Outdoor Club, Warren; www.alleghenyoutdoorclub.org

49 Logan Falls

This hike leads to one of the most dramatic waterfalls in northwestern Pennsylvania. You first walk on an abandoned rail bed that runs alongside Tionesta Creek, one of the nicest streams in the state. You then walk up a ravine alongside Logan Run until you come to the waterfalls. Be sure to take your camera.

Start: Pole barriers at the abandoned rail bed in Mayburg
Distance: 6.0 miles out and back
Hiking time: About 4 hours
Difficulty: Moderate, due to a moderate climb
Schedule: Open year-round
Season: Spring, summer, fall
Trail surface: Abandoned rail bed, stream crossings, forest footpath
Elevation gain: 300 feet
Land status: National forest
Nearest town: Tionesta
Fees and permits: No fees or permits required

Other trail users: Equestrians
Canine compatibility: Leashed dogs permitted
Maps: USGS Mayburg, PA
Trail contacts: *Note:* The Logan Falls Trail is a user-developed trail, not an official Allegheny National Forest trail. You can contact the ANF for general questions: Allegheny National Forest, Warren; (814) 723-5150; www.fs.fed.us/ r9/forests/allegheny. For specific questions regarding the Logan Falls Trail, contact the Allegheny Outdoor Club at their website: www .alleghenyoutdoorclub.org.

Finding the trailhead: From Pittsburgh, drive north on I-79 and take I-80 east to exit 29 at Barkeyville. In Barkeyville, take PA 8 north to Franklin. In Franklin, take US 62 north approximately 50 miles to East Hickory. In East Hickory, turn right on PA 666, drive east approximately 13 miles; turn right on the Mayburg Bridge and cross Tionesta Creek. Turn left on the other side and keep left through the hamlet of Mayburg. Drive about 0.5 mile to the abandoned railroad bed. *DeLorme: Pennsylvania Atlas & Gazetteer.* Page 31 D 5. GPS: N41 35.552' / W79 11.995'

The Hike

Forest County, aptly named for its abundant forests, encompasses the southwestern corner of the 513,000-acre Allegheny National Forest. It is home to 4,800 people and plenty of trees—but there are no malls, fast-food restaurants, movie theaters, or even one stoplight. What Forest County has is some of the most remote and least populated areas in the state. In fact, Forest County has the highest percentage of vacation homes to year-round homes in the United States. What that means is that people from the bustling metropolises of Pittsburgh, Cleveland, Buffalo, and other major cities within a 3-hour drive come to their cabins in Forest County to get away from it all. A number of professional athletes come here to fish or hunt and catch up on their serenity.

To get to this hike, you must come in off US 62 from Tionesta or from PA 6 in Sheffield; either way, be sure to gas up and get your food and supplies before you get

Water, water everywhere at Logan Falls

on PA 666; there are few—if any—year-round services out here. Once you leave the main highway, you are on what one tourist writer calls the "tree tour."

In the booming days of logging the area that was to become the Allegheny National Forest, many of the competing loggers built their own narrow-gauge railroads to get their logs to mill. Our hike begins on one of these abandoned rail beds—the Sheffield to Tionesta Railroad—that carried logs and passengers from Sheffield to Tionesta. This short rail line ran from 1879 to 1942. It was also used to facilitate the Mayburg chemical plant, which, like seventy other wood chemical plants in Pennsylvania, used wood by-products to produce chemicals. As you drive through Mayburg, you can see the abandoned chemical plant.

On this hike you walk 1.7 miles along Tionesta Creek until you intersect Logan Run as it empties into the Tionesta. There is a campsite at this junction. In fact, some kayak and canoe people put in at Sheffield and float downstream to this site. They tie up their crafts, do the hike from there to the falls, then return to the campsite and shove off or spend the night.

At Logan Run turn right and begin a moderate climb along the ravine. Cross Logan Run once, following the red blazes. Be sure to bring your camera. When I do this hike, I bring a good lunch and my camera and plan to spend some time taking

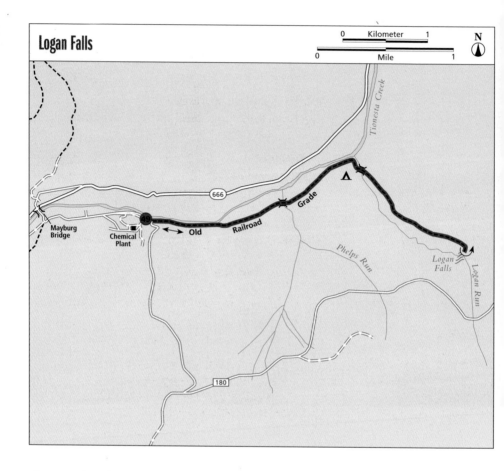

Logan Falls

0   Kilometer   1

0   Mile   1

N

photos and exploring the falls and Logan Run above the falls. After your visit, simply retrace your steps back to your vehicle.

Miles and Directions

0.0   Start at the pole barriers at the abandoned rail bed and walk upstream alongside Tionesta Creek. Follow the red blazes.

0.2   Cross a washout.

1.0   Cross Phelps Run.

1.7   Arrive at Logan Run. The trail turns right.

1.8   Cross Logan Run.

3.0   Arrive at Logan Falls. Follow the red blazes to get closer to the waterfalls. Retrace your steps.

6.0   Arrive back at your vehicle.

Local Information

Pennsylvania Great Outdoors Visitors Bureau, 2801 Maplevale Rd., Brookville 15825; (814) 849-5197; www.visitpago.com

Local Events/Attractions

Pennsylvania State Championship Fishing Tournament, last full weekend in September, Tidioute; (814) 484-3585; e-mail: pascft1959@verizon.net

Campgrounds

Tionesta Recreation Area Campground, Tionesta; (877) 444-6777; www.recreation .gov/camping/tionesta-rec-area-campground/r/campgroundDetails.do?contract Code=NRSO&parkId=73313

Restaurants

George's Little Store, US 62, East Hickory, (814) 463-7660

50 Cook Forest State Park

This hike takes you into the Clarion River Valley and alongside the dark waters of the Clarion River. This descent is followed by a climb out of the gorge to River Valley and a heart-stopping view from an 80-foot fire tower. There is also a natural overlook for the faint of heart. As you loop back to where you began, you'll pass through the Forest Cathedral, a virgin stand of white pine and hemlock that loggers—for some reason—left behind. Be sure and look for the plaque that proclaims the area a National Natural Landmark.

Start: Log Cabin Inn Visitor Center off Vowinkle Road

Distance: 6.6-mile loop

Hiking time: About 4 hours

Difficulty: Moderate to strenuous

Schedule: Open year-round

Season: Spring, summer, fall

Trail surface: Abandoned logging roads, rocky footpaths, and cliff edges

Elevation gain: 1,528 feet

Land status: State park

Nearest town: Clarion

Fees and permits: No fees or permits required

Other trail users: Equestrians, campers, anglers, cross-country skiers

Canine compatibility: Leashed dogs permitted

Maps: USGS Cooksburg, PA

Trail contacts: Cook Forest State Park, 113 River Rd., Cooksburg; (814) 744-8407 or (800) 634-2495; www.cookforest.com

Finding the trailhead: From Brookville, drive north 13 miles on PA 36 to Cooksburg. At the fork in Cooksburg, go right on Vowinkle Road. Drive north 1 mile to the Log Cabin Inn Visitor Center parking area. *DeLorme: Pennsylvania Atlas & Gazetteer:* Page 44 B5. GPS: N41 20.784' / W79 13.098'

The Hike

Cook Forest State Park is a year-round family camping park with endless attractions. You'll find horseback riding stables alongside bumper car parks, a swimming pool, a theater, and a craft center, as well as 226 campsites and 23 cabins. And of course there's fishing, canoeing, and tubing on the Clarion River. In winter there's even sledding, cross-country skiing, and a lighted ice-skating pond.

But don't let all these attractions fool you. Cook Forest has some serious hiking trails. Each year more than 150,000 hikers make their way through the seventeen trails that comprise the park's 30 miles of hiking trails. Moreover, the North Country National Scenic Trail passes through Cook Forest via the Baker Trail. The hike featured here, the Cook Forest Trail, was designed to give a sampling of all the best features the park has to offer. Just follow the orange blazes.

When John Cook came to this area in 1826, he found a true forest cathedral. In old photos you can see giant hemlocks and white pines with 6- or even 8-foot or more diameters. Cook purchased 765 acres and set up a sawmill along Tom's Run. His

It's lonely at the top of this retired fire tower.

descendants continued the operation until the 1920s, when the Cook Forest Association was formed to save the last stand of virgin white pine and hemlock. When the association failed to raise enough money to buy the land, the State of Pennsylvania stepped in and bought 6,055 acres, which has since become Cook Forest State Park.

While the trees are indeed impressive, and a major attribute to the park, there is another major attraction: the highest highlight of this hike, the fire tower. If you make it to the top landing of this 80-foot tower, you'll be 1,600 feet above sea level.

On your way to the tower, you pass through old-growth forest that looks exactly as it did when the first Europeans settled in this area. There's a real primeval feel to this forest. The trail winds between giant hemlocks and moss-covered boulders along the dark, damp forest floor. Then there's the Clarion River, supposedly named by an early settler who thought the ripples of the river sounded like a clarion—a kind of trumpet with a loud, shrill call. After you've sat for a spell with your ear to the river, it's time to move on. From the river it's a healthy climb out of the gorge to the top—a plateau with large, flat boulders forming its edge. It's here, on these boulders, that Fire Tower No. 9 awaits you.

Widest at the base and narrower as it goes up, the tower resembles heavy, fenced-in scaffolding. A powerful, almost constant wind makes you thankful for the handrails.

When workers tried to dig holes to install the tower legs, they encountered solid rock. Rather than abandoning the project, they drilled 4-foot-deep holes into the rock and anchored the tower that way. It certainly worked. The tower was built in 1929, retired from fire protection service in 1966, and has been climbed by thousands of tourists and hikers since.

Once on the top platform of the tower, you have an unobstructed view of the surrounding mountains and valleys. The tower was built high enough so watchers could see over the treetops. If there were a forest fire, you would certainly see it from this perch; of course these days, the forest service uses small airplanes to check for forest fires.

After the tower the fun continues. As you make your way back toward the river, you'll have to walk for a short distance on a cliff edge about 50 feet above the river. Where the trail is most precarious, there are safety rails, wooden steps, and platforms. Just the same, if you drop anything, don't expect to ever see it again.

In terms of sheer grandeur, the end of this hike is far and away the most dramatic. There's an opportunity to cross Tom's Run on a cable bridge, which will put you at the base of the Forest Cathedral. In this section, some of the white pine and hemlock trees are more than 300 years old and more than 180 feet high. In fact, the tallest tree in Pennsylvania is here: The Longfellow Pine stands at 180 feet and 11 inches. Just think, with only four of these trees, you could build a six-room house.

In 1969 Cook Forest was designated a National Natural Landmark. The trail in this section leads you past this plaque and also past a commemorative memorial fountain dedicated to the volunteers who worked to establish Cook Forest. End your hike with a visit to the rustic Log Cabin Inn Visitor Center, where you can learn all about the early logging industry in this part of the state.

Miles and Directions

0.0 Start from the parking area at the Log Cabin Inn Visitor Center. Turn left on the paved road and cross the stream on the traffic bridge. Walk to the sign that reads "Shelter 1." Turn right and cross the road to the Ridge Trail sign. Look for orange blazes and begin an uphill climb.

0.7 Reach the summit. The trail levels off.

0.9 Arrive at the Ridge Camp Campground. Turn left onto a paved road. Immediately after passing the gate, turn left.

1.0 Arrive at PA 36. Cross the road and veer right to the exit sign. Enter the one-way exit road. Come to the gate and turn right, heading back toward PA 36.

1.1 Turn left onto the Mohawk Trail.

1.2 The trail passes through a pair of giant hemlocks.

1.8 Come to a trail junction. Turn right on Tower Road.

2.2 Turn right on the River Trail and begin your descent.

2.8 Turn left on the River Trail.

3.0 Cross a meadow. The trail starts uphill, away from the river.

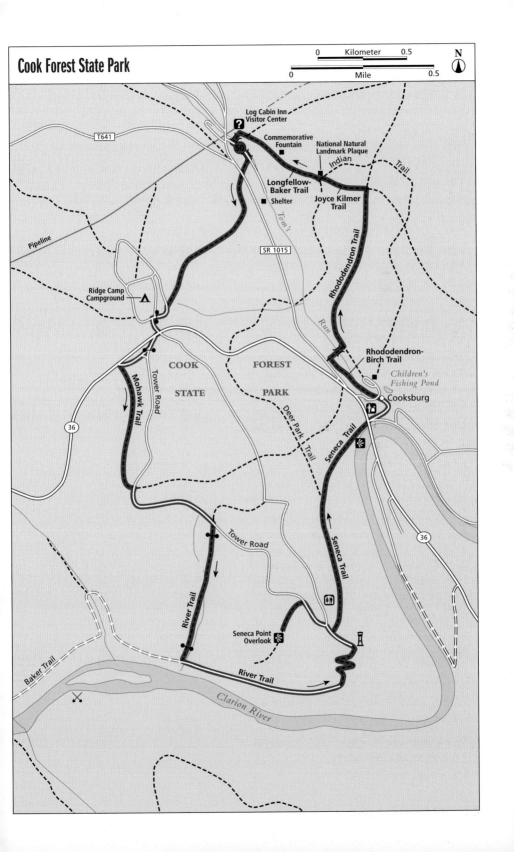

Cook Forest State Park

0	Kilometer	0.5
0	Mile	0.5

N

Log Cabin Inn
Visitor Center

Commemorative
Fountain

National Natural
Landmark Plaque

Indian

Trail

**Longfellow-
Baker Trail**

**Joyce Kilmer
Trail**

Shelter

T641

Tom's

SR 1015

Pipeline

Rhododendron Trail

Run

**Rhododendron-
Birch Trail**

*Children's
Fishing Pond*

Cooksburg

Ridge Camp
Campground

COOK   FOREST

STATE   PARK

Tower Road

Mohawk Trail

36

Deer Park Trail

Seneca Trail

Seneca Trail

Tower Road

River Trail

36

River Trail

Baker Trail

Seneca Point
Overlook

Clarion River

3.2 Encounter two switchbacks.

3.4 Turn left at the sign that reads "Baker Trail and River Trail." Head into the rock outcropping. Come to the flat boulders and the fire tower. Climb the fire tower (if you like). Afterwards, turn right onto the exit road, walk a short distance, and turn left to the Seneca Point Overlook sign.

3.5 Reach the Seneca Point Overlook. Retrace your steps back to the junction of Seneca and Baker Trails. Take the Seneca Trail downhill into the forest.

3.7 Log cabin restrooms are on your left.

4.2 Come to a sign that reads "Deer Park Trail and Baker Trail." Stay on Seneca Trail; follow the orange blazes.

4.5 Arrive at a cliff overlooking Clarion River; the trail parallels the river.

4.8 Cross PA 36. The park office will be on your left.

4.9 Turn left onto the paved road beside the park office.

5.0 The children's fishing pond will be on your right. Take the paved road uphill toward PA 36.

5.1 Turn right onto the Rhododendron-Birch Trail.

5.3 Turn right onto a cable bridge and cross Tom's Run. Turn right into the forest.

5.5 Turn left onto the Rhododendron Trail and enter the Forest Cathedral area.

6.1 Turn left onto the Joyce Kilmer Trail.

6.3 Turn left on the Indian Trail. Note the National Natural Landmark plaque. Turn right onto the Longfellow-Baker Trail then left on the Longfellow-Baker Trail.

6.5 The trail becomes the Longfellow Trail.

6.6 Arrive back at the Log Cabin Inn Visitor Center.

Local Information

Pennsylvania Great Outdoors Visitors Bureau, 2801 Maplevale Rd., Brookville 15825; (814) 849-5197; www.visitpago.com

Local Events/Attractions

Cook Forest State Park half-marathon, March; www.cookforest.com

Accommodations

Gateway Lodge Country Inn Resort & Spa, PA 36, Cooksburg; (814) 744-8017; http://gatewaylodge.com; e-mail: info@gatewaylodge.com

Campgrounds

Cook Forest State Park, campgrounds, cabins; (888) 727-2757 (camping information and reservations); www.cookforest.com

Restaurants

Gateway Lodge Country Inn Restaurant, PA 36, Cooksburg; (814) 744-8017; http://gatewaylodge.com/dining/; e-mail: info@gatewaylodge.com

Organizations

Allegheny Outdoor Club, Warren; www.alleghenyoutdoorclub.org

51 Oil Creek State Park

This hike makes a loop around the Drake Well Museum and oil field, site of the first commercial oil well in the world. It begins with a strenuous uphill climb for a view of the majestic Oil Creek Gorge, followed by a descent into the valley wetlands, where it passes over the tracks of an excursion railroad. The trail then crosses Oil Creek on a cable bridge—also called a swinging bridge because of the way it sways in the breeze. Along the trail you can stop and inspect oilfield ruins and the relics that remain frozen in time.

Start: Jersey Bridge parking area at the northern end of Oil Creek State Park
Distance: 5.9-mile loop
Hiking time: 2.5 to 3 hours
Difficulty: Moderate, due to steep climbs
Schedule: Open year-round
Season: Spring, summer, fall
Trail surface: Dirt roads, rocky forest footpath, grassy meadow, and wetlands boardwalk
Elevation gain: 1,042 feet

Land status: State park
Nearest town: Titusville
Fees and permits: No fees or permits required
Other trail users: Hikers only
Canine compatibility: Leashed dogs permitted
Maps USGS Titusville South, PA
Trail contacts: Oil Creek State Park, 305 State Park Rd., Oil City 16301; (814) 676-5915; www.dcnr.state.pa.us/stateparks/findapark/oilcreek/index.htm

Finding the trailhead: From Youngstown, Ohio, drive east on I-80 to exit 29 at Barkeyville. Drive north on PA 8 through Franklin and Oil City; continue on PA 8 to Titusville. Look for the Drake Well Museum sign on your right. Turn right at the stoplight on Bloss Street and drive 1 mile to the parking area at Jersey Bridge. *DeLorme: Pennsylvania Atlas & Gazetteer.* Page 31 C1. GPS: N41 36.935' / W79 39.501'

The Hike

There are more than 73 miles of hiking and interpretive trails in Oil Creek State Park, the most impressive of which, the Gerard Hiking Trail, is a 36-mile loop that encompasses the entire park. Because this may be a bit ambitious for the average day hiker, there are a number of shorter connecting hikes that allow visitors to map out their own routes. This hike is one of those routes.

As soon as you hit the parking lot, you realize there is so much to do and see in this 7,000-acre park that the tough part is not the climb out of the gorge but choosing an activity for after your hike. This hike, which is set in the northern end of the park, gives you an opportunity to go canoeing, try a little trout fishing, visit the Drake Well Museum, cross the expansive Oil Creek on a cable bridge, explore the world's first oil field, or take a 26-mile round-trip ride on the Oil Creek & Titusville Railroad.

The Swinging Bridge across Oil Creek

The park stretches 13 miles on both sides of Oil Creek, through Oil Creek Gorge. A paved 8.5-foot-wide bicycle path runs from the Jersey Bridge parking area in the north end of the park to Petroleum Centre in the southern end—a distance of 9.5 miles. To get to your hike, you'll have to walk a short stretch of this path—one of the nicest bike paths in the state. The bike trail is built on an old railroad grade that parallels the creek and passes through a broadleaf forest whose canopy provides deep shade from early morning until the sun goes down. The bicycle path is a well-maintained and popular trail. On any given day you're likely to encounter serious runners, mothers pushing jogging strollers, road cyclists, or casual retirees just ambling along.

Once you begin this hike, however, you leave all this behind. It's a serious climb out of the gorge to the top. When you reach the top, glance down at the Drake Well Museum grounds below. You'll notice an original oil pump still pumping away. The well is located more or less at the midpoint of this trail, so the rhythmic clank-clank-clank will keep you company for a good bit of the hike, swelling and fading as you approach and then pass it. While it may be an annoyance to your tranquility, the steady clamoring of an oil rig has always signaled prosperity to folks in this area.

The trail across the ridge top is rocky. After a while you get used to the fact that just about all the ridgetops in the state are rocky. (When these mountains were formed, the earth was folded upward and pushed the rocks out of the top.) Your descent is easier, but no picnic. It consists of a series of knee-jolting switchbacks down an old oilfield road.

Back on level ground, cross the small footbridge to the Oil Creek & Titusville Railroad tracks. Unlike most of the sights in the park, the railroad is still very much operational. There is no fencing and no sign to warn you about the train, which clips right along, so be careful. (*Note:* If you happen to be at this spot when the train comes by, you can see that it's critical to stay a good distance away from the tracks.) Cross the train tracks and enter the creek-side wetlands. Here you can see wild violets, red trilliums, spring beauties, and bedstraw, as well as the ever-present skunk cabbage—which got its name because it smells like decaying meat. While unpleasant to us, its odor is important to the wetland ecosystem because it attracts pollinating insects.

Although there is nothing left to see of it, the trail takes you through Boughton, one of the many settlements that sprung up during the oil boom years. Residents of Boughton worked across Oil Creek at the Boughton Acid Works, now the Boughton Ruins. Cross the tracks and make your way to the cable bridge. Although this isn't the same bridge, it's in the same spot where a cable bridge was built so workers who lived in Boughton could cross the creek to their jobs at the acid works. Across this bridge, shortly after crossing the bicycle trail, you'll find the ruins. Here workers used sulfuric acid to refine oil from the wells. The trail passes a flat, open area that looks like it was the scene of a fire. Sulfuric acid from the old refineries leached into the soil, leaving the area barren. Nothing has grown here since.

From your vantage point on the bridge, take in the view of the clear waters of the wide creek. Oil Creek is the largest trout stream in Pennsylvania. Your chances of seeing a bass or brook trout are pretty good. During the second climb out of the gorge, keep an eye out for a grouping of boulders. You'll notice that some of the oak trees in this area are just plain huge—a few more than 3 feet in diameter. A magnificently manicured park, complete with picnic tables, awaits outside the Drake Well Museum and grounds. Here you'll also find a fully restored, working oilfield. The grounds and museum are fenced off, however, and there is an admission fee. But rest assured, the

WILDCATTING

Back in the 1860s, soon after Col. Edwin Drake drilled the world's first successful oil well, would-be oil barons descended on the area. In no time, drilling rigs popped up, seemingly on every square foot of land. Those entrepreneurs who got to the area first got the prime drilling locations; those who came later were forced farther out into the inhospitable hills. The most unfortunate were forced to drill in the barren Wildcat Hollow, a deep hillside indentation along the banks of Oil Creek.

Ever since then, when an oilman drills for oil in an untested area, he is said to be wild-catting. The oil boom surrounding Drake Well lasted less than twenty years, but the term that began here has survived to become a lasting part of our language.

Oil Creek State Park

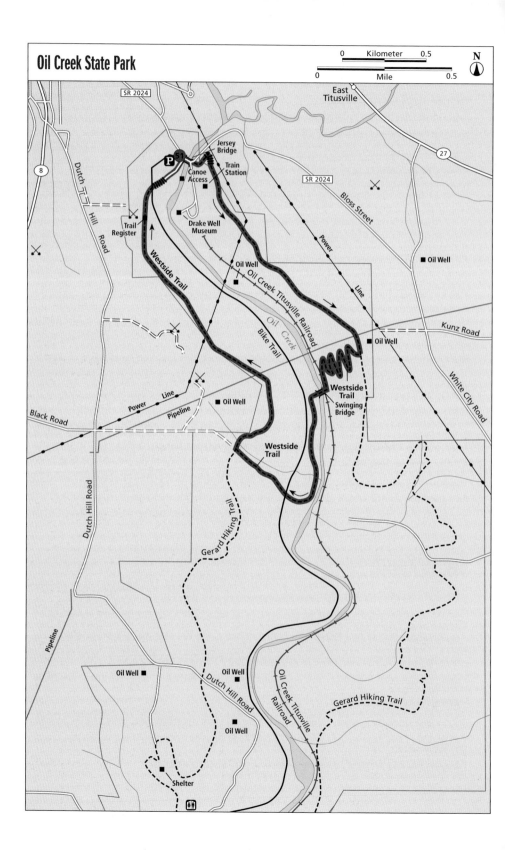

0   Kilometer   0.5

0   Mile   0.5

N

SR 2024

East Titusville

Jersey Bridge

Train Station

8

Dutch Hill Road

Canoe Access

Trail Register

Drake Well Museum

Westside Trail

Oil Well

SR 2024

Bloss Street

27

Power Line

Oil Well

Oil Creek Titusville Railroad

Oil Creek

Bike Trail

Kunz Road

Oil Well

White City Road

Westside Trail

Swinging Bridge

Black Road

Power Line

Pipeline

Oil Well

Westside Trail

Gerard Hiking Trail

Dutch Hill Road

Pipeline

Oil Well

Oil Well

Dutch Hill Road

Oil Creek Titusville Railroad

Gerard Hiking Trail

Oil Well

Shelter

top-rated museum is well worth visiting. There are more than seventy exhibits on the origin of oil, the first oil companies, and well drilling. A movie tells about Colonel Drake and the first oil well. One of the most fascinating aspects of the museum is the enlarged photographs and newspaper clippings of the disastrous fires and floods that befell the area as thousands rushed here to strike it rich. Don't miss it.

Miles and Directions

0.0 Start from the parking area at the Jersey Bridge. Walk to the road and cross Jersey Bridge. Walk within the white-painted bike trail to where the guardrail ends. Cross the road at the end of the guardrails and turn left onto an access road. Turn right onto the access road and cross over the railroad tracks.

0.2 Find a trail sign on your right. Look for yellow blazes.

0.3 Turn right onto the wooden steps.

0.4 Notice a crooked tree with a yellow blaze on the trail.

0.8 Arrive at a power line swath.

1.7 Come to a second power line swath. Arrive at a fork in the trail. Turn right onto the Westside Trail and follow the white blazes.

2.3 Cross Oil Creek & Titusville Railroad tracks a second time. Cross Oil Creek on a swinging bridge. Turn left and come to a sign that reads "Westside Trail." Stay on the Westside Trail.

3.0 Cross the paved bicycle path.

3.3 Pass through Boughton Ruins.

3.5 Arrive at a fork in the trail and a sign that reads "Drake Well Museum: 2 miles." Veer right and continue uphill on the Westside Trail. Follow the yellow blazes.

4.6 Come to a pipeline swath.

5.4 Arrive at a trail register.

5.6 Pass under the green arches. Cross the paved bicycle path to the wooden steps. Follow the Gerard Hiking Trail sign onto the boardwalk and then turn left on an access road.

5.9 Arrive back at the Jersey Bridge parking lot.

Local Information

Oil Region Alliance, 217 Elm St., Oil City 16301; (814) 677-3152; www.oilregion .org/tourism/

Local Events/Attractions

Drake Well Museum, 202 Museum Ln., Titusville; (814) 827-2797; www.drakewell .org

Campgrounds

Oil Creek Campground, 340 Shreve Rd., Titusville; (800) 395-2045; www.oilcreek campground.com

Restaurants

Blue Canoe Brewery, 113 S. Franklin St., Titusville; (814) 827-7181; www.theblue canoebrewery.com

52 Allegheny Gorge

The highlight of this hike is a viewing platform 480 feet above the Allegheny River. The trail follows an old wagon road to the ruins of a nineteenth-century iron ore furnace and then leads you across a plateau to the viewing platform. From there it descends another gorge to a stream with four cable bridges.

Start: State game land parking area at the end of Dewoody Road

Distance: 8.0-mile lollipop

Hiking time: About 4 hours

Difficulty: Difficult, due to steep climbs out of two gorges

Schedule: Open year-round

Season: Spring, summer, fall

Trail surface: Abandoned roads groomed for cross-country skiing, forest footpaths, and rocky washouts

Elevation gain: 1,214 feet

Land status: State game land and state forest

Nearest town: Franklin

Fees and permits: No fees or permits required

Other trail users: Equestrians, cross-country skiers, hunters (in season)

Canine compatibility: Leashed dogs permitted

Trail contacts: Department of Conservation and Natural Resources, Bureau of Forestry, 158 S. Second Ave., Clarion; (814) 226-1901; www.dcnr.state.pa.us

Pennsylvania Game Commission, Northwest Region, PO Box 31, Franklin 16323; (814) 432-3187

Maps: USGS Kennerdell, PA

Special considerations: Hikers on state game land during hunting season—Nov 15 to Dec 15—must wear a minimum of 250 square inches of fluorescent orange.

Finding the trailhead: From Youngstown, Ohio, drive east on I-80 and take exit 29 at Barkeyville. Drive north on PA 8. Take the PA 308 exit, turn left, and go under the thruway. Turn right on Old PA 8, drive 0.4 mile, and turn right on Dennison Run Road. Drive 1.7 miles and turn right on Dewoody Road to the state game land parking area. *DeLorme: Pennsylvania Atlas & Gazetteer.* Page 43 B7. GPS: N41 16.119' / W79 52.328'

The Hike

For the most part, the forest in this area is like any other in the region. There are the ubiquitous hemlock trees, as well as your typical oaks and maples. However, there's one discernible difference. When you're this high above deep gorges, you can feel the height. At this elevation the wind blows all the time. There are so many downed trees in the area that it's a bit disconcerting. Every time the wind blows and the trees rub against each other—making that worrisome creaking, moaning sound—you may catch yourself looking up, just to make sure none of these trees are on their way down.

The hike begins easily enough on two relatively level state game land access roads, but in less than half an hour, you're headed down a steep gorge on a washed-out road alongside Bullion Run to the Bullion Run Iron Ore Furnace. That's right; this road was once considered the best and easiest way to ship materials. Workers back in the

View of the Allegheny River as it flows south to Pittsburgh

1800s used this route to transport dense iron ore and massive logs to the Bullion Run Furnace. Remember this road the next time you feel like complaining about your job.

The smelting process required enormous amounts of wood to make charcoal, which was used to fire the furnace. Limestone was added to the iron ore and heated; the result was iron, which could be poured into a cast. The cast-iron finished products were then loaded onto rafts on the Allegheny River and floated downstream to Pittsburgh.

When you begin your climb back up the canyon from the furnace, turn right onto the South Trail. You may be thinking: This is better than retracing my steps all the way back up to the top of the gorge. It is. But it's still uphill all the way to the forest plateau. At this point on the plateau, the steep and deep Bullion Run Canyon is on your right and the steeper and deeper Allegheny Gorge is straight ahead.

Make your way to the Kennerdell Trail, an old road that has been groomed for cross-country skiing. The first portion of this trail follows the edge of the Allegheny Gorge. You can hear faint sounds of traffic from the village of Kennerdell sweeping up the gorge from across the river. This stretch is an easy walk that leads to the Dennison Point Overlook. The overlook is a railed-in, wooden platform perched on the edge of the gorge, 480 feet above the Allegheny River. It provides a breathtaking view. This is an excellent place to eat your lunch, take photos, and rest up for the rougher section of this hike.

Down the steep canyon you'll find Dennison Run and four cable bridges stretched at intervals across the stream. All is well until you come to the beginning of your climb out of the canyon and face some of the steepest climbing around. But all things, good and bad, must end. Eventually you make it to higher ground, where it's relatively flat and the wind cools you down. From here it's less than 1.0 mile to the parking area and your vehicle.

Miles and Directions

0.0 Start from the state game land parking area south gate. Look for the white blazes.

0.3 Turn left onto an access road. Look for the red blazes.

0.9 Come to the fenced-in deer exclosure. Go through the gate.

1.1 Come to a T intersection and a sign that reads "Bullion Run Iron Furnace." Turn right and cross an access road.

1.3 Arrive at the fence at the south end of the exclosure. Go through the gate.

1.4 Cross the headwaters of Bullion Run on a footbridge.

1.5 Come to the second sign for Bullion Run Iron Furnace.

1.7 Come to the third sign for Bullion Run Iron Furnace.

1.8 Come to the fourth sign for Bullion Run Iron Furnace. Turn left; arrive at the furnace. Retrace your steps back up the hill.

2.0 Arrive back at the third Bullion Run Furnace sign and turn right.

2.2 Turn right again onto the South Trail.

2.3 Bear right at the trail junction. Reach the plateau.

2.6 Cross a series of washouts on four footbridges.

3.1 Come to a fork in the trail. Turn left at the cross-country ski trail sign. Walk a short distance through a rough clearing and turn left onto the ski trail, which is the Kennerdell Trail.

4.1 Pass a sign that directs you to turn right for the overlook.

4.6 Turn right at the sign that reads "Dennison Point Overlook." Arrive at the overlook. Retrace your steps to the sign that reads "Dennison Run." Turn right.

4.7 Pass the sign that reads "No Horses beyond This Point."

5.0 Arrive at an intersection. Turn left onto an access road; follow the red blazes.

5.1 Come to a steep, rugged washout and follow it downhill.

5.4 Turn left at footpath beside Dennison Run.

5.5 Make a hairpin turn to the right. Come to the Dennison Run trail sign. Turn left onto the trail and cross the first suspension bridge over Dennison Run.

5.7 Cross the second suspension bridge.

5.8 Cross the third suspension bridge.

6.0 Arrive at the Bullion Run Iron Furnace sign. Turn left and cross a fourth suspension bridge.

6.1 Turn right onto a bridge over an intermittent tributary stream. Turn left and begin an uphill climb.

6.4 Cross a small footbridge.

6.5 Turn left onto a small bridge over the stream.

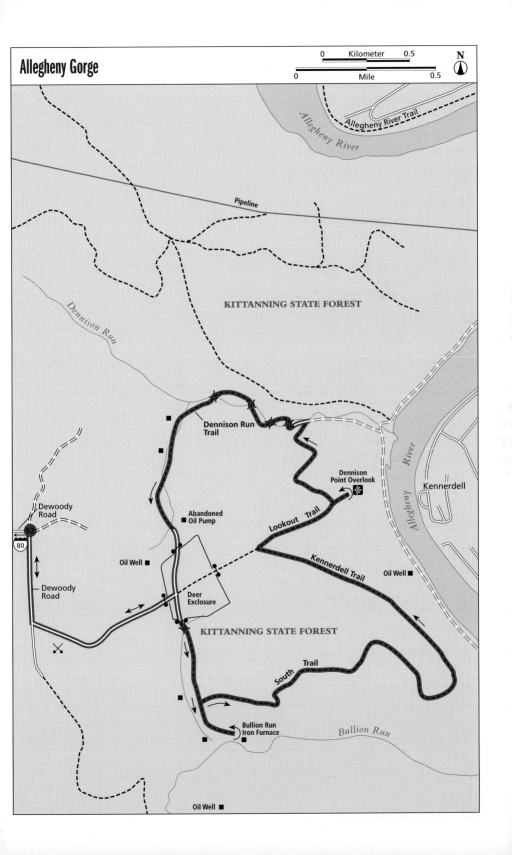

Allegheny Gorge

Kilometer
0   0.5

Mile
0   0.5

N

Allegheny River

Allegheny River Trail

Pipeline

KITTANNING STATE FOREST

Dennison Run

Dennison Run
Trail

Dennison
Point Overlook

Kennerdell

Allegheny River

Dewoody
Road

Abandoned
Oil Pump

Lookout Trail

Oil Well ■

Dewoody
Road

Kennerdell Trail

Oil Well ■

Deer
Exclosure

KITTANNING STATE FOREST

South Trail

Bullion Run

Bullion Run
Iron Furnace

Oil Well ■

6.7 Pass a sign that reads, "No Horses beyond This Point."

6.9 Turn right onto an old road.

7.0 Arrive at the north end of the deer exclosure. Go through the gate.

7.1 Arrive at a major trail intersection and turn right. Exit the exclosure and retrace your steps toward the parking area.

7.7 Turn right onto an access road.

8.0 Arrive back at the parking area.

Local Information

Oil Region Alliance, 217 Elm St., Oil City 16301; (814) 677-3152; www.oilregion .org/tourism/

Local Events/Attractions

De Bence Antique Music World, 1261 Liberty St., Franklin; (888) 547-2377; www .debencemusicworld.com

Accommodations

De Casa Bed & Breakfast, 1501 Liberty St., Franklin; (814) 437-7699; dcasabb.com

Campgrounds

Two Mile Run Campground & Farmhouse, 471 Beach Rd., Franklin; (814) 676-6116; www.twomilerun.net

Restaurants

Leonardo's Restaurant and Pizzeria, 1267 Liberty Rd., Franklin; (814) 432-8421; http://leonardosoffranklin.com

53 Schollard's Wetlands

Springfield Falls is one of the highlights of this hike; the other is the absolutely pristine surroundings along the first stretch. The vast majority of this hike is along remarkably flat terrain, so it's suitable for all types of hikers, including children and the elderly. Be sure to carry your lunch in with you so that you can take advantage of the parklike setting by the falls.

Start: State game land parking lot off Nelson Road

Distance: 5.4 miles out and back

Hiking time: About 2.5 hours

Difficulty: Easy, due to the extremely flat trail

Schedule: Open year-round

Season: Best spring and summer due to hunting seasons

Trail surface: Old railroad bed and paved road

Elevation gain: 406 feet

Land status: State game land

Nearest town: Grove City

Fees and permits: No fees or permits required

Other trail users: Waterfowl enthusiasts, hunters (in season)

Canine compatibility: Dogs permitted (Because of waterfowl and muddy bogs, dogs should be kept on-leash.)

Maps: USGS Mercer, PA; Harlansburg, PA

Trail contacts: Pennsylvania Game Commission, Northwest Region, PO Box 31, Franklin 16323; (814) 432-3187

Special considerations: Hikers on state game land during hunting season—Nov 15 to Dec 15—must wear a minimum of 250 square inches of fluorescent orange.

Finding the trailhead: From I-80, take I-79 south to exit 113 for PA 208. Drive west on PA 208 for 3.7 miles to US 19. Turn left on US 19 and drive 0.7 mile to a fork at Pennsy Road. Bear left on Pennsy Road and drive 1.5 miles to Nelson Road. Turn left onto Nelson Road and continue 0.3 mile to the state game land parking lot. *DeLorme: Pennsylvania Atlas & Gazetteer:* Page 42 C4. GPS: N41 06.887' / W80 11.529'

The Hike

This out-and-back hike can be divided into two distinct sections. The first 2.5 miles, from the beginning to PA 208, is the quieter and more picturesque. It's in this section where you see the diversity of the plants and trees that provide the seeds, wild grapes, and berries that foster the impressive array of wildlife. Notice the variety of trees: shingle, chestnut, white and red oak, dogwood, and cucumber, as well as hemlock and other varieties of pine. You can also observe breeding nests for the wood duck and the Canada goose. The wood ducks' nests are the silver tubular devices with a circular entry hole, resembling something from an old science fiction movie. The nests for Canada geese are open and resemble huge funnels stuffed with straw. They're attached to a pole that's implanted over the water. In either case, the nests are built to keep hungry predators away from the eggs. If you're lucky enough to see a Canada goose roosting, you'll notice its mate circling the pole, functioning as an early-warning system and first line of defense.

Abandoned railroad keeps hikers high and dry.

This longer section of the hike is extremely well kept. The Pennsylvania Game Commission uses this abandoned railroad grade as an access road, so it's high, wide, and dry, and all the underbrush is trimmed away. Although out of sight much of the time, Schollard's Run meanders alongside the trail from bog to bog, heading for Springfield Falls.

When you reach PA Route 208, you leave the idyllic life behind. From here to the falls, the trail is not as well kept; to make matters worse, a grade bridge over Schollard's Run is out. Supposedly you can take this path to get to the falls, but it's tough going—I checked it out. Finding the trail in the marshy field isn't easy, and it doesn't get any better. Because the bridge is out, I had to leave the trail and walk along the stream through thick underbrush. The high stream made it difficult to find a decent spot to cross. For a while there were white markers on a few trees, but those ran out and I was left to simply follow the stream until I reached Falls Road. I do not recommend this route. Instead, I recommend that when you reach PA 208, you turn left, staying on the shoulder. Turn right on SR 2002 and merely walk the 0.25 mile or so to Springfield Falls. There is very little traffic at this point.

Schollard's Wetlands

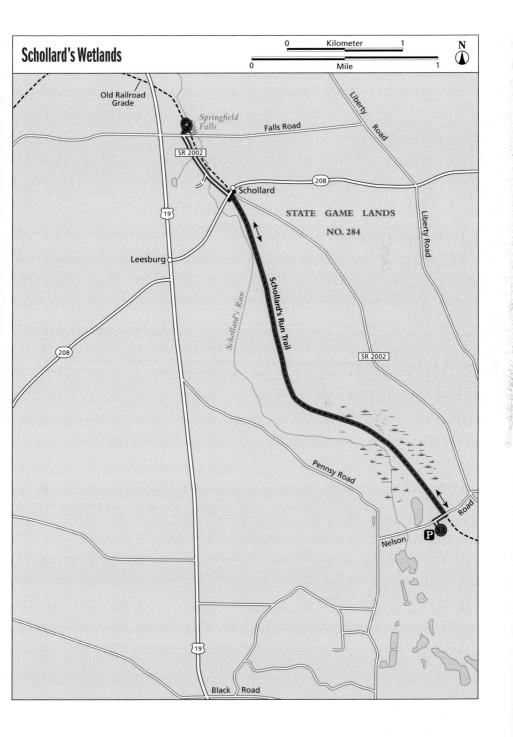

At the stop sign at the intersection of SR 2002 and Falls Road, turn right and walk 100 feet to the falls, which essentially begins under the road. When you get to the falls, enter from your right; access to the left-hand side of the falls is denied by the property owner. Eat your lunch on the boulders above the falls. Rest before simply retracing your steps back to your vehicle.

Miles and Directions

0.0 Start at the state game land parking lot on Nelson Road. Turn right on Nelson Road.

0.1 Arrive at the railroad grade. Turn left.

1.0 Power line veers off to the left.

2.3 Reach PA 208. Turn left.

2.4 Turn right on SR 2002.

2.7 Reach a stop sign on Falls Road. Turn right and walk 100 feet to Springfield Falls. Retrace your steps.

5.4 Arrive back at the Nelson Road parking lot.

Local Information
Visit Mercer County PA; (800) 637-2370; www.visitmercercounty.com

Local Events/Attractions
Wendell August Forge, 620 N. Madison Ave., Grove City; (724) 458-8360; www.wendellaugust.com

Campgrounds
Rocky Springs Campground, 84 Rocky Spring Rd., Mercer; (724) 662-1568; www.rockyspringscampground.com

Restaurants
Rachel's Road House, 1553 Perry Hwy., Mercer; (724) 748-3193; www.springfields.com/rachels-roadhouse/

54 McConnells Mill State Park

After a steep descent into a 400-foot gorge, the trail continues downstream alongside a gushing stream, where giant sandstone boulders have created whitewater rapids. The trail passes through boulders on the slopes—where runoff waters create miniature waterfalls. It then passes a restored mill and a covered bridge. At the turnaround point it crosses the creek on a traffic bridge. On this side of the creek, it is a typical forest footpath, running about 100 feet above the stream.

Start: Alpha Pass Trail trailhead parking lot
Distance: 3.3-mile loop
Hiking time: About 2 hours
Difficulty: Moderate, with strenuous climbs out of the gorge
Schedule: Open year-round; guided tours of McConnells Mill available Memorial Day to Labor Day or off-season by appointment
Season: Spring, summer, fall
Trail surface: Rocky footpath down a deep gorge; wet, slippery rocks
Elevation gain: 346 feet

Land status: State park
Nearest town: New Castle
Fees and permits: No fees or permits required
Other trail users: Canoeists, rafters, tourists
Canine compatibility: Leashed dogs permitted
Maps: USGS Portersville, PA
Trail contacts: McConnells Mill State Park, c/o Moraine State Park, 225 Pleasant Valley Rd., Portersville 16051; (724) 368-8811; www.dcnr.state.pa.us/stateparks/findapark/mcconnellsmill/

Finding the trailhead: From Pittsburgh, drive north on I-79 to exit 99. Drive west on US 422 for 1.7 miles. Turn left and drive south on McConnells Mill Road for 0.6 mile to the Alpha Pass Trail trailhead parking area, on your right. *DeLorme: Pennsylvania Atlas & Gazetteer:* Page 57 A4. GPS: N40 57.610' / W80 10.144'

The Hike

Only 40 miles north of Pittsburgh and surrounded by countless tourist attractions, shopping malls, restaurants, and campgrounds, Slippery Rock Gorge and McConnells Mill State Park provide an excellent way to spend a day. McConnells Mill State Park is both a National and State Natural Landmark comprising 2,529 acres that surround the spectacular Slippery Rock Gorge. The gorge was formed 140,000 years ago when a continental glacier retreated, leaving behind Lakes Prouty, Watts, and Edmund. Waters from these lakes drained swiftly into the channel, carving out the gorge. While little else remains of the glacial melt, the waters are still swift and turbulent.

As you hike the trail in season, you can watch whitewater kayakers and canoeists wend their way downstream between the precariously balanced boulders that litter the stream. Where the creek widens and the water calms, you can watch novice canoeists learn the basics of keeping their craft headed in the right direction.

This covered bridge at McConnells Mill State Park spans Slippery Rock Creek.

The trail passes through the historic section of the park, where you may encounter tourists or schoolchildren touring McConnells Mill and photographing the covered bridge. If it's a hot day, you may see young people from three nearby colleges picnicking or sunbathing on the large flat boulders protruding from the stream. But as soon as you're through this area, visitors on the trail are sparse.

It's hard to estimate how long it takes to do this hike. As its name suggests, the gorge offers up plenty of slippery rocks, where even the most experienced hiker may fall. Recognize that this is a challenging hike, and don't try to rush through it. Interestingly, Slippery Rock Gorge actually got its name not because of the hundreds of slippery rocks along the way but because of one especially slippery shelf of sandstone. This shelf, which is located near the mill, was part of a Native American trail. A nearby oil seep deposited oil in the water, which ran over the shelf and made the passage a slippery one. The rock is still there, but unfortunately it's off-limits to visitors.

Most hikers will want to stop and tour McConnells Mill, a fully restored gristmill. One of its many interesting features is the turbines. The owners abandoned the typical waterwheel—which froze up in winter—in favor of turbines that were placed into the water race, inside the mill where the waters wouldn't freeze. Water was channeled through these underwater turbines, which in turn were connected to gears and rods that distributed the power throughout the mill. Workers made ongoing maintenance checks (underwater, of course), which were always dangerous and sometimes fatal. In fact, it was in mills like this where the expression "put you through the mill" (to give someone a hard time) originated.

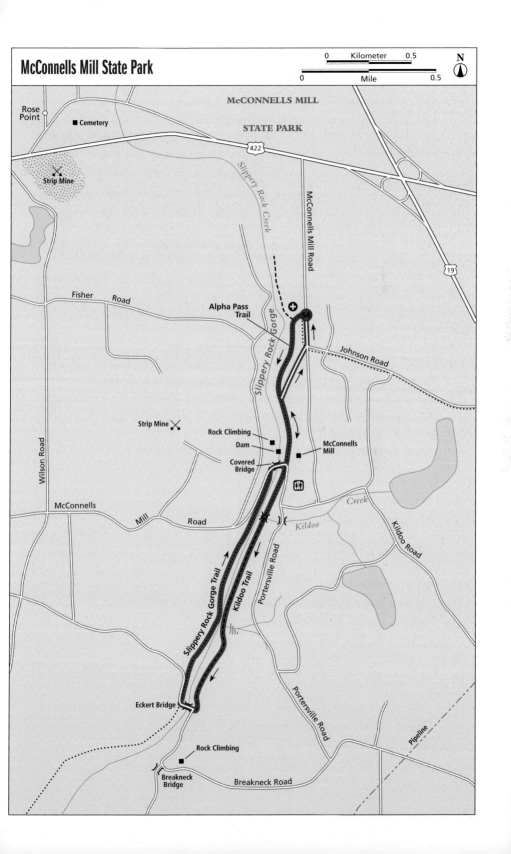

McConnells Mill State Park

0　　Kilometer　　0.5

0　　　　Mile　　　　0.5

N

McCONNELLS MILL

STATE PARK

Rose
Point

■ Cemetery

✕
Strip Mine

422

Slippery Rock Creek

McConnells Mill Road

19

Fisher　Road

Alpha Pass
Trail

Slippery Rock Gorge

Johnson Road

Strip Mine ✕

Rock Climbing

Dam

Covered
Bridge

McConnells
Mill

Wilson Road

McConnells

Mill　Road

Creek

Kildoo

Slippery Rock Gorge Trail

Kildoo Trail

Portersville Road

Kildoo Road

Eckert Bridge

Rock Climbing

Breakneck
Bridge

Breakneck Road

Portersville Road

Pipeline

The Slippery Rock Creek rapids, too, are dangerous. There's no swimming allowed. Stanchions hold white lifesaver devices attached to ropes stationed at intervals along the hiking trails, should there be any need. If you are insistent about living on the edge, there are two places along the trail where rock climbing and rappelling are permitted. The beginner area, the Rim Road Climbing Area, is across the stream from the mill. The advanced area is, appropriately, near Breakneck Bridge.

Miles and Directions

0.0 Start at the Alpha Pass Trail trailhead parking area on McConnells Mill Road and walk to the trailhead of the North Country National Scenic Trail. Follow Alpha Pass Trail arrows down the gorge. Look for blue blazes and take the wooden steps.

0.1 Come to the first lifesaver stanchion. Walk to the boulders at the edge of Slippery Rock Creek. Retrace your steps back to the trail.

0.3 Reach a trail intersection; continue straight.

0.4 Pass a runoff stream. Come to an intersection with a second trail; continue straight.

0.6 Come to McConnells Mill. Walk through the parking lot to the paved Kildoo Trail.

0.9 Cross Kildoo Creek on a small footbridge. The pavement ends.

1.7 Arrive at Eckert Bridge. Turn right and cross over the creek. Turn right at the sign that reads "Old Mill" and head upstream on the Slippery Rock Gorge Trail.

2.7 Arrive at the covered bridge. Cross the stream to McConnells Mill. Walk across the parking lot and continue walking uphill on the road.

3.2 Turn left onto McConnells Mill Road.

3.3 Arrive back at the Alpha Pass Trail trailhead parking area, on your left.

Local Information
Visit Lawrence County, 229 S. Jefferson St., New Castle 16101; (724) 654-8408; visit lawrencecounty.com

Local Events/Attractions
McConnells Mill Heritage Festival, September; (724) 368-3612

Accommodations
Bedford House B&B, 125 Dogwood Way, Pulaski; (724) 964-1050; www.tripadvisor.com … Pulaski B&Bs/Inns

Campgrounds
Moraine State Park, 225 Pleasant Valley Rd., Portersville; (888) 727-2757 (camping information and reservations). Cabins and cottages open year-round.

Restaurants
Iron Bridge Inn, 1438 Perry Hwy., Mercer; (724) 748-3626

Organizations
Wampum Chapter of the North Country National Scenic Trail; northcountrytrail .org/wam/

55 Moraine State Park

This hike provides a good workout as you climb and descend four deep ravines. The trail also makes its way along a glacial lake, into its coves covered with lily pads, and past marshes stuffed full of cattails and wild grapes. At the halfway point you can rest, use the restrooms, and take on water at a full-service marina. There is even a restaurant on the water's edge.

Start: North Country National Scenic Trail parking area on the west side of PA 528
Distance: 10.5-mile circuit
Hiking time: About 6 hours
Difficulty: Difficult, due to a series of climbs in and out of deep ravines
Schedule: Open year-round
Season: Spring, summer, fall
Trail surface: Typical forest footpath and dirt roads
Elevation gain: 1,619 feet

Land status: State park
Nearest town: Butler
Fees and permits: No fees or permits required
Other trail users: Anglers, hunters (in season)
Canine compatibility: Leashed dogs permitted
Maps: USGS Prospect, PA
Trail contacts: Moraine State Park, 225 Pleasant Valley Rd., Portersville 16051; (724) 368-8811; www.dcnr.state.pa.us/stateparks/findapark/moraine/

Finding the trailhead: From Pittsburgh, drive north on I-79. Take exit 99 and drive east on US 422 for 5.8 miles. Turn left onto PA 528 into Moraine State Park and drive north for 4.5 miles to the North Country National Scenic Trail parking area, on your left. *DeLorme: Pennsylvania Atlas & Gazetteer:* Page 57 A5. GPS: N40 58.278' / W80 01.905'

The Hike

If you've ever wondered if you're ready for a major hike or backpacking trip, this hike could be the test. In fact, most of this hike is part of the ambitious North Country National Scenic Trail, which, when completed, will span 4,600 miles from the central plains of North Dakota to the Adirondacks in New York. The 25-mile section that runs through McConnells Mill and Moraine State Parks is a challenging hike. There are a seemingly endless number of climbs and descents along the ridges of this trail.

This route through Moraine State Park covers four major ridges, which means you go up and down each of them on the way out, and up and down again on the way back. While walking uphill is challenging, going down steep grades can be murder on the knees. And unless you can go 6 hours without eating, you'll also have the added burden of carrying food on this hike. Luckily, as far as water is concerned, there is an outdoor drinking fountain at the Davis Hollow Marina restrooms. There's even a down spigot so you can take off your shoes and give your feet a squirt or two.

Continental glaciers, as the name suggests, once stretched from the Atlantic to the Pacific. Where they ended they formed a moraine—a geologic term for an

Everyone needs a break after doing 10.5 miles on this hike.

accumulation of stones, boulders, and other debris carried and deposited by a glacier. Four of these glaciers ended at the area around Moraine State Park. The debris they left behind blocked the natural flow of water, creating a number of glacial lakes and the rugged ridges and valleys that surround them. The largest of these glacial lakes stretched for more than 6 miles. When it receded, it left behind a smaller lake with a series of waterways, creeks, and coves that stretched into valleys like so many crooked fingers.

These odd land formations intrigued English botanist and geologist Frank W. Preston. Beginning in the 1920s, he studied the area, which was then called Muddy Creek Valley, for decades. With support from his friends, Preston formed The Western Pennsylvania Conservancy, which purchased the land and set about to preserve it in all its uniqueness. State agencies later joined forces with the conservancy, and in 1970 Moraine State Park was opened.

One of the centerpieces of the park is the popular 3,222-acre Lake Arthur, built in 1968 by damming Muddy Creek and named for prominent Pittsburgh attorney and naturalist Edmund Watts Arthur. Today dozens of sailboats line the marina, and anglers troll the coves for northern pike, muskellunge, walleye, and other warm-water fish.

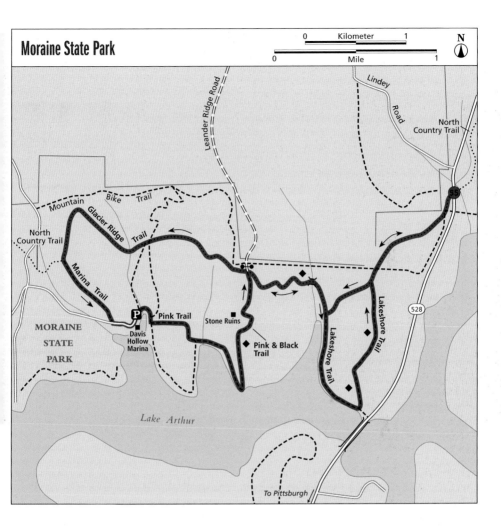

Moraine State Park

0   Kilometer   1

0   Mile   1

N

Leander Ridge Road

Lindey Road

North Country Trail

Mountain Bike Trail

Glacier Ridge Trail

North Country Trail

Marina Trail

528

P

Pink Trail

Stone Ruins

Davis Hollow Marina

MORAINE STATE PARK

Pink & Black Trail

Lakeshore Trail

Lakeshore Trail

Lake Arthur

To Pittsburgh

Miles and Directions

0.0   Start at the North Country National Scenic Trail parking area on PA 528. Walk to the bulletin board and trail marker and follow the blue blazes. Begin a severe uphill climb.

0.8   Come to an intersection with the yellow-blazed 528 Bridge Trail. Continue straight to the Glacier Ridge Trail.

1.7   Begin a serious uphill climb.

1.9   The trail levels off and veers to the left.

2.2   Cross a dirt road and reenter the woods. Pass the signpost for NCNST and the sign on your right for snowmobile and mountain bike trails.

3.3   Come to a junction with the mountain bike trail. Turn right and continue on the Glacier Ridge Trail.

4.2   Turn left on the yellow-blazed Marina Trail toward Davis Hollow Marina.

4.8 Cross a power line swath. Get on an old road and walk parallel to the lake to Davis Hollow Marina.

4.9 Arrive at the marina. Walk east across the parking lot to the walkway at the northern tip of the inlet. Walk on the road around the inlet.

5.1 Turn left on an old road and follow the pink blazes.

6.1 The road turns left, away from lake. Follow the pink blazes and black blazes.

6.6 Pass stone ruins.

6.8 Note the mountain bike trail junction on your right.

6.9 Turn right onto Glacier Ridge Trail and follow the blue blazes.

7.6 Cross second small stream on a wooden footbridge and turn left. Begin an uphill climb.

7.9 Arrive at a trail intersection and sign that reads "528 Bridge." Take the yellow-blazed Lakeshore Trail.

8.0 Cross a marshy area on a wooden footbridge. Turn left and begin a climb.

8.6 Turn left and begin to climb.

8.9 Turn right and follow the yellow blazes.

9.7 Turn right onto Glacier Ridge Trail and cross under a power line.

10.5 Arrive back at the parking area.

Local Information

Butler County Tourism and Convention Bureau, 310 E. Grandview Ave., Zelienople 16063; (866) 856-8444; visitbutlercounty.com

Local Events/Attractions

Regatta at Lake Arthur, first weekend in August, Moraine State Park; (866) 856-8444; www.lakearthurregatta.org

Campgrounds

Moraine State Park, 225 Pleasant Valley Rd., Portersville; (888) 727-2757 (camping information and reservations). Cabins and cottages open year-round.

Organizations

Pennsylvania North Country National Scenic Trail Association; http://northcountry trail.org/trail/states/pennsylvania/

Honorable Mentions

Northwest Pennsylvania

Here are two great hikes in the Northwest region that didn't make the A-list this time around but deserve recognition. Check them out and let us know what you think. You may decide that one or more of these hikes deserves higher status in future editions, or you may have a hike of your own that merits some attention.

O The Erie National Wildlife Refuge

The refuge is 35 miles south of Erie in Crawford County. There are two separate sections: the 5,025-acre Sugar Lake Division and the 3,545-acre Seneca Division. You'll find three short hikes in Sugar Lake and one in Seneca. The refuge, named for the Erie Indians who once inhabited the area, is a bird lover's paradise: More than 230 species of birds have been reported here. The hikes, which total about 7 miles, are easy but can be wet in springtime.

From Meadville, drive east on PA 27 about 12 miles to Guys Mills. Take PA 198 in Guys Mills; drive east for 0.8 mile and turn right for the headquarters. For more information call the Erie National Wildlife Refuge at (814) 789-3585. *DeLorme: Pennsylvania Atlas & Gazetteer.* Page 29 C6

P Chapman State Park

Located in Warren County, Chapman State Park is surrounded by the Allegheny National Forest. There's a network of seven hiking trails within its 805 acres. There's also the 68-acre Chapman Dam and an eighty-three-site campground, as well as a group camping area. The trails, which are mostly old logging roads and railroad beds, make excellent short hikes. If you did all the hikes, the total would be around 11 miles. This is a great little park to visit and relax and get away from it all.

From Warren, drive east on US 6 for about 7 miles to the (only) stoplight in Clarendon. Turn right at the stoplight onto Chapman Dam Road and drive about 5 miles to the park. For more information call Chapman State Park at (814) 723-0250. *DeLorme: Pennsylvania Atlas & Gazetteer.* Page 31 B5

The Art of Hiking

When standing nose to nose with a mountain lion, you're probably not too concerned with the issue of ethical behavior in the wild. No doubt you're just terrified. But let's be honest. How often are you nose to nose with a mountain lion? For most of us, a hike into the "wild" means loading up the SUV with expensive gear and driving to a toileted trailhead. Sure, you can mourn how civilized we've become—how GPS units have replaced natural instinct and Gore-Tex, true-grit—but the silly gadgets of civilization aside, we have plenty of reason to take pride in how we've matured. With survival now on the back burner, we've begun to reason—and it's about time—that we have a responsibility to protect, no longer just conquer, our wild places: that they, not we, are at risk. So please, do what you can. The following section will help you understand better what it means to "do what you can" while still making the most of your hiking experience. Anyone can take a hike, but hiking safely and well is an art requiring preparation and proper equipment.

Trail Etiquette

Zero impact. Always leave an area just like you found it—if not better than you found it. Avoid camping in fragile alpine meadows and along the banks of streams and lakes. Use a camp stove versus building a wood fire. Pack up all of your trash and extra food. Bury human waste at least 100 feet from water sources under 6 to 8 inches of topsoil. Don't bathe with soap in a lake or stream—use prepackaged moistened towels to wipe off sweat and dirt, or bathe in the water without soap.

Stay on the trail. It's true, a path anywhere leads nowhere new, but purists will just have to get over it. Paths serve an important purpose; they limit impact on natural areas. Straying from a designated trail may seem innocent, but it can cause damage to sensitive areas—damage that may take years to recover, if it can recover at all. Even simple shortcuts can be destructive. So, please, stay on the trail.

Leave no weeds. Noxious weeds tend to overtake other plants, which in turn affects animals and birds that depend on them for food. To minimize the spread of noxious weeds, hikers should regularly clean their boots, tents, packs, and hiking poles of mud and seeds. Also brush your dog to remove any weed seeds before heading off into a new area.

Keep your dog under control. You can buy a flexi-lead that allows your dog to go exploring along the trail, while allowing you to reel him in should another hiker approach or should he decide to chase a rabbit. Always obey leash laws and be sure to bury your dog's waste or pack it out in resealable plastic bags.

Respect other trail users. Often you're not the only one on the trail. With the rise in popularity of multiuse trails, you'll have to learn a new kind of respect, beyond the nod and "hello" approach you may be used to. First investigate whether you're on a multiuse trail, and assume the appropriate precautions. When you encounter motorized vehicles (ATVs, motorcycles, and 4WDs), be alert. Though they should always yield to the hiker, often they're going too fast or are too lost in the buzz of their engine to react to your presence. If you hear activity ahead, step off the trail, just to be safe. Note that you're not likely to hear a mountain biker coming, so be prepared and know ahead of time whether you share the trail with them. Cyclists should always yield to hikers, but that's little comfort to the hiker. Be aware. When you approach horses or pack animals on the trail, always step quietly off the trail, preferably on the downhill side, and let them pass. If you're wearing a large backpack, it's often a good idea to sit down. To some animals, a hiker wearing a large backpack might appear threatening. Many national forests allow domesticated grazing, usually for sheep and cattle. Make sure your dog doesn't harass these animals, and respect ranchers' rights while you're enjoying yours.

Getting into Shape

Unless you want to be sore—and possibly have to shorten your trip or vacation—be sure to get in shape before a big hike. If you're terribly out of shape, start a walking program early, preferably eight weeks in advance. Start with a 15-minute walk during your lunch hour or after work and gradually increase your walking time to an hour. You should also increase your elevation gain. Walking briskly up hills really strengthens your leg muscles and gets your heart rate up. If you work in a storied office building, take the stairs instead of the elevator. If you prefer going to a gym, walk the treadmill or use a stair machine. You can further increase your strength and endurance by walking with a loaded backpack. Stationary exercises you might consider are squats, leg lifts, sit-ups, and push-ups. Other good ways to get in shape include biking, running, aerobics, and, of course, short hikes. Stretching before and after a hike keeps muscles flexible and helps avoid injuries.

Preparedness

It's been said that failing to plan means planning to fail. So do take the necessary time to plan your trip. Whether going on a short day hike or an extended backpack trip, always prepare for the worst. Simply remembering to pack a copy of the US Army Survival Manual is not preparedness. Although it's not a bad idea if you plan on entering truly wild places, it's merely the tourniquet answer to a problem. You need to do your best to prevent the problem from arising in the first place. In order to survive—and to stay reasonably comfortable—you need to concern yourself with the basics: water, food, and shelter. Don't go on a hike without having these bases covered. And don't go on a hike expecting to find these items in the woods.

Water. Even in frigid conditions, you need at least two quarts of water a day to function efficiently. Add heat and taxing terrain and you can bump that figure up to one gallon. That's simply a base to work from—your metabolism and your level of conditioning can raise or lower that amount. Unless you know your level, assume that you need one gallon of water a day. Now, where do you plan on getting the water?

Preferably not from natural water sources. These sources can be loaded with intestinal disturbers, such as bacteria, viruses, and fertilizers. *Giardia lamblia*, the most common of these disturbers, is a protozoan parasite that lives part of its life cycle as a cyst in water sources. The parasite spreads when mammals defecate in water sources. Once ingested, *Giardia* can induce cramping, diarrhea, vomiting, and fatigue within two days to two weeks after ingestion. Giardiasis is treatable with prescription drugs. If you believe you've contracted giardiasis, see a doctor immediately.

Treating water. The best and easiest solution to avoid polluted water is to carry your water with you. Yet, depending on the nature of your hike and the duration, this may not be an option—one gallon of water weighs 8.5 pounds. In that case, you'll need to look into treating water. Regardless of which method you choose, you should always carry some water with you in case of an emergency. Save this reserve until you absolutely need it.

There are three methods of treating water: boiling, chemical treatment, and filtering. If you boil water, it's recommended that you do so for 10 to 15 minutes. This is often impractical because you're forced to exhaust a great deal of your fuel supply. You can opt for chemical treatment, which will kill *Giardia* but will not take care of other chemical pollutants. Another drawback to chemical treatments is the unpleasant taste of the water after it's treated. You can remedy this by adding powdered drink mix to the water. Filters are the preferred method for treating water. Many filters remove *Giardia*, organic and inorganic contaminants, and don't leave an aftertaste. Water filters are far from perfect, as they can easily become clogged or leak if a gasket wears out. It's always a good idea to carry a backup supply of chemical treatment tablets in case your filter quits on you.

Food. If we're talking about survival, you can go days without food, as long as you have water. But we're also talking about comfort. Try to avoid foods that are high in sugar and fat, like candy bars and potato chips. These food types are harder to digest and are low in nutritional value. Instead, bring along foods that are easy to pack, nutritious, and high in energy (e.g., bagels, nutrition bars, dehydrated fruit, gorp, and jerky). If you are on an overnight trip, easy-to-fix dinners include rice mixes with dehydrated potatoes, corn, pasta with cheese sauce, and soup mixes. For a tasty breakfast, you can fix hot oatmeal with brown sugar and reconstituted milk powder topped off with banana chips. If you like a hot drink in the morning, bring along herbal tea bags or hot chocolate. If you are a coffee junkie, you can purchase coffee that is packaged like tea bags. You can prepackage all of your meals in heavy-duty resealable plastic bags to keep food from spilling in your pack. These bags can be reused to pack out trash.

Shelter. The type of shelter you choose depends less on the conditions than on your tolerance for discomfort. Shelter comes in many forms—tent, tarp, lean-to, bivy sack,

The Hemlock Run Trail brings you to the crystal clear waters of the Allegheny Reservoir.

cabin, cave, etc. If you're camping in the desert, a bivy sack may suffice, but if you're above tree line and a storm is approaching, a better choice is a three- or four-season tent. Tents are the logical and most popular choice for most backpackers as they're lightweight and packable—and you can rest assured that you always have shelter from the elements. Before you leave on your trip, anticipate what the weather and terrain will be like and plan for the type of shelter that will work best for your comfort level (see "Equipment" later in this section).

Finding a campsite. If there are established campsites, stick to those. If not, start looking for a campsite early—around 3:30 or 4 p.m. Stop at the first decent site you see. Depending on the area, it could be a long time before you find another suitable location. Pitch your camp in an area that's level. Make sure the area is at least 200 feet from fragile areas like lakeshores, meadows, and streambanks. And try to avoid areas thick in underbrush, as they can harbor insects and provide cover for approaching animals.

If you are camping in stormy, rainy weather, look for a rock outcrop or a shelter in the trees to keep the wind from blowing your tent all night. Be sure that you don't camp under trees with dead limbs that might break off on top of you. Also, try to find an area that has an absorbent surface, such as sandy soil or forest duff. This, in addition to camping on a surface with a slight angle, will provide better drainage. By all means, don't dig trenches to provide drainage around your tent—remember, you're practicing zero-impact camping.

If you're in bear country, steer clear of creekbeds or animal paths. If you see any signs of a bear's presence (i.e., scat, footprints), relocate. You'll need to find a campsite

near a tall tree where you can hang your food and other items that may attract bears, such as deodorant, toothpaste, or soap. Carry a lightweight nylon rope with which to hang your food. As a rule, you should hang your food at least 20 feet from the ground and 5 feet away from the tree trunk. You can put food and other items in a waterproof stuff sack and tie one end of the rope to the stuff sack. To get the other end of the rope over the tree branch, tie a good size rock to it, and gently toss the rock over the tree branch. Pull the stuff sack up until it reaches the top of the branch and tie it off securely. Don't hang your food near your tent! If possible, hang your food at least 100 feet away from your campsite. Alternatives to hanging your food are bear-proof plastic tubes and metal bear boxes.

Lastly, think of comfort. Lie down on the ground where you intend to sleep and see if it's a good fit. For morning warmth (and a nice view to wake up to), have your tent face east.

First Aid

I know you're tough, but get 10 miles into the woods and develop a blister and you'll wish you had carried that first-aid kit. Face it, it's just plain good sense. Many companies produce lightweight, compact first-aid kits. Just make sure yours contains at least the following:

- adhesive bandages
- moleskin or duct tape
- various sterile gauze and dressings
- white surgical tape
- Ace bandage

- an antihistamine
- aspirin
- Betadine solution
- first-aid book
- antacid tablets
- tweezers
- scissors
- antibacterial wipes
- triple-antibiotic ointment
- plastic gloves
- sterile cotton tip applicators
- syrup of ipecac (to induce vomiting)
- thermometer
- wire splint

Here are a few tips for dealing with, and hopefully preventing, certain ailments.

Sunburn. Take along sunscreen or sunblock, protective clothing, and a wide-brimmed hat. If you do get a sunburn, treat the area with aloe vera gel, and protect the area from further sun exposure. At higher elevations, the sun's radiation can be particularly damaging to skin. Remember that your eyes are vulnerable to this radiation as well. Sunglasses can be a good way to prevent headaches and permanent eye damage from the sun, especially in places where light-colored rock or patches of snow reflect light up in your face.

Blisters. Be prepared to take care of these hike-spoilers by carrying moleskin (a lightly padded adhesive), gauze and tape, or adhesive bandages. An effective way to apply moleskin is to cut out a circle of moleskin and remove the center—like a doughnut—and place it over the blistered area. Cutting the center out will reduce the pressure applied to the sensitive skin. Other products can help you combat blisters. Some are applied to suspicious hot spots before a blister forms to help decrease friction to that area, while others are applied to the blister after it has popped to help prevent further irritation.

Insect bites and stings. You can treat most insect bites and stings by applying hydrocortisone 1% cream topically and taking a pain medication such as ibuprofen to reduce swelling. If you forgot to pack these items, a cold compress or a paste of mud and ashes can sometimes assuage the itching and discomfort. Remove any stingers by using tweezers or scraping the area with your fingernail or a knife blade. Don't pinch the area—you'll only spread the venom.

Some hikers are highly sensitive to bites and stings and may have a serious allergic reaction that can be life threatening. Symptoms of a serious allergic reaction can include wheezing, an asthmatic attack, and shock. The treatment for this severe type of reaction is epinephrine. If you know that you are sensitive to bites and stings, carry a pre-packaged kit of epinephrine, which can be obtained only by prescription from your doctor.

Ticks. Ticks can carry diseases such as Rocky Mountain spotted fever and Lyme disease. The best defense is, of course, prevention. If you know you're going to be hiking through an area littered with ticks, wear long pants and a long-sleeved shirt. You can apply a permethrin repellent to your clothing and a DEET repellent to exposed skin. At the end of your hike, do a spot check for ticks (and insects in general). If you do find a tick, coat the insect with petroleum jelly or tree sap to cut off its air supply. The tick should release its hold, but if it doesn't, grab the head of the tick firmly—with a pair of tweezers if you have them—and gently pull it away from the skin with a twisting motion. Sometimes the mouth parts linger, embedded in your skin. If this happens, try to remove them with a disinfected needle. Clean the affected area with an antibacterial cleanser and then apply triple-antibiotic ointment. Monitor the area for a few days. If irritation persists or a white spot develops, see a doctor for possible infection.

Poison ivy, oak, and sumac. These skin irritants can be found most anywhere in North America and come in the form of a bush or a vine, having leaflets in groups of three, five, seven, or nine. Learn how to spot the plants. The oil they secrete can cause an allergic reaction in the form of blisters, usually about 12 hours after exposure. The itchy rash can last from ten days to several weeks. The best defense against these irritants is to wear clothing that covers the arms, legs, and torso. For summer, zip-off cargo pants come in handy. There are also nonprescription lotions you can apply to exposed skin that guard against the effects of poison ivy/oak/sumac and can be washed off with soap and water. If you think you were in contact with these plants, wash with soap and water after hiking (or even on the trail during longer hikes). Taking a hot shower with soap after you return home from your hike will also help remove any lingering oil from your skin. Should you contract a rash from any of these plants, use an antihistamine to reduce the itching. If the rash is localized, create a light bleach-water wash to dry up the area. If the rash has spread, either tough it out or see your doctor about getting a dose of cortisone (available both orally and by injection).

Snakebites. Snakebites are rare in North America. Unless startled or provoked, the majority of snakes will not bite. If you are wise to their habitats and keep a careful eye on the trail, you should be just fine. When stepping over logs, first step on the log, making sure you can see what's on the other side before stepping down. Though your chances of being struck are slim, it's wise to know what to do in the event you are.

If a nonvenomous snake bites you, allow the wound to bleed a small amount and then cleanse the wounded area with a Betadine solution (10% povidone iodine). Rinse the wound with clean water (preferably) or fresh urine (it might sound ugly, but it's sterile). Once the area is clean, cover it with triple-antibiotic ointment and a

clean bandage. Remember, most residual damage from snakebites, venomous or otherwise, comes from infection, not the snake's venom. Keep the area as clean as possible and get medical attention immediately.

If you are bitten by a venomous snake, remove the toxin with a suctioning device, found in a snakebite kit. If you do not have such a device, squeeze the wound—DO NOT use your mouth for suction, as the venom will enter your bloodstream through the vessels under the tongue and head straight for your heart. Then clean the wound just as you would a nonvenomous bite. Tie a clean band of cloth snuggly around the afflicted appendage, about an inch or so above the bite (or the rim of the swelling). This is NOT a tourniquet—you want to simply slow the blood flow, not cut it off. Loosen the band if numbness ensues. Remove the band for a minute and reapply a little higher every 10 minutes.

If it is your friend who's been bitten, treat him or her for shock—make the person comfortable, have him or her lie down, elevate the legs, and keep him or her warm. Avoid applying anything cold to the bite wound. Immobilize the affected area and remove any constricting items such as rings, watches, or restrictive clothing—swelling may occur. Once your friend is stable and relatively calm, hike out to get help. Ideally the victim should get treatment within 12 hours, which usually consists of a tetanus shot, antivenin, and antibiotics.

If you are alone and struck by a venomous snake, stay calm. Hysteria will only quicken the venom's spread. Follow the procedure above, and do your best to reach help. When hiking out, don't run—you'll only increase the flow of blood throughout your system. Instead, walk calmly.

Dehydration. Have you ever hiked in hot weather and had a roaring headache and felt fatigued after only a few miles? More than likely you were dehydrated. Symptoms of dehydration include fatigue, headache, and decreased coordination and judgment. When you are hiking, your body's rate of fluid loss depends on the outside temperature, humidity, altitude, and your activity level. On average, a hiker walking in warm weather will lose four liters of fluid a day. That fluid loss is easily replaced by normal consumption of liquids and food. However, if a hiker is walking briskly in hot, dry weather and hauling a heavy pack, he or she can lose one to three liters of water an hour. It's important to always carry plenty of water and to stop often and drink fluids regularly, even if you aren't thirsty.

Heat exhaustion is the result of a loss of large amounts of electrolytes and often occurs if a hiker is dehydrated and has been under heavy exertion. Common symptoms of heat exhaustion include cramping, exhaustion, fatigue, lightheadedness, and nausea. You can treat heat exhaustion by getting out of the sun and drinking an electrolyte solution made up of one teaspoon of salt and one tablespoon of sugar dissolved in a liter of water. Drink this solution slowly over a period of one hour. Drinking plenty of fluids (preferably an electrolyte solution/sports drink) can prevent heat exhaustion. Avoid hiking during the hottest parts of the day, and wear breathable clothing, a wide-brimmed hat, and sunglasses.

Hypothermia is one of the biggest dangers in the backcountry, especially for day hikers in the summertime. That may sound strange, but imagine starting out on a hike in midsummer when it's sunny and 80°F. You're clad in nylon shorts and a cotton T-shirt. About halfway through your hike, the sky begins to cloud up, and in the next hour a light drizzle begins to fall and the wind starts to pick up. Before you know it, you are soaking wet and shivering—the perfect recipe for hypothermia. More advanced signs include decreased coordination, slurred speech, and blurred vision. When a victim's temperature falls below 92 degrees, the blood pressure and pulse plummet, possibly leading to coma and death.

To avoid hypothermia, always bring a windproof/rainproof shell, a fleece jacket, tights made of a breathable synthetic fiber, gloves, and hat when you are hiking in the mountains. Learn to adjust your clothing layers based on the temperature. If you are climbing uphill at a moderate pace, you will stay warm; but when you stop for a break, you'll become cold quickly unless you add more layers of clothing.

If a hiker is showing advanced signs of hypothermia, dress him or her in dry clothes and make sure he or she is wearing a hat and gloves. Place the person in a sleeping bag in a tent or shelter that will protect him or her from the wind and other elements. Give the person warm fluids to drink and keep him awake.

Frostbite. When the mercury dips below 32°F, your extremities begin to chill. If a persistent chill attacks a localized area—say, your hands or your toes—the circulatory system reacts by cutting off blood flow to the affected area, the idea being to protect and preserve the body's overall temperature. And so it's death by attrition for the

affected area. Ice crystals start to form from the water in the cells of the neglected tissue. Deprived of heat, nourishment, and now water, the tissue literally starves. This is frostbite.

Prevention is your best defense against this situation. Most prone to frostbite are your face, hands, and feet, so protect these areas well. Wool is the material of choice because it provides ample air space for insulation and draws moisture away from the skin. Synthetic fabrics, however, have recently made great strides in the cold weather clothing market. Do your research. A pair of light silk liners under your regular gloves is a good trick for keeping warm. They afford some additional warmth, but more importantly they'll allow you to remove your mitts for tedious work without exposing the skin.

If your feet or hands start to feel cold or numb due to the elements, warm them as quickly as possible. Place cold hands under your armpits or bury them in your crotch. If your feet are cold, change your socks. If there's plenty of room in your boots, add another pair of socks. Do remember, though, that constricting your feet in tight boots can restrict blood flow and actually make your feet colder more quickly. Your socks need to have breathing room if they're going to be effective. Dead air provides insulation. If your face is cold, place your warm hands over your face, or simply wear a head stocking.

Should your skin go numb and start to appear white and waxy, chances are you've got or are developing frostbite. Don't try to thaw the area unless you can maintain the warmth. In other words, don't stop to warm up your frostbitten feet only to head back on the trail. You'll do more damage than good. Tests have shown that hikers who walked on thawed feet did more harm, and endured more pain, than hikers who left the affected areas alone. Do your best to get out of the cold entirely and seek medical attention—which usually consists of performing a rapid rewarming in water for 20 to 30 minutes.

The overall objective in preventing both hypothermia and frostbite is to keep the body's core warm. Protect key areas where heat escapes, like the top of the head, and maintain the proper nutrition level. Foods that are high in calories aid the body in producing heat. Never smoke or drink when you're in situations where the cold is threatening. By affecting blood flow, these activities ultimately cool the body's core temperature.

Altitude sickness (AMS). High lofty peaks, clear alpine lakes, and vast mountain views beckon hikers to the high country. But those who like to venture high may become victims of altitude sickness, also known as acute mountain sickness (AMS). Altitude sickness is your body's reaction to insufficient oxygen in the blood due to decreased barometric pressure. While some hikers may feel lightheaded, nauseous, and experience shortness of breath at 7,000 feet, others may not experience these symptoms until they reach 10,000 feet or higher.

Slowing your ascent to high places and giving your body a chance to acclimatize to the higher elevations can prevent altitude sickness. For example, if you live at sea level and are planning a weeklong backpacking trip to elevations between 7,000 and 12,000 feet, start by staying below 7,000 feet for one night, then move to between 7,000 and 10,000 feet for another night or two. Avoid strenuous exertion and alcohol to give your body a chance to adjust to the new altitude. It's also important to eat light food and drink plenty of nonalcoholic fluids, preferably water. Loss of appetite at altitude is common, but you must eat!

Most hikers who experience mild to moderate AMS develop a headache and/or nausea, grow lethargic, and have problems sleeping. The treatment for AMS is simple: Stop heading uphill. Keep eating and drinking water, and take meds for the headache. You actually need to take more breaths at altitude than at sea level, so breathe a little faster without hyperventilating. If symptoms don't improve over 24 to 48 hours, descend. Once a victim descends about 2,000 to 3,000 feet, his or her symptoms will usually begin to diminish.

Severe AMS comes in two forms: high altitude pulmonary edema (HAPE) and high altitude cerebral edema (HACE). HAPE, an accumulation of fluid in the lungs, can occur above 8,000 feet. Symptoms include rapid heart rate, shortness of breath at rest, AMS symptoms, dry cough developing into a wet cough, gurgling sounds, flu-like or bronchitis symptoms, and lack of muscle coordination. HAPE is life threatening, so descend immediately, at least 2,000 to 4,000 feet. HACE usually occurs above 12,000 feet but sometimes occurs above 10,000 feet. Symptoms are similar to HAPE but also include seizures, hallucinations, paralysis, and vision disturbances. Descend immediately—HACE is also life threatening.

Hantavirus Pulmonary Syndrome (HPS). Deer mice spread the virus that causes HPS, and humans contract it from breathing it in, usually when they've disturbed an area with dust and mice feces from nests or surfaces with mice droppings or urine. Exposure to large numbers of rodents and their feces or urine presents the greatest risk. As hikers, we sometimes enter old buildings, and often deer mice live in these places. We may not be around long enough to be exposed, but do be aware of this disease. About half the people who develop HPS die. Symptoms are flu-like and appear about two to three weeks after exposure. After initial symptoms, a dry cough and shortness of breath follow. Breathing is difficult. If you even think you might have HPS, see a doctor immediately!

Natural Hazards

Besides tripping over a rock or tree root on the trail, there are some real hazards to be aware of while hiking. Even if where you're hiking doesn't have the plethora of venomous snakes and plants, insects, and grizzly bears found in other parts of the United States, there are a few weather conditions and predators you may need to take into account.

Lightning. Thunderstorms build over the mountains almost every day during summer. Lightning is generated by thunderheads and can strike without warning, even several miles away from the nearest overhead cloud. The best rule of thumb is to start leaving exposed peaks, ridges, and canyon rims by about noon. This time can vary a little depending on storm buildup. Keep an eye on cloud formation, and don't underestimate how fast a storm can build. The bigger the clouds get, the more likely a thunderstorm will happen. Lightning takes the path of least resistance, so if you're the high point, it might choose you. Ducking under a rock overhang is dangerous, as you form the shortest path between the rock and ground. If you dash below tree line, avoid standing under the only or the tallest tree. If you are caught above tree line, stay away from anything metal you might be carrying, Move down off the ridge slightly to a low, treeless point and squat until the storm passes. If you have an insulating pad, squat on it. Avoid having both your hands and feet touching the ground at once, and never lie flat. If you hear a buzzing sound or feel your hair standing on end, move quickly—an electrical charge is building up.

Flash floods. On July 31, 1976, a torrential downpour unleashed by a thunderstorm dumped tons of water into the Big Thompson watershed near Estes Park in Colorado. Within hours, a wall of water moved down the narrow canyon, killing 139 people and causing more than $30 million in property damage. Flash floods can appear out of nowhere from a storm many miles away. While hiking or driving in canyons or ravines, keep an eye on the weather. Always climb to safety if danger threatens. Flash floods usually subside quickly, so be patient, and don't cross a swollen stream.

Bears. Most of the United States (outside of the Pacific Northwest and parts of the Northern Rockies) does not have a grizzly bear population, although some rumors exist about sightings where there should be none. Black bears are plentiful, however. Here are some tips in case you and a bear scare each other. Most of all, avoid scaring a bear. Watch for bear tracks (five toes) and droppings (sizable with leaves, partly digested berries, seeds, and/or animal fur). Talk or sing where visibility or hearing is limited. Keep a clean camp, hang food, and don't sleep in the clothes you wore while cooking. Be especially careful in spring to avoid getting between a mother and her cubs. In late summer and fall, bears are busy eating berries and acorns to fatten up for winter, so be extra careful around berry bushes and oak brush. If you do encounter a bear, move away slowly while facing the bear, talk softly, and avoid direct eye contact. Give the bear room to escape. Since bears are very curious, a bear might stand upright to get a better whiff of you; it may even charge you to try to intimidate you. Try to stay calm. If a bear does attack you, fight back with anything you have handy. Unleashed dogs have been known to come running back to their owners with a bear close behind. Keep your dog on a leash, or leave it at home.

Mountain lions. Mountain lions appear to be getting more comfortable around humans as long as deer (their favorite prey) are in an area with adequate cover. Usually elusive and quiet, lions rarely attack people. If you meet a lion, give it a chance to escape. Stay calm and talk firmly to it. Back away slowly while facing the lion. If you run, you'll only encourage the curious cat to chase you. Make yourself look large by opening a jacket, if you have one, or waving your hiking poles. If the lion behaves aggressively, throw stones, sticks, or whatever you can while remaining tall. If a lion does attack, fight for your life with anything you can grab.

Moose. Because moose have very few natural predators, they don't fear humans like other animals do. You might find moose in sagebrush and wetter areas of willow, aspen, and pine, or in beaver habitats. Mothers with calves, as well as bulls during mating season, can be particularly aggressive. If a moose threatens you, back away slowly and talk calmly to it. Keep your pets away from moose.

Other considerations. Hunting is a popular sport in the United States, especially during rifle season in October and November. Hiking is still enjoyable in those months in many areas, so just take a few precautions. First, learn when the different hunting seasons start and end in the area in which you'll be hiking. During this time frame, be sure to wear at least a blaze orange hat, and possibly put an orange vest over your pack. Don't be surprised to see hunters in camo outfits carrying bows or muzzleloading rifles around during their season. If you would feel more comfortable without hunters around, hike in national parks and monuments or in state and local parks where hunting is not allowed.

Navigation

Whether you are going on a short hike in a familiar area or planning a weeklong backpack trip, you should always be equipped with the proper navigational equipment—at the very least a detailed map and a sturdy compass.

Maps. There are many different types of maps available to help you find your way on the trail. Easiest to find are USDA Forest Service maps and Bureau of Land Management (BLM) maps. These maps tend to cover large areas, so be sure they are detailed enough for your particular trip. You can also obtain national park maps as well as high-quality maps from private companies and trail groups. These maps can be obtained either from outdoor stores or ranger stations.

US Geological Survey (USGS) topographic maps are particularly popular with hikers—especially serious backcountry hikers. These maps contain the standard map symbols such as roads, lakes, and rivers, as well as contour lines that show the details of the trail terrain like ridges, valleys, passes, and mountain peaks. The 7.5-minute series (1 inch on the map equals approximately 0.4 mile on the ground) provides the closest inspection available. USGS maps are available by mail (USGS Information Services, PO Box 25286, Denver, CO 80225) or online at http://store.usgs.gov. If you want to check out the high-tech world of maps, you can purchase topographic maps on CD-ROM. These software-mapping programs let you select a route on your computer, print it out, then take it with you on the trail. Some software mapping programs let you insert symbols and labels, download waypoints from a GPS unit, and export the maps to other software programs.

The art of map reading is a skill that you can develop by first practicing in an area you are familiar with. To begin, orient the map so that it is lined up in the correct direction (i.e., north on the map is lined up with true north). Next, familiarize yourself with the map symbols and try match them up with terrain features around you, such as a high ridge, mountain peak, river, or lake. If you are practicing with a USGS map, notice the contour lines. On gentler terrain these contour lines are spaced farther apart; on steeper terrain they are closer together. Pick a short loop trail, and stop frequently to check your position on the map. As you practice map reading, you'll learn how to anticipate a steep section on the trail, a good place to take a rest break, and so on.

Compasses. First off, the sun is not a substitute for a compass. So, what kind of compass should you have? Here are some characteristics you should look for: a rectangular base with detailed scales, a liquid-filled protective housing, a sighting line on the mirror, luminous alignment and back-bearing arrows, a luminous north-seeking arrow, and a well-defined bezel ring.

You can learn compass basics by reading the detailed instructions included with your compass. If you want to fine-tune your compass skills, sign up for an orienteering class or purchase a book on compass reading. Once you've learned the basic skills of using a compass, remember to practice these skills before you head into the backcountry.

If you are a klutz at using a compass, you may be interested in checking out the technical wizardry of the GPS (Global Positioning System) device. The GPS was developed by the Pentagon and works off twenty-four NAVSTAR satellites, which were designed to guide missiles to their targets. A GPS device is a handheld unit that calculates your latitude and longitude with the easy press of a button. The Department of Defense used to scramble the satellite signals a bit to prevent civilians (and spies!) from getting extremely accurate readings, but that practice was discontinued in May 2000; GPS units now provide nearly pinpoint accuracy (within 30 to 60 feet).

There are many different types of GPS units available, ranging in price from $100 to $400. In general, all GPS units have a display screen and keypad where you input information. In addition to acting as a compass, the unit allows you to plot your route, easily retrace your path, track your traveling speed, find the mileage between waypoints, and calculate the total mileage of your route.

Before you purchase a GPS unit, keep in mind that these devices don't pick up signals indoors, in heavily wooded areas, on mountain peaks, or in deep valleys.

Pedometers. A pedometer is a small, clip-on unit with a digital display that calculates your hiking distance in miles or kilometers based on your walking stride. Some units also calculate the calories you burn and your total hiking time. Pedometers are available at most large outdoor stores and range in price from $20 to $40.

Trip Planning

Planning your hiking adventure begins with letting a friend or relative know your trip itinerary so he or she can call for help if you don't return at your scheduled time. Your next task is to make sure you are outfitted to experience the risks and rewards of the trail. This section highlights gear and clothing you may want to take with you to get the most out of your hike.

Day Hikes

- camera
- compass/GPS unit
- pedometer
- day pack
- first-aid kit
- food
- guidebook
- headlamp/flashlight with extra batteries and bulbs
- hat
- insect repellent
- knife/multipurpose tool
- map
- matches in waterproof container and fire starter
- fleece jacket
- rain gear
- space blanket
- sunglasses
- sunscreen
- swimsuit

- watch
- water
- water bottles/water hydration system

Overnight Trip

- backpack and waterproof rain cover
- backpacker's trowel
- bandanna
- bear repellent spray
- bear bell
- biodegradable soap
- pot scrubber
- collapsible water container (2- to 3-gallon capacity)
- clothing—extra wool socks, shirt and shorts
- cook set/utensils
- ditty bags to store gear
- extra plastic resealable bags
- gaiters
- garbage bag
- ground cloth
- journal/pen
- nylon rope to hang food
- long underwear
- permit (if required)
- rain jacket and pants
- sandals to wear around camp and to ford streams
- sleeping bag
- waterproof stuff sack
- sleeping pad
- small bath towel
- stove and fuel
- tent
- toiletry items
- water filter
- whistle

Equipment

With the outdoor market currently flooded with products, many of which are pure gimmickry, it seems impossible to both differentiate and choose. Do I really need a tropical-fish-lined collapsible shower? (No, you don't.) The only defense against the maddening quantity of items thrust in your face is to think practically—and to do so before you go shopping. The worst buys are impulsive buys. Since most name brands will differ only slightly in quality, it's best to know what you're looking for in terms of function. Buy only what you need. You will, don't forget, be carrying what you've bought on your back. Here are some things to keep in mind before you go shopping.

Clothes. Clothing is your armor against Mother Nature's little surprises. Hikers should be prepared for any possibility, especially when hiking in mountainous areas. Adequate rain protection and extra layers of clothing are a good idea. In summer, a wide-brimmed hat can help keep the sun at bay. In the winter months the first layer you'll want to wear is a "wicking" layer of long underwear that keeps perspiration away from your skin. Wear long underwear made from synthetic fibers that wick moisture away from the skin and draw it toward the next layer of clothing, where it then evaporates. Avoid wearing long underwear made of cotton, which is slow to dry and keeps moisture next to your skin.

The second layer you'll wear is the "insulating" layer. Aside from keeping you warm, this layer needs to "breathe" so you stay dry while hiking. A fabric that provides insulation and dries quickly is fleece. It's interesting to note that this one-of-a-kind fabric is often made out of recycled plastic. Purchasing a zip-up jacket made of this material is highly recommended.

The last line of layering defense is the "shell" layer. You'll need some type of waterproof, windproof, breathable jacket that will fit over all your other layers. It should have a large hood that fits over a hat. You'll also need a good pair of rain pants made from a similar waterproof, breathable fabric. Some Gore-Tex jackets cost as much as $500, but you should know that there are more affordable fabrics out there that work just as well.

Now that you've learned the basics of layering, you can't forget to protect your hands and face. In cold, windy, or rainy weather, you'll need a hat made of wool or fleece and insulated, waterproof gloves that will keep your hands warm and toasty. As mentioned earlier, buying an additional pair of light silk liners to wear under your regular gloves is a good idea.

Footwear. If you have any extra money to spend on your trip, put that money into boots or trail shoes. Poor shoes will bring a hike to a halt faster than anything else. To avoid this annoyance, buy shoes that provide support and are lightweight and flexible. A lightweight hiking boot is better than a heavy, leather mountaineering boot for most day hikes and backpacking. Trail running shoes provide a little extra cushion and

are made in a high-top style that many people wear for hiking. These running shoes are lighter, more flexible, and more breathable than hiking boots. If you know you'll be hiking in wet weather often, purchase boots or shoes with a Gore-Tex liner, which will help keep your feet dry.

When buying your boots, be sure to wear the same type of socks you'll be wearing on the trail. If the boots you're buying are for cold weather hiking, try them on while wearing two pairs of socks. Speaking of socks, a good cold weather sock combination is to wear a thinner sock made of wool or polypropylene covered by a heavier outer sock made of wool. The inner sock protects the foot from the rubbing effects of the outer sock and prevents blisters. Many outdoor stores have some type of ramp to simulate hiking uphill and downhill. Be sure to take advantage of this test, as toe-jamming boot fronts can be very painful and debilitating on the downhill trek.

Once you've purchased your footwear, be sure to break them in before you hit the trail. New footwear is often stiff and needs to be stretched and molded to your foot.

Hiking poles. Hiking poles help with balance and, more importantly, take pressure off your knees. The ones with shock absorbers are easier on your elbows and knees. Some poles even come with a camera attachment to be used as a monopod. And heaven forbid you meet a mountain lion, bear, or unfriendly dog—the poles can make you look a lot bigger.

Backpacks. No matter what type of hiking you do, you'll need a pack of some sort to carry the basic trail essentials. There are a variety of backpacks on the market, but let's first discuss what you intend to use it for. Day hikes or overnight trips?

If you plan on doing a day hike, a day pack should have some of the following characteristics: a padded hip belt that's at least 2 inches in diameter (avoid packs with only a small nylon piece of webbing for a hip belt); a chest strap (the chest strap helps stabilize the pack against your body); external pockets to carry water and other items that you want easy access to; an internal pocket to hold keys, a knife, a wallet, and other miscellaneous items; an external lashing system to hold a jacket; and a hydration pocket for carrying a hydration system (which consists of a water bladder with an attachable drinking hose).

For short hikes, some hikers like to use a fanny pack to store just a camera, food, a compass, a map, and other trail essentials. Most fanny packs have pockets for two water bottles and a padded hip belt.

If you intend to do an extended, overnight trip, there are multiple considerations. First off, you need to decide what kind of framed pack you want. There are two backpack types for backpacking: the internal frame and the external frame. An internal frame pack rests closer to your body, making it more stable and easier to balance when hiking over rough terrain. An external frame pack is just that, an aluminum frame attached to the exterior of the pack. An external frame pack is better for long backpack trips because it distributes the pack weight better and you can carry heavier loads. It's easier to pack, and your gear is more accessible. It also offers better back ventilation in hot weather.

The most critical measurement for fitting a pack is torso length. The pack needs to rest evenly on your hips without sagging. A good pack will come in two or three sizes and have straps and hip belts that are adjustable according to your body size and characteristics.

When you purchase a backpack, go to an outdoor store with salespeople who are knowledgeable in how to properly fit a pack. Once the pack is fitted for you, load the pack with the amount of weight you plan on taking on the trail. The weight of the pack should be distributed evenly, and you should be able to swing your arms and walk briskly without feeling out of balance. Another good technique for evaluating a pack is to walk up and down stairs and make quick turns to the right and to the left to be sure the pack doesn't feel out of balance. Other features that are nice to have on a backpack include a removable day pack or fanny pack, external pockets for extra water, and extra lash points to attach a jacket or other items.

Sleeping bags and pads. Sleeping bags are rated by temperature. You can purchase a bag made of synthetic fiber, or you can buy a goose down bag. Goose down bags are more expensive, but they have a higher insulating capacity by weight and will keep their loft longer. You'll want to purchase a bag with a temperature rating that fits the time of year and conditions you are most likely to camp in. One caveat: The techno-standard for temperature ratings is far from perfect. Ratings vary from manufacturer to manufacturer, so to protect yourself you should purchase a bag rated 10 to 15 degrees below the temperature you expect to be camping in. Synthetic bags are more resistant to water than down bags, but many down bags are now made with a Gore-Tex shell that helps to repel water. Down bags are also more compressible than synthetic bags and take up less room in your pack, which is an important consideration if you are planning a multiday backpack trip. Features to look for in a sleeping bag include a mummy-style bag, a hood you can cinch down around your head in cold weather, and draft tubes along the zippers that help keep heat in and drafts out.

You'll also want a sleeping pad to provide insulation and padding from the cold ground. There are different types of sleeping pads available, from the more expensive self-inflating air mattresses to the less expensive closed-cell foam pads. Self-inflating air mattresses are usually heavier than closed-cell foam mattresses and are prone to punctures.

Tents. The tent is your home away from home while on the trail. It provides protection from wind, snow, rain, and insects. A three-season tent is a good choice for backpacking and can range in price from $100 to $500. These lightweight and versatile tents provide protection in all types of weather, except heavy snowstorms or high winds, and range in weight from 4 to 8 pounds. Look for a tent that's easy to set up and will easily fit two people with gear. Dome type tents usually offer more headroom and places to store gear. Other tent designs include a vestibule where you can store wet boots and backpacks. Some nice-to-have items in a tent include interior pockets to store small items and lashing points to hang a clothesline. Most three-season tents also come with stakes so you can secure the tent in high winds. Before you purchase a tent, set it up and take it down a few times to be sure it is easy to handle. Also, sit inside the tent and make sure it has enough room for you and your gear.

Cell phones. Many hikers are carrying their cell phones into the backcountry these days in case of emergency. That's fine and good, but please know that cell phone coverage is often poor to nonexistent in valleys, canyons, and thick forest. More importantly, people have started to call for help because they're tired or lost. Let's go back to being prepared. You are responsible for yourself in the backcountry. Use your brain to avoid problems, and if you do encounter one, first use your brain to try to correct the situation. Only use your cell phone, if it works, in true emergencies.

Hiking with Children

Hiking with children isn't a matter of how many miles you can cover or how much elevation gain you make in a day; it's about seeing and experiencing nature through their eyes.

Kids like to explore and have fun. They like to stop and point out bugs and plants, look under rocks, jump in puddles, and throw sticks. If you're taking a toddler or young child on a hike, start with a trail that you're familiar with. Trails that have interesting things for kids, like piles of leaves to play in or a small stream to wade through during summer, will make the hike much more enjoyable for them and will keep them from getting bored.

You can keep your child's attention if you have a strategy before starting on the trail. Using games is not only an effective way to keep a child's attention but also a great way to teach him or her about nature. Play hide and seek, where your child is the mouse and you are the hawk. Quiz children on the names of plants and animals. If your children are old enough, let them carry their own day pack filled with snacks and water. So that you are sure to go at their pace and not yours, let them lead the way. Playing follow the leader works particularly well when you have a group of children. Have each child take a turn at being the leader.

With children, a lot of clothing is key. The only thing predictable about weather is that it will change. Especially in mountainous areas, weather can change dramatically in a very short time. Always bring extra clothing for children, regardless of the season. In winter, have your children wear wool socks and warm layers, such as long underwear, a fleece jacket and hat, wool mittens, and good rain gear. It's not a bad idea to have these along in late fall and early spring as well. Good footwear is also important. A sturdy pair of high-top tennis shoes or lightweight hiking boots is the best bet for little ones. If you're hiking in summer near a lake or stream, bring along a pair of old sneakers that your child can put on when he or she wants to go exploring in the water. Remember when you're near any type of water, always watch your child at all times. Also, keep a close eye on teething toddlers, who may decide a rock or leaf of poison oak is an interesting item to put in their mouth.

From spring through fall, you'll want your kids to wear a wide-brimmed hat to keep their face, head, and ears protected from the hot sun. Also, make sure your children wear sunscreen at all times. Choose a brand without PABA—children have sensitive skin and may have an allergic reaction to sunscreen that contains PABA. If you are hiking with a child younger than 6 months, don't use sunscreen or insect repellent. Instead, be sure that the head, face, neck, and ears are protected from the sun with a wide-brimmed hat, and that all other skin exposed to the sun is protected with the appropriate clothing.

Remember that food is fun. Kids like snacks, so it's important to bring a lot of munchies for the trail. Stopping often for snack breaks is a fun way to keep the trail interesting. Raisins, apples, granola bars, crackers and cheese, cereal, and trail mix all

make great snacks. If your child is old enough to carry his or her own backpack, fill it with treats before you leave. If your kids don't like drinking water, you can bring boxes of fruit juice.

Avoid poorly designed child-carrying packs—you don't want to break your back carrying your child. Most child-carrying backpacks designed to hold a 40-pound child will contain a large carrying pocket to hold diapers and other items. Some have an optional rain/sun hood.

Hiking with Your Dog

Bringing your furry friend with you is always more fun than leaving him behind. Our canine pals make great trail buddies because they never complain and always make good company. Hiking with your dog can be a rewarding experience, especially if you plan ahead.

Getting your dog in shape. Before you plan outdoor adventures with your dog, make sure he's in shape for the trail. Getting your dog into shape takes the same discipline as getting yourself into shape; luckily, your dog can get in shape with you. Take your dog with you on your daily runs or walks. If there is a park near your house, hit a tennis ball or play Frisbee with your dog.

Swimming is also an excellent way to get your dog into shape. If there is a lake or river near where you live and your dog likes the water, have him retrieve a tennis ball or stick. Gradually build your dog's stamina up over a two- to three-month period. A good rule of thumb is to assume that your dog will travel twice as far as you will on the trail. If you plan on doing a 5-mile hike, be sure your dog is in shape for a 10-mile hike.

Training your dog for the trail. Before you go on your first hiking adventure with your dog, be sure he has a firm grasp on the basics of canine etiquette and behavior. Make sure he can sit, lie down, stay, and come. One of the most important commands you can teach your canine pal is to "come" under any situation. It's easy for your friend's nose to lead him astray or possibly get him lost. Another helpful command is the "get behind" command. When you're on a hiking trail that's narrow, you can have your dog follow behind you when other trail users approach. Nothing is more bothersome than an enthusiastic dog that runs back and forth on the trail and disrupts the peace of the trail for others. When you see other trail users approaching you on the trail, give them the right-of-way by quietly stepping off the trail and making your dog lie down and stay until they pass.

Equipment. The most critical pieces of equipment you can invest in for your dog are proper identification and a sturdy leash. Flexi-leads work well for hiking because they give your dog more freedom to explore but still leave you in control. Make sure your dog has identification that includes your name and address and a number for your veterinarian. Other forms of identification for your dog include a tattoo or a microchip. You should consult your veterinarian for more information on these last two options.

The next piece of equipment you'll want to consider is a pack for your dog. By no means should you hold all of your dog's essentials in your pack—let him carry his own gear! Dogs that are in good shape can carry 30 to 40 percent of their own weight.

Most packs are fitted by a dog's weight and girth measurement. Companies that make dog packs generally include guidelines to help you pick out the size that's right for your dog. Some characteristics to look for when purchasing a pack for your dog include a harness that contains two padded girth straps, a padded chest strap, leash attachments, removable saddle bags, internal water bladders, and external gear cords.

You can introduce your dog to the pack by first placing the empty pack on his back and letting him wear it around the yard. Keep an eye on him during this first introduction. He may decide to chew through the straps if you aren't watching him closely. Once he learns to treat the pack as an object of fun and not a foreign enemy, fill the pack evenly on both sides with a few ounces of dog food in resealable plastic bags. Have your dog wear his pack on your daily walks for a period of two to three weeks. Each week add a little more weight to the pack until your dog will accept carrying the maximum amount of weight he can carry.

You can also purchase collapsible water and dog food bowls for your dog. These bowls are lightweight and can easily be stashed into your pack or your dog's. If you are hiking on rocky terrain or in the snow, you can purchase footwear for your dog that will protect his feet from cuts and bruises.

Always carry plastic bags to remove feces from the trail. It is a courtesy to other trail users and helps protect local wildlife.

The following is a list of items to bring when you take your dog hiking: collapsible water bowls, a comb, a collar and a leash, dog food, plastic bags for feces, a dog pack, flea/tick powder, paw protection, water, and a first-aid kit that contains eye ointment, tweezers, scissors, stretchy foot wrap, gauze, antibacterial wash, sterile cotton tip applicators, antibiotic ointment, and cotton wrap.

First aid for your dog. Your dog is just as prone—if not more prone—to getting in trouble on the trail as you are, so be prepared. Here's a rundown of the more likely misfortunes that might befall your little friend.

- **Bees and wasps.** If a bee or wasp stings your dog, remove the stinger with a pair of tweezers and place a mudpack or a cloth dipped in cold water over the affected area.

- **Porcupines.** One good reason to keep your dog on a leash is to prevent it from getting a nose full of porcupine quills. You may be able to remove the quills with pliers, but a veterinarian is the best person to do this nasty job because most dogs need to be sedated.

- **Heat stroke.** Avoid hiking with your dog in really hot weather. Dogs with heat stroke will pant excessively, lie down and refuse to get up, and become lethargic and disoriented. If your dog shows any of these signs on the trail, have him lie down in the shade. If you are near a stream, pour cool water over your dog's entire body to help bring his body temperature back to normal.

- **Heartworm.** Dogs get heartworms from mosquitoes, which carry the disease in the prime mosquito months of July and August. Giving your dog a monthly pill prescribed by your veterinarian easily prevents this condition.

- **Plant pitfalls.** One of the biggest plant hazards for dogs on the trail are foxtails. Foxtails are pointed grass seed heads that bury themselves in your friend's fur, between his toes, and even get in his ear canal. If left unattended, these nasty seeds can work their way under the skin and cause abscesses and other problems. If you have a long-haired dog, consider trimming the hair between his toes and giving him a summer haircut to help prevent foxtails from attaching to his fur. After every hike, always look over your dog for these seeds—especially between his toes and his ears.

  Other plant hazards include burrs, thorns, thistles, and poison oak. If you find any burrs or thistles on your dog, remove them as soon as possible before they become an unmanageable mat. Thorns can pierce a dog's foot and cause a great deal of pain. If you see that your dog is lame, stop and check his feet for thorns. Dogs are immune to poison oak but they can pick up the sticky, oily substance from the plant and transfer it to you.

- **Protect those paws**. Be sure to keep your dog's nails trimmed so he avoids getting soft tissue or joint injuries. If your dog slows and refuses to go on, check to see that his paws aren't torn or worn. You can protect your dog's paws from trail hazards such as sharp gravel, foxtails, lava scree, and thorns by purchasing dog boots.

- **Sunburn.** If your dog has light skin, he is an easy target for sunburn on his nose and other exposed skin areas. You can apply a nontoxic sunscreen to exposed skin areas that will help protect him from overexposure to the sun.

- **Ticks and fleas.** Ticks can easily give your dog Lyme disease, as well as other diseases. Before you hit the trail, treat your dog with a flea and tick spray or powder. You can also ask your veterinarian about a once-a-month pour-on treatment that repels fleas and ticks.

- **Mosquitoes and deerflies.** These little flying machines can do a job on your dog's snout and ears. Your best bet is to spray your dog with fly repellent for horses to discourage both pests.

- **Giardia.** Dogs can get giardia, which results in diarrhea. It is usually not debilitating, but it's definitely messy. A vaccine against giardia is available.

- **Mushrooms.** Make sure your dog doesn't sample mushrooms along the trail. They could be poisonous to him, but he doesn't know that.

When you are finally ready to hit the trail with your dog, keep in mind that many national parks and wilderness areas do not allow dogs on trails. Your best bet is to hike in national forests, BLM lands, and state parks. Always call ahead to see what the restrictions are.

Clubs & Organizations

Keystone Trails Association

From the KTA website: "The Keystone Trails Association, a volunteer-directed, public service organization, is a federation of membership organizations and individuals dedicated to providing, preserving, protecting and promoting recreational hiking trails and hiking opportunities in Pennsylvania, and to represent and advocate the interests and concerns of the Pennsylvania hiking community."

The KTA also publishes a monthly newsletter for its members.
Keystone Trails Association
101 N. Front St., Third Floor
Harrisburg, PA 17101
(717) 238-7017
www.kta-hike.org
E-mail: info@ktaihike.org

Southeast Pennsylvania

Allentown Hiking Club
www.allentownhikingclub.org

Appalachian Mountain Club: Delaware Valley Chapter
www.amcdv.org

Batona Hiking Club
www.batonahikingclub.org

Berks Community Hiking Club
Berkshiker.blogspot.com

Blue Mountain Eagle Climbing Club
www.bmecc.org

Chester County Trail Club
www.cctrailclub.org

Friends of the Wissahickon
www.fow.org

Horse-Shoe Trail Club
www.hstrail.org

Lancaster Hiking Club
http://lancasterhikingclub.angelfire.com

Lebanon Valley Hiking Club
Contact: Sharon Southall (717) 274-5509

Mason-Dixon Trail System
www.mason-dixontrail.org

Philadelphia Trail Club
www.philadelphiatrailclub.org

Schuylkill County Conservancy
www.schuylkillconservancy.org

Northeast Pennsylvania

Pocono Outdoor Club
www.poconooutdoorclub.org

Susquehanna Trailers Hiking Club
http://susquehanna_trailers.tripod.com

North Central Pennsylvania

Alpine Club of Williamsport
www.lycoming.org/alpine

Asaph Trail Club
www.wildasaphoutfitters.com

Mid State Trail Association
www.hike-mst.org

Ridge and Valley Outings Co-op
E-mail: monoprint@gmail.com

Sierra Club: Otzinachson Group
https://otzinachson.wordpress.com

Susquehannock Trail Club
www.stc-hike.org

South Central Pennsylvania

Cumberland Valley Appalachian Trail Club
www.cvatclub.org

Mountain Club of Maryland
http://mcomd.org

Potomac Appalachian Trail Club
www.patc.net

Susquehanna Appalachian Trail Club
www.satc-hike.org

York Hiking Club
http://yorkhikingclub.com

Southwest Pennsylvania

North Country Trail Association: Wampum Chapter
www.northcountrytrail.org/wam

Rachel Carson Trails Conservancy
www.rachelcarsontrails.org

The Western Pennsylvania Conservancy
waterlandlife.org

Warrior Trail Association, Inc.
E-mail: Llew.Williams@L-3Com.com

Northwest Pennsylvania

Allegheny Outdoor Club
www.alleghenyoutdoorclub.org

Butler Outdoor Club
www.butleroutdoorclub.org

Hike Index

About the Author

John L. Young was born and raised in Altoona. He has a degree in journalism and is a former newspaper reporter and columnist. His outdoor and travel articles have appeared in *Ohio Magazine, Pennsylvania Magazine,* and *Pursuits,* a publication of the Pennsylvania Tourism Office. His books include the true-life novel *From Pithole to Paradise,* two historical true-crime stories: *Murder at the Airport Inn* and *Murder in the Courtroom,* and the career guide *Unemployed No More.* He is the author of two other FalconGuides: *Hiking the Poconos* and *Best Hikes Near Philadelphia.*

His love affair with the woods and mountains of Pennsylvania began at age 12 when he started deer hunting with his father and brother at their camp on Tussey Mountain in Huntington County; even before then, he remembers swimming in the icy waters of nearby Spruce Creek. John has hiked the Oak Creek Canyon area of Sedona, Arizona, searching for the fabled vortexes, and the Presidential Range of the White Mountains in New Hampshire. His hobbies include outdoor photography, cross-country skiing, bicycling Pennsylvania's rail trails, trail maintenance, and of course hiking. His indoor interests include reading and table tennis. John lives with his wife, Debra, a retired school district administrator and college guidance counselor, in a small farming community in Warren County, just north of the Allegheny National Forest. He is a member of the Allegheny Outdoor Club.

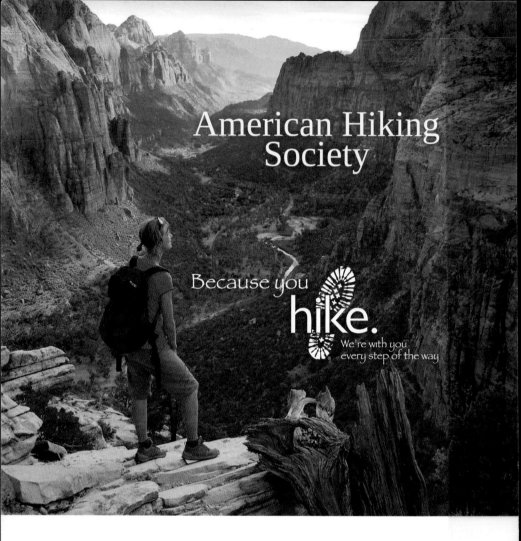

American Hiking
Society

Because you
hike.
We're with you
every step of the way

As a national voice for hikers, **American Hiking Society** works every day:

- Building and maintaining hiking trails
- Educating and supporting hikers by providing information and resources
- Supporting hiking and trail organizations nationwide
- Speaking for hikers in the halls of Congress and with federal land managers

Whether you're a casual hiker or a seasoned backpacker, become a member of American Hiking Society and join the national hiking community! You'll enjoy great member benefits and help preserve the nation's hiking trails, so tomorrow's hike is even better than today's. We invite you to join us now!

American Hiking Society